PRINCIPLES OF COMMUNICATION

PRINCIPLES OF COMMUNICATION

VIJAYA SOMASUNDARAM

AUTHORSPRESS

Worldwide Circulation through Authorspress Global Network

First Published in 2005

by

Authorspress

Q-2A Hauz Khas Enclave, New Delhi-110 016 (India)

Phone: (0) 9818049852

E-mail: authorspressgroup@gmail.com

Website: www.authorspressbooks.com

Principles of Communication

ISBN 81-7273-258-9

Printed in India at Tarun Offset, Delhi

Contents

1

Fundamentals of Communication

Communication is the process of exchanging information usually via a common system of symbols. It occurs only when there are two associated information producing processes, and the output from one process is the functional inverse of the other process's output. It is at the core of all human relationships. Humans communicate in order to share knowledge and experiences. Common forms of human communication include sign language, speaking, writing, gestures, and broadcasting. Communication can be interactive, transactive, intentiona l, or unintentional; it can also be verbal or non-verbal. In addition, communication can be intrapersonal or interpersonal. There are a number of theories of communication that attempt to explain human communication".

1.1 Defining Communication

Defining communication is not an easy task since it is a complex blend of numerous entities. We will incorporate major areas of the concept by defining it as: *Communication is the process of sending, receiving, and interpreting messages through which we relate to each other and to our larger world as well.*

The first important concept in this definition is "process." By process, we mean that communication is not a single act but a series of interconnected acts moving through time. This means, first of all, that communication is ongoing. It begins when two or more parties (senders and receivers) come into contact with each other and continues until the parties break contact. The parties may be two people, a group of people, a large audience and a speaker, or even individuals communicating with themselves via "interpersonal communication".

Since it exists in time, communication is irreversible. Once the process begins, it cannot go back to its beginnings and start all over. A common experience is that we, from time to time, say things we wish we had not said. Perhaps the words slipped out in the heat of an argument, perhaps we said something as a joke that turned out to be more hurtful than funny. Much as we would like to recall the message, to counteract its negative effect, we cannot. We can try to reframe the message, but we cannot "erase the tape." Since communication is ongoing and irreversible, it is also an activity in which the elements are interdependent. Each part of an interchange influences what follows. Each portion builds on what went before it.

Communication is more like a game than it is like a play in which the lines are all known in advance. In communication, one person makes a statement, sends a greeting, answers the phone, calls a meeting to order. Others respond to that initiation. That response calls forth another response and that response, yet another. What each party contributes to the interchange adds to the situation and at the same time changes it. The final result and shape of the interchange is not known until its very end.

What passes between the parties in communication are messages. Messages are signals sent with the intent of creating understanding in the receiver. While the concept of messages is familiar to us, we need to realise the wide variety of messages that exist. On a personal level, we send verbal and non-verbal messages through our voices and our bodies. The number of ways we have created to communicate is testimony to human ingenuity. We send written transmissions through a wide variety of communication channels: letters, faxes, newspapers, magazines, advertising brochures, etc. We send aural messages through telephones, radios, and various types of musical devices. We reach one person through conversation; we reach millions through mass communication. Some even communicate through the use of drums, flags, fireworks, mirror flashes, waggling airplane wings, and firing shots across the bow.

Interpretation is the act of bringing to understanding. Whatever messages we receive, we try to make sense of them. As long as sender and receiver use the same language and operate in familiar settings, responses are easy to make. When the context of communication begins to include the unfamiliar, then interpretation is more difficult and, in some cases, impossible. One would think that people speaking English could readily understand each other. Americans, for example, have general agreements on the meanings of words such as "napkin", "dear", and "lavatory". The first is something we put in our laps when we eat; the second is someone or something toward which we feel affection; the third is a sink. Should one be travelling in the British Isles, however, one might discover to one's embarrassment that those terms in British English are interpreted as "diaper", "expensive", and "commode".

As meaning is not automatic and as interpretation is necessary in communication, misunderstanding is always a possibility in communication. Both sender and receiver may be thoroughly convinced that they have done all that is necessary for effective communication yet discover later that the messages are still garbled and confusion exists.

Communication is a linking of selves in some ways, be those ways serious or superficial. The quality and type of our relationships are highly dependent on the quality and type of our communication. Saying "good morning" to someone and having that person respond with "good morning" seems simple enough. When we think, though, of the number of "good mornings" that occur in a university housing unit, a family, or a huge industrial complex, the number becomes staggering. Each of those greetings adds another strand to the web of relationships in those organisation.

The thousands of messages that pass back and forth between thousands of people create their environments, the worlds in which they will functions as individuals or groups.

When we move from simple greetings to all the social communication, conflicts, group discussion, and decision making that occurs in a family, much less a corporation, we have a mind-boggling amount of communication to consider. All of the communication contributes to the nature of that unit.

Communication also shapes our relationship to our larger world, be it local or international. As children, our parents communicate to us what kinds of behaviour are acceptable or not acceptable, including how our communication should be patterned. Friends and institutions such as schools, clubs, athletic teams, and religious organisations further shape our consciousness and foster patterns of interaction.

When we move beyond the personal, we rely on mass media. Our perceptions and judgements of events are often dependent on how newspapers, radio, and television communicate an event. The naive conception of these media is that they simply report the facts of a case. Upon closer inspection, we discover that the stories communicate a viewpoint, one of the many possible viewpoints available to observers.

The communicative process of sending, receiving, and interpreting involves us at all levels, from the intimacy of our private lives to the world view of our political lives. Messages do not simply come to us. They are shaped by their senders, and we, in turn, shape them through our perceptions.

1.2 The Communication Act

Every communication involves a sender, a message, and a receiver.

1.2.1 The Sender

Communication begins in the sender's mind as a mental image, either an idea, a wish, or a feeling (or some combination of all three). These thoughts are transformed into symbols that can carry information. Those symbols make up the message. The most common symbols in communication are:

i) *Words*: spoken or printed
ii) *Images*: drawings, photos
iii) *Posture or Body Language*: gaze, touch, smile, physical proximity
iv) *Objects*: flowers, gifts, food, money
v) *Behaviors*: doing a favour, giving a kiss, ignoring an appointment

We choose symbols that:

i) represent our thoughts and feelings.
ii) we think will accomplish our goals.
iii) we are most comfortable using.
iv) have been previously successful.
v) we think the other person(s) will understand.
vi) our social relationships allow.

1.2.2 The Receiver

The sender's encoding of her or his mental images into the symbols that make up the message is only half of a communication act. The other half is the inverse process in the receiver: taking in the symbols that make up the message and decoding them into her or his own mental images. Thus, a communication act requires two transformations:

i) in the sender, the transformation of mental images into symbols
ii) in the receiver, the transformation of symbols into mental images

1.2.3 Literal and Meta Messages

Every communication act carries two types of message or potential meaning:

i) *The literal message:* conveyed by the symbols themselves, as in the words "It's raining."

ii) *The metamessage* ("meta" is the Greek word for "beyond", "additional", or "transcendent") carries implicit messages about the reason for the communication, how the message is to be interpreted, and the nature of the relationship of the sender and receiver.

1.3 Traditions of Communication Theory

Communication theory emerged as a distinct intellectual topic only in the mid-twentieth century. The term, communication theory, was first used in the 1940's by electrical engineers with reference to the mathematical analysis of signals. Claude Shannon and Warren Weaver's *The Mathematical Theory of Communication*, and Norbert Wiener's *Cybernetics*, for many readers augured the dawn of a new science of communication. The technical vocabulary of information transmission and feedback entered the common language and was taken up by social scientists, especially in the booming interdisciplinary field of communication research.

The rapid spread of this vocabulary was one manifestation of a long crescendo of societal interest in problems of communication, punctuated by wars and technological advances, throughout the last century. Communication was recurrently at the center of public debates about democracy, propaganda, mass media, popular culture, and human relations. Early in the century, communication as a formal category of knowledge was still largely identified with commercial and military transportation.

As late as 1928, the Library of Congress subject classification featured the word communication(s) in only two headings: "communication and traffic" and "communications, military". With the growth of electronic media, communication(s) more frequently referred to processes of information transmission through technological channels (the initial subject of communication theory). Around mid-century, however, as the quantity of published works on communication exploded, the emphasis in defining the term shifted decisively. Communication was now commonly defined as an interactive process that performs essential functions in every field of social practice. Subject categories related to communication now included communication in worship, communication in business, political communication, mass communication, communication in the family, and so on.

Communication theory, having germinated in the groves of academe in the late 1940's, grew like a weed by sinking roots into every intellectual tradition or trend in any way related to communication. Ideas from physical science and engineering, linguistics, anthropology, sociology, psychology, and philosophy were absorbed and reinterpreted as theories of communication. While continuing to grow in this fashion, the subject even now has not yet matured as a coherent body of thought. Communication theory has not grown historically forward, out of its traditions, but, in a sense, historically backward, by retrospectively appropriating a series of traditions, one of which is rhetorical theory.

Currently, at least seven major traditions of communication theory can be distinguished, rhetoric being the oldest. From classical rhetoric comes the idea that communication can be studied and cultivated as a practical art of discourse. Whereas the art of rhetoric still refers primarily to the theory and practice of public, persuasive communication, the communication arts more broadly encompass the whole range of communication practices including interpersonal, organisational, and cross-cultural communication, technologically mediated communication, and practices specific to various professions and fields. Modern rhetorical theory has elaborated and problematised the epistemological, sociological, and political dimensions of the classical tradition in ways that further contribute to communication theory. In theories of epistemic and constitutive rhetoric, for example, rhetorical theory has developed its own versions of the constitutive model.

A second tradition of communication theory, originated in its modern form by Locke, is semiotics, the study of signs. Semiotic theory conceptualises communication as a process that relies on signs and sign systems to mediate across the gaps between subjective viewpoints. For semiotic theory, communication problems result from barriers to understanding that arise from the slippage between sign-vehicles (physical signs such as spoken or written words, or graphic images) and their meanings, the structure of sign systems, and particular ways of using (or misusing) signs. Distinct traditions of semiotics grew from the late-nineteenth century writings of the American pragmatist philosopher Charles S. Peirce, and the early twentieth century work of the Swiss linguist Ferdinand de Saussure. The Peirceian tradition analysed the cognitive and mental functions of signs as a basis for distinguishing among types of signs (icon, index, symbol) and dimensions of semiosis (syntactics, semantics, pragmatics). The Saussureian tradition, which led to structuralist and poststructuralist theory, focused instead on the systematic structure of language and other sign systems. Although Locke's semiotic theory was the fountainhead of the transmission model, post-structuralist theories, such as Jacques Derrida's theory of deconstruction, conceptualise communication as a process in which meanings are not fixed by the linguistic system but billow up and float in shifting winds of discourse. In a post-structuralist view, we do not exist independently of signs, with our essentially real personal identities and subjective viewpoints, and "use" signs in order to communicate. We exist meaningfully only in and as signs.

A third, phenomenological tradition conceptualises communication as the experience of self and other in dialogue. Such twentieth-century theorists of dialogue as Martin Buber, Hans-George Gadamer, Emanuel Levinas, and Carl Rogers can be broadly identified with this tradition. The problem of communication for phenomenology, as for semiotics, is that of a gap between subjective viewpoints. One cannot directly experience another consciousness, and the potential for intersubjective understanding is thereby limited. The two traditions approach this problem in quite different ways, however. Whereas semiotics looks to the mediational properties of signs, phenomenology looks to the authenticity of our ways of experiencing self and other. The basis for communication lies in our common existence with others in a shared world that may be constituted differently in experience.

Authentic dialogue requires open self-expression and acceptance of difference while seeking common ground. Barriers to communication can arise from self-unawareness, non-acceptance of difference, or strategic agendas that preclude openness to the other. The phenomenological tradition in modern philosophy stems from Edmund Husserl's transcendental phenomenology, which was an analysis of the essential structure of conscious experience. Husserl's protégé and critic Martin Heidegger, in Zein und Zeit, held that our being has no essence apart from the interpretive self-understanding that unfolds through time as we engage with the particular world in which we find ourselves. This hermeneutic phenomenology influenced subsequent existentialist, hermeneutic, and post-structuralist theories that have emphasised the constitutive properties of dialogue. Dialogue, in these theories, is not a essentially a sharing of pre-existing inner meanings; it is engagement with others to negotiate meaning.

Fourth, a cybernetic tradition of communication theory grew from the mid-twentieth century work of Shannon, Wiener, Gregory Bateson, and a host of other writers in many fields. This is actually one of the newest traditions of communication theory, although, as we have noted, it was the first communication theory explicitly named and widely known as such. Cybernetics conceptualises communication as information processing. All complex systems, including computers and telecommunication devices, DNA molecules and cells, plants and animals, the human brain and nervous system, social groups and organisations, cities, and entire societies, process information, and in that sense communicate. Cybernetic theory downplays the differences between human communication and other kinds of information processing systems. Information storage, transmission, and feedback, network structures, and self-organising processes occur in every sufficiently complex system. Problems of communication can arise from conflicts among subsystems or glitches in information processing like positive feedback loops that amplify noise. Proponents of second-order cybernetics have recast cybernetic theory within a constitutive model of communication. Second-order cybernetics reflexively includes the observer within the system observed and emphasises the necessary role of the observer in defining, perturbing, and, often in unpredictable ways, changing a system by the very act of observing it.

Social psychology, a fifth tradition of communication theory, conceptualises communication as social interaction and influence. Communication always involves individuals with their distinctive personality traits, attitudes, beliefs, and emotions. Social behaviour both displays the influence of these psychological factors and modifies them as participants influence each other, often with little awareness of what is happening. Influence can be essentially a transmission process from source to receiver. If, however, interaction reciprocally changes the participants and leads to collective outcomes that would not otherwise have occurred, communication becomes a constitutive social process. Whether conceived on a transmission or a constitutive model, the problem of communication from a sociopsychological perspective is how to manage social interaction effectively in order to achieve preferred and anticipated outcomes. This requires an understanding, solidly grounded in scientific theory and research, of how the communication process works. Social scientific communication research has always been closely identified with social psychology, so it is not surprising that classic mid-century theories of group dynamics, persuasion, and cognitive dissonance, were quickly absorbed into communication theory, and joined by many later theories in a flow of cross-disciplinary borrowing that continues unabated.

Sociocultural communication theory, which derives from twentieth century sociological and anthropological thought, is a sixth tradition. Sociocultural theory conceptualises communication as a symbolic process that produces and reproduces shared meanings, rituals, and social structures.

As John Dewey noted in *Democracy and Education*, society exists not only by but in communication. That is, society exists not only by using communication as a necessary tool for transmitting and exchanging information. To communicate as a member of society is to participate in those coordinated, collective activities and shared understandings that constitute society itself.

There is a tension in sociocultural theory between approaches that emphasise macro-social structures and processes and those that emphasise micro-social interaction. On the macro side, structural and functionalist views emphasise the necessary role of stable social structures and cultural patterns in making communication possible. On the micro side, interactionist views emphasise the necessary role of communication as a process that creates and sustains social structures and patterns in everyday contexts of social interaction. From either view, communication involves the coordination of activities among social actors, and communication problems are directly manifested in difficulties and breakdowns of coordination. Communication problems have apparently become more pressing and difficult under modern conditions of societal diversity, complex interdependence, and rapid change. A reasonable conjecture from a sociocultural point of view is that communication theory developed in modern society as a way of understanding and addressing this new condition in which communication seems to be at once the disease that causes most of our social problems, and the only possible cure.

A seventh tradition of communication theory, and the last to be discussed here, is a critical tradition that defines communication as a reflexive, dialectical discourse essentially involved with the cultural and ideological aspects of power, oppression, and emancipation in society. Dialectic, like its counterpart rhetoric, was first conceptualised in ancient Greece. In the philosophical practice of Socrates as portrayed in Plato's *Dialogues*, dialectic was a method of argumentation through question and answer that, by revealing contradictions and clarifying obscurities, led the interlocutors to higher truth. The dialectical materialism of Karl Marx initiated the modern conception of dialectic as an inherently social process connecting political economy to cultural practice. In orthodox Marxist theory, ideology and culture were determined by class interests, and dialectic at the level of ideas primarily reflected the underlying struggle between economic classes. Latuer-day Marxism, notably in the mid-twentieth century critical theory of the Frankfort School, has tended to see a larger role, less directly dependent on economic class relationships, for cultural and ideological debate. The goal of critical theory is then to promote emancipation and enlightenment by lifting ideological blinders that otherwise serve to perpetuate ignorance and oppression. More recently, the German social theorist Jürgen Habermas has reconstructed critical theory around key concepts including communicative action and systematically distorted communication. Communicative action, or discourse that seeks mutual understanding, for Habermas inherently involves certain transcendental validity claims that social actors must be free to contest openly in order for authentic communication to occur.

Communication is systematically distorted by power imbalances that affect participation and expression, and critical theory can serve emancipatory interests by reflecting upon the sources of systematically distorted communication. Recent movements in the critical tradition such as postmodernism and critical cultural studies tend to reject both Marxist economic determinism as well as Habermas's universalistic ideal of communicative action, but continue to conceptualise communication in ways that emphasise ideology, oppression, critique, and reflexivity. Post-modernist cultural critique primarily addresses ideological discourses of race, class, and gender that suppress differences, preclude or devalue the expression of certain identities, and limit cultural diversity. In post-modernist theory, ideal communication is not, as it was for Plato, a dialectical discourse that leads the way to higher, universal truths. Post-modernism nevertheless implies a similar model of communication: that of a dialectical discourse that can, if only in limited ways, liberate the participants and expand human possibilities.

These seven traditions include the most prominent intellectual sources that currently influence communication theory but the seven traditions do not, of course, cover the field exhaustively. Ideas about communication are too numerous, diverse, and dynamically evolving to be captured entirely by any simple scheme. The field could certainly be mapped in other ways that would distinguish the main traditions differently. Moreover, no matter how the traditions may be defined, they will not be found to have developed independently of one another. Contemporary theory draws from all of the traditions in various ways but is often hard to classify neatly in any one of them. Blends and hybrid varieties are common. Post-structuralist theory, for example, draws from both semiotics and phenomenology, is often regarded as a kind of rhetorical theory, and has significantly influenced recent sociocultural and critical theory. Similarly, traces of every other tradition of communication theory can be found in recent rhetorical theory. The academic discipline of communication studies has become like a cauldron in which ideas from across the traditions of communication theory are mixed and stirred in different combinations to make intellectual stock for current debates.

1.4 Transmission and Constitutive Models of Communication

In the simplistic transmission model that is so often taken for granted in everyday discourse, communication is conceptualised as a process in which meanings, packaged in symbolic messages like bananas in crates, are transported from sender to receiver. Too often the bananas are bruised or spoiled in transport and so we have the ubiquitous problem of miscommunication: The message sent is not the message received, the sender's meaning does not come across. In order to improve communication, according to this model, we need better packaging and speedier transportation of messages. Good communication is basically a technical problem.

Sophisticated versions of the transmission model acknowledge that ideas cannot literally be put into words and transported. In a cliché expression, meanings are in people, not in words. The English empiricist philosopher John Locke, in his *Essay Concerning Human Understanding*, famously articulated this view. According to Locke, words have no natural meanings. The association of words with ideas in the mind is a voluntary act of the individual person. Although social convention establishes a rough correlation between words and ideas, however conscientiously we follow these conventional rules of language we ultimately have no way of knowing whether the corporeal signs we choose to represent our thoughts will excite similar thoughts in the mind of another person. The inherent limitations of language thus make perfect communication well-nigh impossible. Yet, good communication is imperative; for communication is the bond that holds society together and the conduit through which knowledge is disseminated through society and conveyed to future generations. Locke warned against common abuses of language (such as confusing words with things) and proposed a series of remedies to improve communication.

Variations of the transmission model, whether simplistic or sophisticated, still typify everyday thinking and much of the academic literature about communication, but communication theorists recently have favoured an alternative, constitutive model. According to these critics, the transmission model misleadingly assumes that the essential elements of communication—distinct individuals, their private thoughts and feelings, and technical means of communication (shared codes, channels of transmission, etc.)—must all be fixed in place before the act of communication occurs.

The constitutive model posits instead that the elements of communication, rather than being fixed in advance, are reflexively constituted within the act of communication itself. Communication is defined as an ongoing process that symbolically forms and re-forms our personal identities, our social relations, our common world of meaningful objects and events, our ideas and feelings, and our routine ways of expressing these socially constructed realities. No longer merely a technical question of how to get one's meaning across without distortion, the problem of communication has complex moral and political dimensions in a constitutive model. The field of communication expands to include all aspects of the creation and negotiation of meaning in society.

A constitutive model posits that the social practice of communication is ultimately inseparable from the ideas about communication embedded in ordinary language. The reality of communication as a distinct, meaningful kind of activity is socially created, shaped, and sustained by our routine ways of talking about communication. These ordinary ideas and ways of talking have emerged in history, and the traditions of intellectual thought now designated as "communication theory" have emerged along with them. Communication theory is thus inextricably bound up with the cultural evolution of communication as a social practice.

Formal theories of communication recurrently have drawn from, reflected upon, and influenced the vernacular language of communication, and so the everyday practice of communication. The idea of communication as transmission, emerged in modern Europe as a reflection on practices (related to private property and trade, transportation, empire, the spread of literacy and print media, etc.) that were central to life in bourgeois society, and has been bolstered by subsequent advances in communication technology. Now, as communication theorists have recently argued, the idea of communication as a constitutive social process is emerging as a reflection on practices (related to global interdependence, cultural diversity, ideas of democracy and human rights, etc.) that are becoming central to life in our own world.

Communication theory now shapes its own field of practices, which play an increasingly important role in education and other formal institutions of society. Communication skills, and a savvy awareness of communication techniques, are considered essential to success in business, the professions, public affairs, and personal relationships. We speak of communication in an eclectic terminology drawn from discourses of human relations and therapy, information processing, marketing, and entertainment, as well as rhetoric and the social sciences.

The subtext of current debates in communication theory is a debate on how to shape the language that constitutes the field of communication practices in society. One of the virtues of the constitutive model is that it sensitises us to the political stakes that are always involved in such debates. Every form of communicative practice, including ones that fly the banner of the constitutive model, reflects the perspectives of some social groups more than others. Cultural conservatives, for example, may understandably dislike the constitutive model with its overtones of cultural and moral relativism, while globalising elites may like it for their own reasons.

In the expanded field of communication implied by the constitutive model, rhetoric, depending on how it is defined, may be subsumed as a particular kind of communication, criticised as a misguided outgrowth of the transmission model, or identified with communication as a whole.

1.5 Functions of Communication

Communication can perform a variety of different functions. Persuasion or social influence, socialisation, social support, information processing, conflict, decisionmaking, and entertainment are a few of the more widely studied functions of communication.

Persuasion, a large topic in itself, bonds communication studies to rhetoric in one important way. Aristotle defined rhetoric as the art of discovering the available means of persuasion in any given case. Experimental social psychological research on persuasion and attitude change has often been linked to this Aristotelian tradition and characterised as "scientific rhetoric"—an effort to create a more solid, scientific basis for the art of persuasion. Numerous scientific experiments have investigated the persuasive effects of logical and emotional appeals, one-sided and two-sided arguments, source credibility (or ethos), audience characteristics, media of transmission, and a host of other variables. Social psychological theories have been presented as scientific alternatives to traditional rhetoric. Leon Festinger's theory of cognitive dissonance, for example, not only offered a seemingly new explanatory principle for persuasion but opened entirely new fields of study such as selective exposure (the tendency to seek information that supports one's current attitudes) and self-persuasion (or counter-attitudinal advocacy, as it was uncharmingly called). A more recent line of research has investigated "compliance-gaining" behaviour, the strategies people use to influence each other in interpersonal situations.

With the growing popularity of the human potential movement and associated therapeutic conceptions of communication in the 1960's and 1970s, the traditional focus of communication research on persuasion and social influence processes was criticised. As an alternative to such manipulative, "rhetorical" uses of communication, research was needed to promote more humane and therapeutic functions of communication such as interpersonal bonding, group cooperation, and conflict resolution. Lines of research have developed in each of these areas and have produced substantial bodies of knowledge. One such area, for example, is the study of social support and comforting communication. Some of these studies have investigated behaviours that function to express emotional supportiveness under given conditions, or variables that predict the ability to produce sophisticated comforting messages.

Social scientific communication researchers have often favoured a functional approach because it focuses attention on measurable outcomes of communication, and attempts to explain how outcomes are influenced by variables and processes that occur across a wide range of communicative situations. For example, certain cognitive processes and message characteristics may help to explain the efficiency with which information is gained from communication, whether in the context of a political campaign in the mass media, the socialisation of new members in an organisation, a classroom lesson, or a group discussion among friends.

1.6 Codes, Media and Channels

Codes, media and channels are not so much different kinds of things as they are different perspectives on the same range of phenomena.

Code refers to the way a sign system is structured to constitute a particular correlation of signs to meanings. Medium (in current usage often confused with its Latin plural form, media) refers to a particular configuration of physical, technological, and institutional characteristics that constitute a distinct form of communication such as face-to-face interaction, commercial television, or electronic mail.

Channel refers to a selection from a particular array of options for sending and receiving information. One array of channels comprises the five senses of vision, hearing, touch, etc.; another array comprises the telephone, fax, postal letter, e-mail, or face-to-face interview as options for business communication; still another array might be a set of available television channels. The use of different channels may or may not involve the use of different media and codes for communication.

Language, of course, is a primary code (or, in different perspectives, a medium or channel) of human communication, and is a vast field of research in its own right. The commonplace distinction between verbal and non-verbal channels (or codes) is often criticised by experts in non-verbal communication, who point out that verbal and non-verbal behaviours are closely intertwined and function together in the communication process.

Kinesics (gesture, facial expression, and body movement), proxemics (the use of space), haptics (touch), and paralanguage (vocal pitch, intonation, etc.) are some codes of face-to-face communication that have been studied. On the wider scene of societal culture, every distinguishable field of cultural practice, in so far as it is meaningful, can be said to embody its own particular codes or sign system. Semiotic analysis reveals systematic codes that govern the social meaning of clothing, food, mythic stories, character types in television genres, or kinds of shots in film or video. For example, whether a television scene is filmed in close-up, medium, or long shots can contribute, in conjunction with other codes, to the portrayal of different kinds of social relationships (the longer the shot, the more public the relationship).

A branch of media theory known, in its more extreme formulations, as technological determinism holds that communication media shape our consciousness of the world, and that the dissemination of new media through society can bring about new forms of consciousness and culture.

Marshall McLuhan, undoubtedly the most publicly famous technological determinist, popularised several catch phrases ("the medium is the message," "the Guttenberg galaxy," "the Global Village") that have persisted in common usage. McLuhan speculated that the new electronic media, especially television, were causing cultural and epistemological changes no less profound than the revolutionary changes in consciousness that came with the transition from oral to literate culture and the introduction of the printing press in earlier eras. The simplistic notion that changes in media technology directly cause changes in consciousness has never been widely accepted by communication theorists.

McLuhan's ideas, however, along with the less popularised works of Harold Innis, Walter Ong, and other scholars of media history, continue to stimulate thought on the cultural implications of new communication media. The recent tidal waves of technological change in computing and telecommunications have triggered new waves of speculation on the changes in culture and consciousness that may come in the wake of this so-called digital revolution.

1.7 The Seven C's of Communication

The sevenC's of communication are the necessary and sufficient elements for experiencing communication. They apply to both oral and written and even casual communication. The communication process can be improved especially by using the sevenC's simultaneously. The sevenC's are:

i) Completeness
ii) Conciseness
iii) Consideration
iv) Concreteness
v) Clarity
vi) Courtesy
vii) Correctness.

1.7.1 Completeness

Completeness refers to the extent that a message contains all the facts the reader/listener needs, for the desired reaction. Message receivers desire complete information to their questions. A business message is complete when it contains all the facts, needed or asked for. Assess completeness through the eyes of the receiver.

Some benefits of completeness are given below:

i) They are more likely to bring the desired results.
ii) Additional messages are not required.
iii) Builds goodwill.
iv) It shows concern for others.
v) Avoid litigations due to missing information.
vi) Complete communication is more effective.

To achieve completeness:

i) Provide all necessary information
ii) Answer all questions asked
iii) Give something extra, when desirable.

1.7.2 Conciseness

Conciseness is conveying a message in the fewest possible words. It helps the message stand out. It facilitates emphasis. In business, conciseness saves time and expenses. It focuses on the lead points. To achieve conciseness:

i) Avoid verbosity.
ii) Eliminate repetition.
iii) Be specific/relevant.

1.7.3 Consideration

Consideration refers to the preparation of the message keeping the receiver in mind. This indicates the end-user notion. Fine-tune your message keeping the reader/listener in full vision. This requires being empathic, understanding and sensitive. Ways of indicating consideration are to substitute 'you' for 'our', 'we'. Express interest in the other. Mention positive/ pleasant aspects of the other person Show good ethical judgements. Focus on 'you' instead of 'I' or 'we'.

1.7.4 Concreteness

Concreteness involves being specific, definite and clear as far as possible. Put action into your verbs. Use vivid image-building words.

To achieve concreteness:

i) use words that are specific, definite and vivid.
ii) avoid words that are vague and general. The meaning of words should be direct and explicit.

1.7.5 Clarity

Clarity implies getting the message across clearly. The possibility of misunderstanding is to be eliminated.

To achieve clarity:

i) Choose short, crisp, familiar terms or words.
ii) Construct simple, short but complete and meaningful sentences.
iii) Make it easy to read and listen to.
iv) Use examples and illustrations, whenever possible.
v) Avoid technical and business jargons, as far as possible.

vi) Keep sentences short in length. Make each sentence relevant. Let each sentence lead to the next. Keep the flow of the message going.

vii) Emphasise that which you need to convey in a forceful manner.

1.7.6 Courtesy

Courtesy includes friendly/sincere and pleasant messages. Courteous messages strengthen friendships, builds goodwill. Courtesy builds goodwill and gains new friends. Courtesy involves consideration in the tone of communication.

To achieve courtesy:

i) Be sincerely tactful, thoughtful and appreciative.

ii) Omit expressions that irritate, hurt or belittle.

iii) Grant mistakes and apologise in a good natural way.

iv) Use tact instead of bluntness.

v) Being intentionally blunt or abrupt, implies, discourtesy.

1.7.7 Correctness

Correctness refers to the accuracy and authenticity of the messages. In terms of both content and style correctness needs to be present in all communication. This implies:

i) Use of the right level of a language.

ii) Checking the accuracy of facts/figures.

iii) Maintaining acceptable working mechanics.

iv) Eliminating errors in typing, grammar, etc.

v) Use, of non-evaluating statements.

1.8 Elements of Effective Communication

Communication is the most important skill in life. Successful relationships depend on it, as does success in the workplace.

The ability to effectively communicate with others is an essential skill for everyone. However, the importance of this skill is frequently downplayed, and poor communication behaviour is often justified. Poor communication is frequently a symptom of a problem but seldom a cause. It is a gross generalisation of a highly complex series of interactions between organisations, groups, or individuals requiring both knowledge and learned skills of those attempting to communicate effectively.

Effective communication involves meanings that go beyond words and require an understanding of perceptions, gestures, folklore, and family and community dynamics. All of these elements can affect whether and how well a message is received. When communicating, either by fax, email, telephone, text, memo or letter, the one thing you should ask yourself is 'Can this message or instruction be easily understood by the person receiving it?' Can you be sure that those receiving your message actually understand what you are saying? The most important limitations on people's perceptions are often based on cultural and emotional differences. Most of us, generally speaking, perceive what we expect to perceive. In other words, we see what we expect to see and to a very large extent hear what we want to hear. The fact that the unexpected communication may be resented is not the issue; what often happens is that the message has not actually been received at all. It has been neither seen nor heard. It has been ignored.

When we communicate, there are always demands. Communications demand that the recipient becomes someone, does things and believes something. Effective communication is good for motivation. If the communication gels with the aspirations, the values and the point of view of the recipient, it is a powerful thing. However, if it goes against the goals and ambitions, etc., of that particular individual it is highly likely that the communication will either not be received at all or meet stiff resistance. Throughout the course of history, historians have tried to garner information that identifies the relationships between people based on perceptions of the bits of available information. Most of us who see people regularly in our daily work are often unaware of what we say to others without thinking of what we are actually saying to them.

All communication requires a transmitter or sender and a receiver. If both the transmitter and receiver are tuned to each other, operating properly and without noise or distortion in the system, the message gets through, or at least this is normally true when we are transmitting and receiving electronically. When human beings are involved, however, there is almost always noise and distortion bedeviling the interactive process, often caused by unrecognised differences in spontaneous responses derived from life experiences, lack of knowledge especially cross-cultural knowledge, failure to interpret correctly available clues, inaccurate perception, biases, or failure to differentiate between what someone said and what he/she meant.

1.8.1 Effective Verbal Communication

1.8.1.1 Attitude towards Communication

Your attitude is the first thing people pick up on in face-to-face communication. Just as laughing, yawning, and crying are infectious, attitude is infectious. Before you say a word, your attitudes can infect the people who see you with the same behaviour. Somehow just by looking or feeling, you can be infected by another person's attitude, and vice versa. When you are operating from inside a really useful attitude, such as enthusiasm, curiosity, and humility, your body language tends to take care of itself and sends out unmistakable signals of openness.

1.8.1.2 Effective Speaking

Perhaps the greatest single stumbling block to real communication is the one-sided nature of speaking. Most of us think of "communicating" as a one-way process. Two monologues do not make a dialogue, however. Exchange between you and your targeted prospect is the key to effective communication. So, listening is an active pursuit for selling your ideas. What makes people listen? The three basic factors are:

i) Self-interest;

ii) Who's speaking; and

iii) How they say it.

Understanding the basic principles of how we communicate and why we listen — what works, what doesn't, and why — starts you on the road to a realistic appraisal of what you want to say and how you plan to say it.

1.8.1.3 The Power of Listening

Typically, our education has afforded us the opportunity to study grammar, rhetoric, public speaking, expository writing, or other related skills. However, these output skills of communication alone do not prevent problems of communication, for communication is a two-way street involving input as well. Most of the preoccupation with communication has focused on output and we still find on every hand courses in composition, effective speaking, and the arts of plain and fancy talk. Not surprisingly, experts writing about communication have begun to see that a large part of the problem is caused by faulty listening. As the noted general semanticist S.I. Hayakawa stated some years ago, "It does not avail the speakers to have spoken well if we as listeners have failed to understand, or if we come away believing them to have said things they didn't say at all." Listening is a problem when ineffective, and a source of power and a leadership skill when effective. Improvement in our ability to listen effectively will go a long way in improving communication.

It goes without saying that listening means not just maintaining a polite silence while you rehearse in your mind the speech you are going to make the next time you can grab a conversational opening. Listening also means more than just hearing words. In order to understand someone, you often must make an effort to know what the speaker means in terms of his or her spontaneous responses derived from his or her perceptions and life experiences, and not just in terms of your own spontaneous responses. In his article, "How to Listen to Other People", Hayakawa writes:

"Listening means trying to see the problem the way the speaker sees it—which means not sympathy, which is feeling for him, but empathy, which is experiencing with him. Listening requires entering actively and imaginatively into the other fellow's situation and trying to understand a frame of reference (life experiences) different from your own." Carl Rogers and F. J. Roethlisberger, in their treatment of *Barriers and Gateways to Communication* reiterated the importance of empathetic listening, saying that in order to communicate with understanding you have "to see the expressed idea and attitude from the other person's point of view, to sense how it feels to him, to achieve his frame of reference (based on his life experiences and perceptions) in regard to the thing he (or she) is talking about." recognising the speaker's frame of reference (understanding his or her Perceptions and Life experiences).

The first item of importance to be derived from this concept of effective listening is this: we must occasionally remind ourselves that a speaker may have perspectives quite different from our own and that what he or she means by a statement might be very different from what we would mean if we used the same words! Our common language is such that ordinary words mean different things to different people. It is an unreasonable demand on the part of the listener to expect everyone else to use words with the precise meaning he or she would use, were he or she speaking.

To listen effectively, we must listen reflectively and with empathy. Thus far we have said that communication may be impeded if we fail to allow for the possibility of a speaker having different experiences and perspectives from our own. Empathetic listening requires a sensitivity that goes beyond the speaker's words to get at the meaning behind the words. If we fail to understand the speaker's frame of reference and insist on hearing everything he or she says in terms of our own, the reason may be our mistaken assumption that words, independent of the people who are using them, have unambiguous meaning. It is the listeners job to understand what the speaker means, not what the words mean!

1.8.1.4 Problem of Evaluating the Communication Process

Rogers and Roethlisberger proposed that a major barrier to mutual interpersonal communication is our very natural tendency to judge, to evaluate, to approve (or disapprove) the statement of the other person or the other group. They illustrated the point as follows:

Suppose someone, commenting on this discussion, makes the statement, "I didn't like what the man said." How will you respond? Almost invariably your reply will either be approval or disapproval of the attitude expressed. Either you respond, "I didn't like it either; I thought it was terrible," or else you tend to reply, "Oh, I thought it was really good." In other words, your primary reaction is to evaluate it from your point of view, your own frame of reference.

This is an example of your spontaneous perceptual evaluative filters, derived from your life experiences and perceptions, in action.

By evaluating in this manner, the listener has only brought his or her spontaneous response derived from his or her frame of reference to bear on the matter. Instead of communication with understanding, the interaction consists of two ideas, two feelings, two judgements missing each other in psychological space and in this situation the psychological distance between the two remains unbridged. In the instance noted above, for example, the evaluative response has failed to inform the listener why the person didn't like the discussion or what the discussion apparently meant from his or her point of view.

In order for communication to flow rather than break down, we must be able to understand what the speaker means, and this often means making an attempt to understand his or her meaning and his or her spontaneous responses (life experiences and perspectives) rather than evaluating his or her statements by using our own spontaneous meanings or definitions, derived from our own life experiences and perspectives. Among other things, this implies that listening does not mean waiting alertly for the flaws in the other fellow's arguments so that later you can cut him down. In regard to the tendency to evaluate rather than listen empathetically, Hayakawa (op. cit.) suggests a general rule: "Refrain from agreement or disagreement with a speaker, refrain from praise or censure of his (or her) views, until we are sure that we thoroughly understand what those views are."

1.8.1.5 Pathways to Better Communication

The point has been made that good listening is reflective, empathetic listening: listening with an awareness that the speaker may be operating with different life experiences and perspectives leading to a different set of spontaneous responses or frame of reference, and trying to understand those experiences and perspectives and that set of spontaneous responses or frame of reference in order to glean the speaker's meaning. This doesn't imply that we have to agree with a speaker, rather it suggests that we have to see reflectively and empathetically his or her meaning through his or her eyes before we can agree or disagree. Writers on the subject of effective communication have suggested certain procedures for improving understanding:

i) A good listener does not merely remain silent; he or she asks questions. However, these questions must avoid all implications, whether in tone of voice or in wording, of scepticism or challenge or hostility, i.e., we must avoid putting the speaker in the position of defending his or her perspectives. Our questions must clearly be motivated by curiosity about the speaker's views (and perspectives). Such questions, which may be called "questions for clarification", usually take the form, "Would you expand on that point about...?" or "What exactly is your recommendation again?" or "Would you mind restating that argument about...?"

ii) Before commenting upon a statement, the listener can try to restate to the speaker's satisfaction what the speaker has just said. Hayakawa writes: "Perhaps the most useful kind of question at this stage is something like 'I am going to restate in my words what I think you mean. Then, would you mind telling me if I've understood you correctly?'" or, if talking with someone of more recent vintage, try 'Hey man, let's see if I got that.'

Rogers suggests that as an experiment the reader might do the following: the next time you expect to get into an especially difficult or heated argument with someone, institute this rule for your behavior—"I can speak for myself only after I have first restated the ideas and feelings of the other speaker accurately and to that person's satisfaction." If this is done sincerely, in a true effort to understand not only what the other person says but what he or she feels and what his or her perspectives are, the usual response to this behaviour is that the other person begins to make some effort to understand your point of view.

These techniques in themselves will not guarantee effective listening, but they should help the listener to avoid some of the terminological tangles resulting from incongruent or conflicting spontaneous responses derived from the unique life experiences and perspectives of the speaker and listener that is at the root of poor communication. Recognising and respecting the speaker's frame of reference, can help sidestep the hostilities, resentments and defensiveness that arise through misunderstanding.

Improvement in the quality of listening can go a long way toward avoiding the misunderstandings that often are the basis for ineffective communication. Effective listening is reflective empathetic listening. Before responding to a statement, a listener is advised to be certain he or she has reflectively understood the statement in the speaker's terms. This requires a sensitivity to the speaker's life experiences, perspectives and frame of reference, which may be quite different from the listener's. The listener must be able to see things through the eyes of the speaker before he or she can be sure he or she has understood. Listening empathetically, however, may not be as easily achieved as it might sound. Writers on the subject have noted that in addition to a willingness and the necessary skills, empathetic listening requires courage. As Rogers writes:

> If you really understand another person in this way, if you are willing to enter his private world and see the way life appears to him (or her with his or her life experiences and perspectives) without any attempt to make evaluative judgements (based on your own life experiences and perspectives), you run the risk of being changed yourself (you may modify your own frame of reference). You might see it his (or her) way; you might find yourself influenced in your attitudes or your personality (and your perspectives).

Rogers' point above, that good communication can seem too dangerous, suggests the curious turn of thought that misunderstandings and poor communication, in some circumstances, might be functional for preserving intact our intrinsic perspectives and biases. Writers on the subject of communication typically adopt the point of view that poor communication is a problem everyone laments, and that as far as everyone is concerned, we would be better off with communicative clarity. There are some writers, however, notably Charlotte Kursh, who suggest that it is a mistake to view good communication as a panacea. In her article, "The Benefits of Poor Communication", she challenges the assumption that better communication will necessarily reduce strife and conflict. She writes:

> A better understanding of the situation might serve only to underline the differences rather than to resolve them. Indeed, many of the techniques thought of as bad communication were apparently developed with the aim of bypassing or avoiding confrontation, and some of them continue to be reasonably successful in this aim.

Kursch's point is that the assumption that the attainment of maximum clarity as measured by some more or less objective standard is always in the interest of at least one of the parties to an interaction, and often of both, may not always be correct. The heated rhetorical clashes, with all their implied misunderstandings of each other's position, between, say, the Arabs and the Israelis, may prove quite functional: the speakers might not be at all interested in understanding each other; rather, suggests Kursh, they have their eyes on "pleasing the crowds" that are their constituents. The fuzziness, the lack of clarity, the meaninglessness of the ordinary political speech can be an important tool in getting a working majority-and a consensus, however arrived at, may be vital for the well-being or even existence of a nation.

The possibility that poor communication may be functional is raised not with the purpose of advocating it; rather, it is raised to point out the importance of recognising that the cause of misunderstanding and poor communication may go far beyond the problems of speaking and listening well, to the fundamentally different life experiences and intrinsic values of the individual, group, organisation, or nation thus yielding quite different spontaneous responses. In these circumstances, there is not a problem in communications but a fundamental conflict in deep-rooted life experiences, cultures and perspectives. Where good communication and understanding is called for, skilful reflective listening without making evaluative judgements will go a long way toward accomplishing it.

1.8.2 Effective Non-verbal Communication

1.8.2.1 Congruence between Verbal and Physical Signals

If we are even minimally sensitive, most of us have some skill at interpreting the many sets of signals we receive from facial expressions, hand movements and other body movements exhibited by other people. What people mean, as contrasted with what they are saying, is often most explicitly revealed through complex sets of body language signals. Obvious examples of these "constellations" that most of us, within our own culture, are able to interpret correctly, are:

i) Male-female "magnetism" which results in a complex set of "signals" that may or may not be consistent with the words spoken.

i) An authoritarian boss, "taught" to be a participative manager, signals through grimaces, frowns, changes in eye contact, folding arms, or other body language signs whenever a subordinate, whose ideas he or she does not respect, ventures one.

i) One person involved in an intense conversation with another notices that the other party signals through loss of eye contact, expressions of annoyance, changes in posture and other signs that the psychological distance, and sometimes even the physical distance, between them has increased.

All of these are examples of complete sets of clues that some of us "read" accurately and others, less sensitive to physical manifestations influencing communication, hardly notice. Body language talks; sometimes more clearly than the words we say. If you have ever had the experience of trying to communicate with someone who does not speak your language, and when you are forced to get your message across through gestures and facial expressions, you will begin to understand the power of body language. Or, if you have had to rely on only telephone conversations with an important other person and cannot see their expressions (with consequent miscommunication), or in the case of the blind who have to receive all their signals through interpretation of voice inflection, then you will recognise that these are all manifestations of the importance of physical accompaniments to verbal signals.

Body language is one means of communication; one language among others, including the language we speak, and the language of space, time, and things. It is also largely unconscious and spontaneous. We usually don't particularly notice it, in ourselves or others, and therefore we often miss an important element of the total communication process

These non-verbal messages may either confirm or deny the verbal messages accompanying them (or be neutral or unintended or misinterpreted). As an important part of the total communications package, we need to learn to "read" the complex sets of physical elements in messages sent and to resolve any conflicts we perceive between the physical and verbal signals.

A complication: sets of non-verbal signals vary immensely, not only between individuals but between cultures and in connection with the context of the total communication. Take this ubiquitous symbol in the society:

A smile. What does it mean when it is:

a) accompanied by a gun in your ribs and the admonition to "stick 'em up"?
b) accompanied by the phrase "have a nice day", said routinely by the supermarket checker?
c) preceded by the message from your boss that you have just goofed badly and need to watch your step?
d) exhibited by a used car salesman trying to sell you a clunker?

To complicate matters further, what does a smile mean in different cultures, to say nothing of different kinds of smiles: a thin-lipped smile from a Texas rancher; a toothsome smile from a Japanese businessman; an indulgent smile from a Boston Brahmin dowager; a diffident smile from a shy Pakistani woman; an eye-twinkling smile from an Irishman? These signals are given in interrelated sets or constellations and, in context within our own culture, may be easily "read" by most of us if we pay attention to our spontaneous intuitive responses. Single signs or small sets of other facial and bodily signals are easily misinterpreted, especially if we are unfamiliar with the individual's background and life experiences. Eye contact is an especially difficult aspect of body language to read across different cultures.

How we look and how we are looked at has a lot to do with our needs for approval, acceptance, trust and love — and we usually react accordingly. Looking is a non-tactile way to "touch" another. Looking away or not looking at all is a clear-cut sign of disinterest-of distancing oneself from another. Avoiding eye contact is a way of hiding true feelings, especially discomfort or guilt. People who feel insecure about themselves will avoid eye contact in a threatening situation but seek it when the situation is to their advantage. In such a way, characteristics of self-concept can be expressed through body language. The meanings of eye contact and avoidance differ across culture and social class.

There are many other sets of clues available to the astute observer; we express feelings with our hands, arms, legs, and total body posture. Once again, it is important to emphasise that these clues can be correctly interpreted only in context and only in constellations or large sets. As Holtz puts it: "No position, expression, or movement can be considered in isolation. Communication is a "multi-channel" system. Body language is but one channel, interdependent with our use of time, space, things, and verbal language. For one concerned about more accurate communication and consequent better judgements and decisions, awareness of and increasing skill in interpreting body language appears to be an appropriate and useful adjunct to the tool kit.

1.8.3 Communicating with Time, Space and Status

In his books *The Silent Language*, and *The Hidden Dimension*, the famous applied anthropologist Edward Hall demonstrated graphically how people inhabiting different cultures use time, space and things to communicate messages and how people in those cultures, lacking knowledge of the differences, often miscommunicate. Dealing particularly with the American society, he demonstrated the many ways we send messages non-verbally, and in subsequent years a number of authors have extended his insights and applied them to management. There are two important lessons we can learn from Hall and others who have built on his ideas:

i) People around the world view time very differently than we do; they are equally or even more sensitive to spatial discriminations, and things carry many different messages to people in other parts of the world than they do for us.

ii) Different parts of many countries and different people in the same country often view time, space, and things differently.

1.8.3.1 Dimensions of Time

We have many ways of talking about time. We have time, keep time, buy time and save time; we mark time, spend it, sell it and waste it; we kill time, pass time, take time and make time. In the world of business and industry, we are concerned with overtime and flextime. We speak of "bankers hours" and consider the implications of the four-day work week. We worry about workaholic managers who spend too much time on the job and about malingering workers who spend too little.

In many parts of the world, and particularly in connection with work, junior managers are very concerned about being "on time". And how we handle on-time-ness communicates a good deal about relative status. An executive who has summoned subordinates to a meeting expects them to be on time for the meeting, but is not over-concerned about keeping them waiting if he or she is busy. The subordinates, on the other hand, will often arrive ahead of the time set even if it means they will cool their heels in the boss's waiting room until he or she is ready for them. People of equal status sometimes will use time in somewhat subtle ways to communicate relative status.

The amount of time we are willing to give another person also communicates a message, sometimes positive, sometimes negative. Consider the manager who interacts frequently with subordinates in their offices in a friendly or supportive way, contrasted with the manager who rarely leaves his office and only calls people in to critique their work. Or a boss who spends many hours coaching a subordinate, but gives little time to anyone else in the office. A signal has been given: with positive connotations to the recipient of the manager's time and a negative message to everyone else.

The way different cultures and sub-cultures deal with time is often affected by elements peculiar to the culture. In Spain and Latin America, most work stops for at least two hours in the heat of the afternoon while people enjoy siesta. To make up for the hiatus, work continues until late in the evening and the dinner hour is advanced to 10:00 pm. When visitors from other cultures where a much more relaxed attitude toward timeliness prevails come to the United States, their US hosts may escort them on tightly scheduled visits that fit the hosts' concept of maximising the effective use of time. The visitors often find it difficult to understand why it is necessary to be on time for appointments and find themselves exhausted at the end of a day of rigidly scheduled visits. Lack of sensitivity to other people's ways of viewing time can trap us into inappropriate behaviour toward them. Clearly the ways we handle time communicates many different messages about how we feel; not infrequently unconscious and unintended messages that account for many of the problems in communication between people.

1.8.3.2 Language of Space

We communicate a good deal about ourselves and how we feel about others by how we use space. The best example of this, apparent to all who work in organisations, involves the strong values connected with the size and locations of offices. Although there are sometimes ambiguities caused by purposeful or accidental flouting of the basic values, almost anyone can walk into many plants or offices for the first time and accurately estimate the relative status of those working there by observing the circumstances of their workplace.

There are five basic values that most of us assume when concerned about work space:

1. *More is better than less:* Many a battle has been fought by executives over the size of their offices. While the acute concern felt by most people about office size has its amusing aspects, most organisations have found it expedient to be very exacting about office space that accurately reflects the rank of the person occupying it.

2. *Private is better than public*: Secretaries work in open spaces, junior managers often in cubicles enclosed only by room dividers or in offices with several other inhabitants, while senior managers have private offices where doors can be closed.
3. *Higher is better than lower*: Senior executives usually have their offices in upper floors of office buildings. At the U.S. Department of State in Washington, when people speak about the "seventh floor", they are referring to the offices of the Secretary and Undersecretary. In other organisations, "Let's go upstairs with this" means "Let's go see the boss". Being "kicked upstairs" means an ineffective manager is being given the boot from a sensitive operating position to the implied (but false) status of an empty office in the executive suite.
4. *Near is better than far*: At a large government laboratory, the executive offices are referred to as "Mahogany Row". The Director's suite of offices is at one end of Mahogany Row, the Associate Director's office is next in line and the rank of other executives is directly related to how near their offices are to the Director's.
5. *In is better than out*: We speak of the "in group". An executive's office may be located, for business reasons, far from the seat of power; even, in large organisations, in another city. However, when he or she visits headquarters, if he or she sits near the boss at the conference table, that executive is "in".

While much of the above noted uses of space and the values connected with them are similar to those of other cultures, the needs, values and customs connected with interpersonal space vary considerably from one culture to another. Hall has identified the often fascinating cross-cultural differences, and indeed the differences between people from the same cultures, in regard to their feelings about and behaviour regarding what he calls their "bubble of personal space". Degrees of tolerance for closeness to others varies tremendously between individuals, sometimes related to race or ethnic factors, sometimes to status or social position and sometimes to both.

The phrase "keep your distance" is germane to this phenomenon. While Latin or Arab males frequently embrace or talk nose-to-nose, British and Nordic males prefer to converse, even intimately, at a "respectable" distance. When those of one persuasion intrude on the "territory" of those who feel differently, sometimes amusing and sometimes tragic or dysfunctional results can be observed. In the United States, an insecure manager usually prefers to keep a desk or equivalent space between himself and a subordinate, while perfectly comfortable with closer contact with peers. So, communication can be facilitated or can break down as a consequence of sensitivity to the "proper" uses of space and time.

1.8.3.4 Things Signal Status

People of high status sometimes try to lessen the manifestations of their higher levels in their society by downplaying the importance of things; people of lower status rarely do so. In most cultures, the possession of things connotes status, wealth, education, and taste; all in contrast to things possessed by those less fortunate. Some relish and even flaunt the former; others feel guilty about or wish to hide their good fortune. Those who possess less sometimes want to signal more than they have to the world, for example, the economically deprived individual who drives a Cadillac. Or, we see the opposite, for example, the wealthy individual who prefers a modest home and a "compact" car.

Like time and space, things emit signals that are part and parcel of the complex communication process. People who wish to communicate effectively need to pay as much attention to these signals as to those received from effective listening to verbal messages and knowledgeable observation of sets of clues from body language. People who operate in sub-cultures of the India and in cultures other than our own need to recognise the difficulties in expression verbally, physically and with regard to time, space, and things. People everywhere are extraordinarily sensitive to the values embodied in their cultures. Those who wanted to communicate effectively wiil takes all the facets of communication into account when interacting with individuals and groups and when making important decisions.

1.9 Barriers of Effective Communication

The communication process encompasses every single part of our daily being. The use of both verbal and non-verbal communication is the very basis of how we converse, both on a personal and on a business level. Effective communication is an important process in everyday life. People must be able to communicate effectively with each other on both a personal as well as business level. Breakdowns in the communication processes can lead to benign misunderstandings, or worse, a major disaster.

Communication barriers can arise at any of the stages in the communication process.

i) *At sender level:* During the presentation of the thought or ideas of the message.
ii) *At the encoding level:* During the formulation of the message.
iii) *At the transmission level*: In encoding and sending the message.
iv) *At the receiver's level*: In decoding and receiving the message.
v) *At the feedback level:* During the completion of the communication process.

Recognising barriers to effective communication is a first step in improving communication style. Barriers to communication are of different types. Some of them are discribed below in brief.

1.9.1 Encoding Barriers

The process of selecting and organising symbols to represent a message requires skill and knowledge. Obstacles listed below can interfere with an effective message.

i) *Lack of sensitivity to receiver*: A breakdown in communication may result when a message is not adapted to its receiver. Recognising the receiver's needs, status, knowledge of the subject, and language skills assists the sender in preparing a successful message.

ii) *Lack of basic communication skills*. The receiver is less likely to understand the message if the sender has trouble choosing the precise words needed and arranging those words in a grammatically-correct sentence.

iii) *Insufficient knowledge of the subject*. If the sender lacks specific information about something, the receiver will likely receive an unclear or mixed message. Have you shopped for an item such as a computer, and experienced how some salespeople can explain complicated terms and ideas in a simple way? Others cannot.

iv) *Information overload*. If you receive a message with too much information, you may tend to put up a barrier because the amount of information is coming so fast that you may have difficulty comfortably interpreting that information. If you are selling an item with 25 terrific features, pick two or three important features to emphasise instead of overwhelming your receiver with an information avalanche.

v) *Emotional interference*. An emotional individual may not be able to communicate well. If someone is angry, hostile, resentful, joyful, or fearful, that person may be too preoccupied with emotions to receive the intended message.

1.9.2 Transmitting Barriers

Things that get in the way of message transmission are sometimes called "noise." Communication may be difficult because of noise and some of these problems:

i) *Physical distractions.* A bad cellular phone line or a noisy restaurant can destroy communication. If an e-mail message or letter is not formatted properly, or if it contains grammatical and spelling errors, the receiver may not be able to concentrate on the message because the physical appearance of the letter or e-mail is sloppy and unprofessional.

ii) *Conflicting messages.* Messages that cause a conflict in perception for the receiver may result in incomplete communication. For example, if a person constantly uses jargon or slang to communicate with someone from another country who has never heard such expressions, mixed messages are sure to result. Another example of conflicting messages might be if a supervisor requests a report immediately without giving the report writer enough time to gather the proper information.

iii) *Channel barriers.* If the sender chooses an inappropriate channel of communication, communication may cease. Detailed instructions presented over the telephone, for example, may be frustrating for both communicators. If you are on a computer technical support help line discussing a problem, it would be helpful for you to be sitting in front of a computer, as opposed to taking notes from the support staff and then returning to your computer station.

iv) *Long communication chain.* The longer the communication chain, the greater the chance for error. If a message is passed through too many receivers, the message often becomes distorted. If a person starts a message at one end of a communication chain of 10 people, for example, the message that eventually returns is usually liberally altered.

1.9.3 Decoding Barriers

The communication cycle may break down at the receiving end for some of these reasons:

i) *Lack of interest*. If a message reaches a reader who is not interested in the message, the reader may read the message hurriedly or listen to the message carelessly. Miscommunication may result in both cases.

ii) *Lack of knowledge*. If a receiver is unable to understand a message filled with technical information, communication will break down. Unless a computer user knows something about the Windows environment, for example, the user may have difficulty organising files if given technical instructions.

iii) *Lack of communication skills*. Those who have weak reading and listening skills make ineffective receivers. On the other hand, those who have a good professional vocabulary and who concentrate on listening, have less trouble hearing and interpreting good communication. Many people tune out who is talking and mentally rehearse what they are going to say in return.

iv) *Emotional distractions*. If emotions interfere with the creation and transmission of a message, they can also disrupt reception. If you receive a report from your supervisor regarding proposed changes in work procedures and you do not particularly like your supervisor, you may have trouble even reading the report objectively. You may read, not objectively, but to find fault. You may misinterpret words and read negative impressions between the lines. Consequently, you are likely to misunderstand part or all of the report.

v) *Physical distractions*. If a receiver of a communication works in an area with bright lights, glare on computer screens, loud noises, excessively hot or cold work spaces, or physical ailments, that receiver will probably experience communication breakdowns on a regular basis.

1.9.4 Responding Barriers

The communication cycle may be broken if feedback is unsuccessful.

i) *No provision for feedback.* Since communication is a two-way process, the sender must search for a means of getting a response from the receiver. If a team leader does not permit any interruptions nor questions while discussing projects, he may find that team members may not completely understand what they are to do. Face-to-face oral communication is considered the best type of communication since feedback can be both verbal and non-verbal. When two communicators are separated, care must be taken to ask for meaningful feedback.

ii) *Inadequate feedback.* Delayed or judgmental feedback can interfere with good communication. If your supervisor gives you instructions in long, compound-complex sentences without giving you a chance to speak, you may pretend to understand the instructions just so you can leave the stress of the conversation. Since you may have not fully understood the intended instructions, your performance may suffer.

1.10 Strategies for Effective Communication

While there are many subtleties to communication between people, some basic skills can help you to be a more effective communicator. Some inprotant strategies for effective communication are listed below:

i) *Focus on what you know.* Describe your own feelings rather than evaluating others. Express yourself in terms of information, observations, and specific issues, rather than making assumptions about other people or situations.

ii) *Focus on the issue, not the person.* Try not to take everything personally, and similarly, express your own needs and opinions in terms of the job at hand. Solve problems rather than attempt to control others. For example, rather than criticising a co-worker's personality, express your concerns in terms of how to get the job done more smoothly in the future.

iii) *Be genuine rather than manipulative.* Be yourself, honestly and openly. Be honest with yourself, and focus on working well with the people around you, and acting with integrity.

iv) *Empathise rather than remain detached.* Although professional relationships entail some boundaries when it comes to interaction with colleagues, it is important to demonstrate sensitivity, and to really care about the people you work with. If you don't care about them, it will be difficult for them to care about you when it comes to working together.

v) *Be flexible towards others.* Allow for other points of view, and be open to other ways of doing things. Diversity brings creativity and innovation.

vi) *Value yourself and your own experiences.* Be firm about your own rights and needs.

vii) Undervaluing yourself encourages others to undervalue you, too. Offer your ideas and expect to be treated well.

viii) *Present yourself as an equal rather than a superior.* Even when you are in a position of authority, focus on what you and the other person each have to offer and contribute to the job or issue.

ix) *Use confirming responses.* Respond to other in ways that acknowledge their experiences.

x) *Thank them for their input.* Confirm their right to their feelings, even if you disagree. Ask questions, express positive feeling; and provide positive feedback when you can.

xi) *Be consistent between verbal and non-verbal cues.* Non-verbal cues tend to be more convincing than verbal messages. For example, if you are expressing a serious concern to someone, do not grin broadly while discussing it, or the listener may not know whether to take you seriously or not.

1.10.1 Strategies for Effective Listening

i) *Stop.* Focus on the other person, their thoughts and feelings. Consciously focus on quieting your own internal commentary, and step away from your own concerns to think about those of the speaker. Give your full attention to the speaker.

ii) *Look.* Pay attention to non-verbal messages, without letting yourself be distracted. Notice body language and non-verbal cues to allow for a richer understanding of the speaker's point. However, avoid getting distracted from the verbal message.

iii) *Listen.* Listen for the essence of the speaker's thoughts: details, major ideas and their meanings. Seek an overall understanding of what the speaker is trying to communicate, rather than reacting to the individual words or terms that they use to express themselves.

iv) *Be empathetic.* Imagine how you would feel in their circumstances. Be empathetic to the feelings of the speaker, while maintaining a calm centre within yourself. You need not be drawn into all of their problems or issues, as long as you acknowledge what they are experiencing.

v) *Ask questions.* Use questions to clarify your understanding, as well as to demonstrate interest in what is being said.

1.10.2 Strategies for Improved Perception

i) *Analyse your own perceptions.* Question your perceptions, and think about how they are formed. Check in with others around you regularly, and be aware of assumptions that you are making. Seek additional information and observations. You may just need to ask people if your perceptions are accurate.

ii) *Observe carefully and attentively.* Look for detail, but keep the bigger picture in mind. For instance, it is important not to ignore or glossover the details of a situation or the subtle aspects of a person. However, it is important to see any one moment as part of a larger context. People have lives outside of work, for example, and any small part of a project ultimately is linked to a system much larger than itself.

iii) *Interpret consciously*. Recognise the meanings you attach to what you perceive, and know that not everyone will attach the same meanings to the same things or situations. Ask yourself why you associate those meanings with what you do.

iv) *Work on improving your perception*. Increase your awareness of barriers to perception, and which ones you tend towards. Check in with yourself regularly. Seek honest, constructive feedback from others regarding their perceptions of you as a means of increasing your selfawareness.

v) *Focus on others*. Develop your ability to focus on other people, and understand them better by trying to gather knowledge about them, listening to them actively, and imagining how you would feel in their situation.

1.11 Areas of Communication Study

As an essential part of human activities, communication invites study, study which provides us with insights into ourselves as human beings. The complexities of the field, as do the complexities of any area, lead us to divide it into smaller units. These divisions are made more for convenience, though, than in recognition of any clear-cut boundaries. When we speak of "areas of communication", we are talking about the different contexts in which communication may occur. The following are not an exhaustive listing of areas of communication study, but they provide a survey of the different ways in which we may approach the study of communication.

1.11.1 Public Communication

Perhaps the best known area of communication, and certainly one of the first ones studies, is public communication or public speaking. This communication is marked by an individual addressing an audience which may number from several to thousands. Examples of public speaking are political speakers and speakers at service organisations, convocations, lectures, religious services, and dedication ceremonies.

Public speaking was a topic of high important to the Greeks 2,400 years ago, and the people who wrote then are still studied today for what they can tell us about the process of communication. Plato and Aristotle were the most important of these people, but they were only two of a number of people talking about talk and how we influence each other through communication. One of their main concerns was how cases should be argued in courts of law. Aristotle provided us with a classic description of rhetoric when he labelled it as "the faculty of discovering in any given case the available means of persuasion". Another way of phrasing this idea is to say that rhetoric is "finding all the available means of persuasion in a given situation." The study of communication and rhetoric has extended in an unbroken line from that time to this.

Public speaking is an integral part of our lives. Most professions, be they technical or artistic, will demand that we make presentations to audiences. Architects show plans to clients. Agronomists tell farmers of developments in seeds. Financial officers diagnose their company's fiscal health. The study of public communication puts us in front of audiences, develops confidence, and makes us aware of the importance of organising our thoughts well for effective communication.

Scholars in rhetoric and public communication look, naturally enough, at public discourse. These may be examined from an historical context in which one studies the forces that produced the speech, or they may be studied from other viewpoints such a style, type, or philosophy. In looking at speeches and speaking, rhetorical scholars look at the processes by which we accommodate ourselves to our changing political and intellectual environments. Rhetorical scholars are interested in what one calls "adjusting ideas to people and people to ideas". This view of rhetoric allows us to examine such diverse areas as presidential rhetoric, ceremonial rhetoric, and social movements.

1.11.2 Interpersonal Communication

When we deal with people individually or in small groups, we engage in what is generally designated interpersonal communication. Interpersonal communication could include such situations as talking with a friend, going through a job interview, arguing with a roommate, negotiating with sales personnel, and comforting a friend or family member. Interpersonal communication is often labelled dyadic communication since much of it is between two people. Three people communicating would, naturally enough, be triadic communication.

Numerically, the next step is interpersonal communication is small group communication. Small groups may form for a number of purposes. some, such as social groups, exist for the sake of the relationships within the group while other small groups exists primarily for the accomplishment of tasks. Sales meetings, quality circles, board meetings, and study groups, and even bridge foursomes and tailgate parties would qualify as small groups.

Interpersonal communication research examines how we respond top each other in various settings and under varying conditions. Studies might detail the kind of communication that goes on between friends between married couples, between superiors and subordinates, and between parents and children. Studies might also look at how we communication through the way we use our bodies or the way in which we learn how to take turns in conversations. Those interested in small groups might study the lifecycles of groups as they form, function, then disband. Others examine the patterns of communication within groups or how groups contribute to a larger whole such as a business or organisation, an approach closely linked to organisational communication.

1.11.3 Organisational Communication

Organisational communication centers on the process of sending, receiving, and interpreting messages within and between organisations. As W. Charles Redding has observed, organisations consist of interdependent, goal-oriented activities of people who work together within a system or rules, norms, and routines. People band together in organisation to accomplish their purposes: businesses make money and service organisations relieve problems. Goals, however, are not always singular or explicit. To achieve their objectives, organisational members perform a variety of tasks, one that are linked to the activities of other members. The size of organisations may range from small, such as a neighbourhood day care center, to a multinational corporation.

Another important aspect about organisations is that they are formed and maintained through communication. In effect, an organisation has a life of its own. The activity of organising continues even when particular individuals leave or retire from a company. Organisations rely on communication and the coordination of activities to form work units that change over time. Large corporations such as Ford, Exxon, RCA, and Beatrice have employed thousands of people and experienced many changes in their operations, but these businesses typically survive despite the inflow and outflow of people. Hence, organisation are dynamic activities rather than static collections of people.

Studies in organisational communication focus on many elements of the organising process. Areas of study include modes and channels of communication, interaction between superior and subordinates, and formal and informal relationships among organisational members. Other researchers look at the use of communication to socialise new members, to make decisions, to resolve conflicts, and to shape the environment and climate of organisations. Who uses written communication and who uses face-to-care communication and for what type of messages? With the proliferation of personal computers and computer networks, researchers now study the influence of computer interaction on the communication patterns of an organisation.

Organisations require constant adjustments of people, resources, and goals. Thus, mediation and conflict management are a large part of the study of organisational communication. Communication in organisations also establishes a sense of "culture' through sharing stories of organisational events, using particular language patterns such as military or technical jargon, and telling tales of company history. This culture may reflect an atmosphere or climate which casts an organisation as "a big happy family", "a dull sweatshop", or even "a strange zoo". Communication is also an integral part of the process organisations go through as they shape and adapt to their external environments.

1.11.4 Mass Communication

Another major area of communication and communication study is mass communication. Two major considerations determine whether or not communication is considered mass communication. The first, and most obvious, is that mass communication involves large numbers of people. Instead of a personal audience or a small group, or even a large audience for a public speech, mass communication reaches far more people and is audience is dispersed rather than collected in one place. While hundreds or even thousands may come together for a public speech, thousands more can watch a newscast without leaving their homes.

The second major characteristic of mass communication is that it is mediated communication. something comes between the sender and the final receiver of the message. Rather than the first-hand directness of interpersonal communication, mass communication distances senders and receivers. The "something" that comes between sender and receiver is both mechanical and human. Mass communication is dependent on both senders and receivers possessing the appropriate technology such as cameras, tape, film, editing equipment and receiving equipments (radios, television sets, etc.). Mass communication also imposes the shaping consciousness of a third party between the event and the receiver.

We can see the mediation process in mass communication by following a typical story. A reporter attends a meeting to report the university's board of trustees' decision on an important issue such as raising tuition. The television tape of the meeting is edited, the reporter writes the commentary, and the board's decision is recounted in a minute or so of the evening news. People watching the programme receive the news of the meeting but do it through a television set rather than obtaining the information directly from the reporter. Further, the account of the meeting has been shaped by the perceptions of the reporter and the format of television news. this is not to say that the reported story is untrue, but that, rather, the story will necessarily reflect one viewpoint of the many available.

A great deal of discussion has been generated in the study of mass communication on the influence of the medium on its audience and on society. Numerous studies have been done, for example, on the effects of television violence on people who watch such programming. Other researchers examine how people use mass communication, what needs it satisfies in people's lives. Others look at how messages are shaped by the medium. Some study the effect of mass media on society. Studies, for example, have determined that the more people watch television, the more they think they are likely to be the victim of a crime.

On a broader scale, Marshall McLuhan's well know claim that "the medium is the message" suggests that the advent of electronic mass communication in our society has had more impact on us than all the individual messages communicated through the medium. Other scholars focus on the impact of these individual messages. For example, many claim that much of the opposition to the Vietnam war arose because the American public saw the gore and bloodshed of the fighting in color on the evening news.

1.11.5 Public Affairs and Issue Management

Coming into prominence is another area of communication studies, public affairs and issue management. The field is allied to public relations but is much larger than the techniques of running campaigns and writing press releases. Issue management is an outgrowth of the traditional study of rhetoric.

Public affairs and issue management investigates how organisation affect and are, in turn, affected by aspects of the communicative environment. Some of these aspects include government regulatory agencies, politicians, consumers, competitor, and other organisations. The area studies how organisations seek to adjust to the demands of their publics and how they seek to adjust the publics' views of the organisations. Organisations may be for-profit or not-for-profit and in corporate, political, and private contexts.

An oil tanker runs aground in Alaska and dumps thousands of gallons of crude oil into the ocean, polluting the ocean, destroying wildlife, and fouling the beaches. The oil company responds to the situation as do the municipal, state, and federal governments and environmental groups. Issue management would examine the ways in which each of these groups defines the situation and how each group argues for and counterargues to convince the public of the rightness of its stance.

While much of the work in public affairs and issue management is in reaction to crises of various kinds, not all is reactive. One aspect of issue management involves planning ahead to help shape public opinions in the direction desired by the organisation. A hospital, for example, might foresee a need for a routine raise in revenue because of projected rises in salaries, maintenance costs, supplies, and equipment. Prior to raising its charges, the hospital would make a strong effort to explain its situation to the community via press releases, seminars, speeches, and newsletters. The communication could stress the high quality of the hospital's care, its dedication to maintaining high standards, and the rising cost of providing quality health care. If the campaign were successful, the public would be more accepting of the increased charges than if the charges were put into effect with no explanation.

1.11.6 Performance Studies

The last area of study we will discuss is performance studies which, like public speaking, is one of the oldest areas of communication. Besides writing the Rhetoric, Aristotle also wrote a *Poetics* in which he examined how we are moved emotionally when we watch stories being enacted. "Performance" in the sense of "performance studies" means those ways of behaving that are set apart from ordinary communication and are "preceded by rehearsal or preparation". Theatre is, of course, an area of performance study, but performance goes much further than the formalities of the stage. We perform in various ways in our own lives. We tell jokes. We recount our experiences imitate people to make a point about how our day went. Religious life is permeated by performance be it in sermons, testimonials, or the celebration of the mass.

One area of performance study is oral interpretation, the performance of literature. The performer studies and empathises with a poem, an essay, or a work of fiction. The performer then reads or recites the literature in a way that the audience understands the ideas and emotions of the piece. Research in performance studies may examine how performers approach different kinds of literature and the demands of different types of literature. Others in the field examine how performance is used in daily life, how gender affects performance, and how folklore is created and transmitted.

1.11.7 Current Trends in Communication Studies

The discipline of communication has grown enormously in recent decades and continues to evolve. Some of the more important current trends in communication studies can be encapsulated in four emerging themes: technology, culture, discourse, and practice.

The first theme is technology. The present era is one of dizzying technological change, so rapid that we lack a conceptually stable language with which to describe it. Information has become a fungible commodity, transferable from any medium to any other. Twenty years ago the television and the telephone were clearly two distinct technologies. Twenty years from now the proliferating array of telecommunication devices may be classified quite differently.

Technological change is reshuffling the levels and functions of communication. Competence and critical awareness in the use of new media become important goals of communication education, but the contents of this learning are difficult to codify and expensive to keep up to date. Every tradition of communication theory is challenged to conceptualise new technology. The rhetoric of visual images, the phenomenology of virtual reality, the social psychology of e-mail, sociocultural community in cyberspace, and, perhaps most importantly, critical analysis and debunking of the ideology underlying much of the hype that currently surrounds technology, become topics for investigation.

A second emerging theme is culture. Culture converges with technology in critical cultural studies of technological practices, ethnographic studies of virtual communities, and so on. But culture is also an important theme in its own right. With increasing global interdependence, cultural diversity and change become visible everywhere and raise inescapable questions. Cross-cultural diffusion raises questions of neo-imperialist cultural domination. Intercultural communication loses its distinct character as we become more aware of the interplay of cultural identity and difference in all communication. Gender, class, racial, ethnic, and national identities are always at stake, whether in media representations or workplace interactions. The performance of these identities, and their often subtle negotiation, become critical elements of communicative practice in multicultural societies.

Much traditional communication theory and research has been implicitly ethnocentric and patriarchal. "We" studied the communication behaviour of males, and occasionally of females in comparison with a male standard, and seldom questioned whether such categories might be defined differently except in "other" cultures. This approach is no longer intellectually or politically acceptable. Traditional ethnographic studies of communication in various cultural communities continue to be important. But every branch of communication studies is now challenged to address the cultural dimensions of communication and to recognise its own constitutive role in the production of culture.

A third trend is to conceptualise communication as discourse. Discourse is language in use, or more broadly, the interactive production of meaning. The theme of discourse is significant in several dimensions. In one dimension it represents an effort to understand in greater detail the process by which communication actually occurs, beyond merely summarising the process in abstract models and categories. It is no longer enough to count the number of experts who appear on television talk shows or to classify the types of advice they provide. The trend now is to ask exactly how "expertise" is constituted in the discourse among participants on stage and in the audience, and how this negotiation of the expert role relates to other discourses on matters such as legitimate knowledge and authority, selfhood, and the boundary between private and public spheres. In another dimension, discourse represents a point of convergence between rhetoric and other traditions of communication theory. It brings a rhetorical perspective to our understanding of forms of communication that were not traditionally thought of as rhetoric. And it enriches the rhetorical perspective with insights and techniques from pragmatics, conversation analysis, cultural studies, and other fields. In a third dimension, discourse represents a movement toward understanding communication as practice—that is, as meaningful, situated, morally accountable action.

Practice, then, is a fourth theme that encapsulates current trends in communication. In recent years it has become more academically respectable—and more intellectually interesting—to admit that communication is a practical discipline. Throughout the field, applied studies, critical studies, community-based action research, attention to normative, ethical, and educational issues, and, in general, the idea that academic work ought to address socially relevant practical concerns, are both more common and more esteemed in high places than they used to be. The forces that have contributed to this shift are numerous, but the tradition of rhetoric as a practical art within communication studies is surely one of them. Contrary to what might be expected, the trend toward practice has not been accompanied by a rejection of theory.

Communication theory is now flourishing as never before. Rather, the traditional separation of practice from theory has been challenged by alternative views. Some of those alternative views have been informed by an Aristotelian tradition of practical philosophy in which the art of rhetoric was closely associated with political praxis. In this tradition, practice requires judgement as well as skill, and both judgement and skill can be informed and cultivated with the help of theory that is specifically designed to serve those ends. The challenge to communication studies is not to elevate practice over theory, but to develop more practical theories for the cultivation of better and more reflective communication practices.

Communication theory has sometimes aspired to transcend the mundane. Communication on a very abstract plane is universal. Planet and moon, flower and bee, lover and beloved, all communicate. All exist in reciprocal relations. All emit and respond to signals according to laws of physics and laws of information. Cybernetics reveled in such analogies, which inspired visions of a fundamental communication theory to rival the theories of Newton and Einstein.

If that mid-twentieth century vision was grandiose, the reality has been grand enough in some ways. The abstract model of communication as information and signal transmission is a hallmark of the Information Age. It has been usefully applied in engineering and science, biology, psychology, and social science. Ironically, its role in the theory and practice of human discourse has been more limited and may even have diminished, relatively speaking, despite the current vogue of communication technology and the associated efflorescence of cyber-talk. In a transmission model of communication, human interaction is merely one among many examples of information processing, less attractive to science than others, perhaps, because it is so complex and difficult to analyse. In the constitutive model that communication theorists now tend to prefer, information theory is merely one among many examples of metadiscourse, one way of constituting "communication" within the act of communication.

Practical metadiscourse, or reflexive discourse-about-discourse, occurs abundantly in human interaction. In everyday conversation, "the second point I want to make" could be a bit of metadiscourse used to bracket and introduce a segment of talk. "That's a promise" could be a bit of metadiscourse used to constitute what has just been said as a promise. "There was too much noise in the channel" could be a bit of metadiscourse used to make an excuse for a failure of communication. That last example happens to draw from the language of information theory. It illustrates one way in which theoretical metadiscourse—the formal discourse of communication theory—can be used in practical metadiscourse. Theory becomes a resource for constituting communication as an object of discussion in a particular way, for some practical purpose.

The entire field of communication—the discourse about models of communication, traditions of communication theory, disciplines, functions, codes, media, levels, contexts, technology, culture, discourse, and practice—is a vast metadiscourse that constitutes "communication" as an object for systematic study and critical reflection for many different purposes. Of the various ways in which rhetoric can be related to communication, one of the most currently useful may be to conceptualise communication theory as a rhetoric of communication. Classical rhetorical theory, provides a rich storehouse of topical categories, lines of argument, and figures of speech useful for crafting persuasive messages on public affairs. Rhetorical stases assist the communicator in defining the issues under dispute in a given situation, and rhetorical topoi assist in finding arguments with which to address those issues.

Just as rhetorical theory provides resources for participating in discourses on public affairs, communication theory provides resources for practical metadiscourse, that is, for participating in discourses on communication. This suggests one way of connecting communication theory to practice: Communication theory is to the practice of communication as rhetorical theory is to the practice of public affairs. Rhetorical theory can affect public affairs indirectly, by informing what Thomas B. Farrell has called the norms of rhetorical culture—the climate of beliefs and habits that shapes the discourses in which we negotiate and conduct public affairs. So, communication theory can affect the practice of communication in society indirectly, by informing the practical metadiscourse in which we negotiate and conduct communication. Thus, academic communication studies, including rhetorical studies, can participate actively in societal discourses that ultimately constitute what we might call the norms of communicative culture.

Selected References

Arnold, Carroll C., and John Waite Bowers, (eds.), *Handbook of Rhetorical and Communication Theory*, Boston, 1984.

Barnouw, Erik, et.al., (eds.), *International Encyclopedia of Communications*, New York and Oxford, 1989.

Berger, Charles R., and Steven H. Chaffee, (eds.), *Handbook of Communication Science*, Newbury Park, California, 1987.

Bittner John, *Fundamentals of Communication*, Prentice Hall, Englewood Cliffs, 1985.

Burgoon Michael, et.al., *Human Communication,* Sage Publications, London, New Delhi, 1994.

Carey, James. W., *Communication as Culture: Essays on Media and Society*. Winchester, Massachusetts, 1989.

Hauser, Marc D., *The Evolution of Communication*, Cambridge, Massachusetts, 1996.

McQuail Dennis, *Communication*, Longman, London and New York, 1984.

Pilotta, Joseph J., and Algis Mickunas, *Science of Communication: Its Phenomenological Foundation*, Hillsdale, New Jersey, 1990.

2

Process of Communication

Communication is central to all human social behaviour. Humans cannot socially interact unless they communicate through shared symbols. Through sharing common symbols, people can communicate information, ideas, and emotions. Individuals use symbols—words, gestures, pictures—to transmit messages-information, ideas, emotions—to others. When people give similar meanings to the symbols, they communicate. Similar meanings arise from a common social and cultural background. The members of a community service club have a common social and cultural background. The service club members have shared many experiences. The meanings which they assign to word, gesture, and picture symbols are likely to be quite similar.

Communication covers a wide topic area. Any definition of a topic as broad as communication would be too general, too complex, or too fragmented to be of much use to a community leader. We can explain various aspects of communication with definitions, but they would not be unified. One way to define communication is to explain the process of communication. Applying the term process to communication means that it is an ongoing event. In our social interaction with others, we are communicating. Communication, therefore, is the process whereby we attempt to transmit our thoughts, ideas, wishes, or emotions to others.

The goal of communication is the acceptance of the sender's message by the receiver. If the receiver understands the meaning of a message which asks for action, but fails to act, the goal of communications is not achieved. But if the receiver does respond to the message by taking the appropriate action, the goal of the communication has been achieved.

Communication is not something that one person does to another person. Communication is a continuous, ever-changing, circular, process of interaction. Over the years, many theorists have developed models of communication. Communication models give us a way to visualise, or make more concrete, an abstract process. They simplify the complexities of communication. They help us to understand the important components of the communication process and the relationships among them.

The significant elements of the communication process include the source, message, channel, receiver, feedback, noise, and context or environment. The process of communication cannot function effectively and efficiently if problems or barriers exist in any one of these elements of the model. A source transmits a message through a channel to a receiver.

The source brings to the communication event her communication skills, her attitudes, her knowledge, the social system to which she belongs, and her culture. The source encodes, or creates the message by putting ideas into words and actions. The message includes verbal elements (content) and non verbal elements (delivery)—what the speaker says and how she says it. The message must have qualities that will lead the receiver to perceive the meaning the source intended. Hence, words, phrasing, and the way they are organised become significant aspects of the verbal message. Additionally, the way that sources use their voice and body become important aspects of the non verbal message.

Channel refers to the means by which the message gets from sender to receiver. Some theorists conceptualise the channels as one's senses. Although each person may use them differently, each of us who is not sensory impaired communicates through all five senses: sound, sight, touch, smell, taste. When you hear someone speak, you use the aural or sound channel. When you look at the speaker's facial expressions, you use your sight. When you shake the speaker's hand afterwards, you use touch to convey meaning. When you smell the speaker's cologne, you use another channel. When you eat the refreshments the speaker has provided, you use your sense of taste. Other theorists consider channels as the technology used to deliver the message, for example the air waves (for face-to-face oral communication), the telephone line, the internet, the written channel, or a human intermediary. From this perspective, the channel is the medium which carries the message from source to receiver. Communication is likely to be more effective if multiple senses are involved and the medium has the capability to convey the intended meaning.

The receiver, like the source, brings to the communication situation all of his or her communication skills, attitudes, knowledge, social system, and culture. The receiver decodes, or translates, the source's message attaching meaning and understanding to the message (verbal and nonverbal). When the source and receiver differ significantly in their frame of reference (for example, in attitudes, knowledge, social system, and culture), the decoding process is likely to result in messages different from the ones intended. While decoding or processing the message, the receiver then becomes the source of a new message by providing feedback.

Feedback is any verbal or non verbal response to a source: a question from the audience, a puzzled look, nods of agreement. If receivers do not provide feedback (or sources do not allow or pay attention to feedback) the effectiveness of the communication process decreases.

Noise is anything that interferes with the process. Noise may be external or internal to the receiver. External noise is sometimes referred to as physical noise because it presents a physical barrier that prevents the message from getting through to the receiver. For example, if someone else coughs and the audience fails to hear part of the message, the noise is external to the listener. Internal noise can be physiological or psychological. If a listener is distracted by a thought about lunch or an up-coming exam (psychological noise), a lack of concentration will interfere with reception of the speaker's message. If the listener has a cold and her ears are "stopped up" the physiological problem might interfere with the reception of the message.

One cannot consider a communication event without taking into account the role of the context. The context or environment is the situation in which the communication occurs and includes the physical context, social context, number of people involved, relationship of participants, surrounding events, culture, rituals, and noise.

The physical context is the place in which the communication occurs. Think for a moment about listening to a local politician in the football stadium parking lot after a game versus listening in a convention hall. The temperature outdoors, the time of day, the surrounding people, and the accompanying activities all affect your reception of the message.

The social context can influence communication. If you are asked to "say a few words", the social expectations will be different at a fund raising dinner for the local Humane Society than at a going-away party for a co-worker. Such factors as the level of formality, use of appropriate language, familiarity with the audience members, use of humour, content of the message, appropriate dress, and other factors may be influenced by social context.

2.1 A Linear View of Communication Process

In the early days of studying communication as a social science, researchers created models to illustrate the communication process. Their first attempts resulted in a linear communication model, which depicts communication as something a sender 'does to' a receiver. According to the linear model in Figure 2.1, asender (the person creating the message) encodes (puts thoughts into symbols, usually words) a message (the information being transmitted), sending it through a channel (the medium through which the message passes) to a receiver (the person attending to the message) who decodes (makes sense of the message), while contending with noise (distractions that disrupt transmission).

The widespread use of this model has affected the way we think and talk about communication. There is a linear, machine like quality to familiar phrases such as "We're having a communication breakdown" and "I don't think my message is getting through."

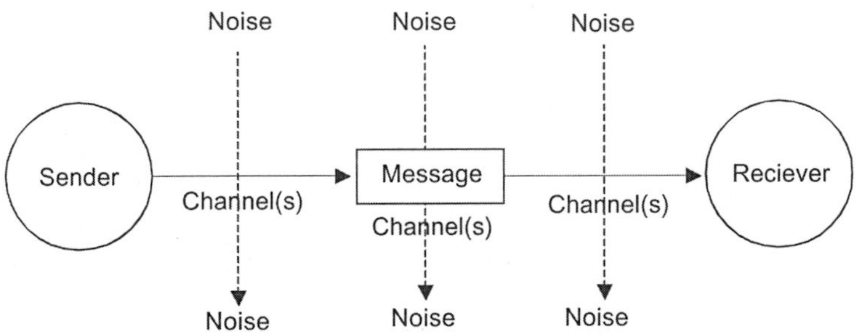

Figure 2.1. Linear communication model

These familiar phrases (and the thinking they represent) obscure some important differences between mechanical and human communication. Does interpersonal communication really "break down," or are people still exchanging information even when they're not talking to each other? Is it possible to "get a message through" to someone loudly and clearly, but still not get the desired reaction? Here are some other questions to consider about the 'shortcomings of the linear model:

i) When you're having a conversation with a friend, is there only one sender and one receiver, or do both of you send and receive messages simultaneously?

i) Do you purposely encode every message you send, or are there behaviours you engage in unconsciously that still communicate messages to others?

i) Does communication take place in a vacuum, or is a message's meaning affected by larger factors such as culture, environment, and relational history?

These and other questions have led scholars to create models that better represent communication.

2.2 Transactional Communication Process

A transactional communication model updates and expands the linear model to better capture communication as a uniquely human process. Some concepts and terms from the linear model are retained in the transactional model, while others are enhanced, added, or eliminated.

The transactional model uses the word communicator instead of sender and receiver. This term reflects the fact that people send and receive messages simultaneously and not in a unidirectional or back-and-forth manner, as suggested by the linear model. A transactional model also shows that communicators often occupy different environments—fields of experience that affect how they understand others' behaviour. In communication terminology, environment refers not only to a physical location but also to the personal experiences and cultural background that participants bring to a conversation.

Consider just some of the factors that might contribute to different environments:

i) Person A might belong to one ethnic group and person B to another.

ii) A might be rich and B poor.

iii) A might be rushed and B have nowhere to go.

iv) A might have lived a long, eventful life and B might be young and inexperienced.

v) A might be passionately concerned with the subject and B indifferent to it.

Notice how the model in Figure 2.2 shows that the environments of individuals A and B overlap. This area represents the background that the communicators have in common. As the shared environment becomes smaller, communication becomes more difficult.

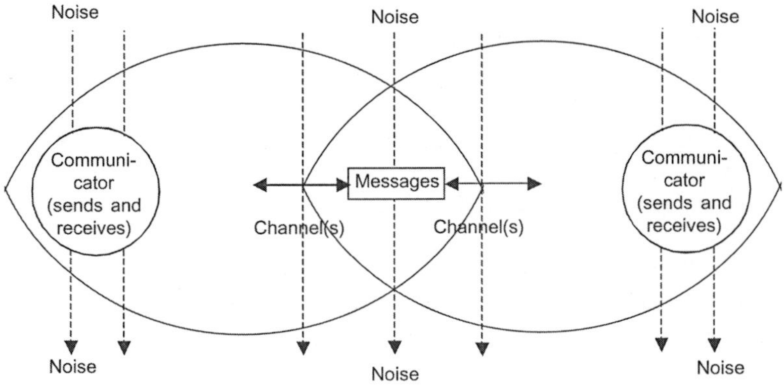

Figure 2.2. Transactional communication model

Consider a few examples in which different perspectives can make understanding difficult:

i) Bosses who have trouble understanding the perspective of their employees will be less effective managers, and workers who do not appreciate the challenges of being a boss are more likely to be uncooperative (and probably less suitable for advancement).

ii) Parents who have trouble recalling their youth are likely to clash with their children, who have never known and may not appreciate the responsibility that comes with parenting.

iii) Members of a dominant culture who have never experienced how it feels to be "different" may not appreciate the concerns of people from minority co-cultures, whose own perspectives make it hard to understand the cultural blindness of the majority.

Communication channels retain a significant role in the transactional model, as they did in the linear model. Although it is tempting to see channels simply as neutral conduits for delivering a message, a closer look reveals the important role they play.

The transactional model also retains the concept of noise but with a broader focus. In the linear model, the focus is on noise in the channel what is known as external noise. For instance, loud music or too much cigarette smoke in a crowded room might make it hard for you to pay attention to another person. The transactional model shows that noise also resides within communicators. This includes physiological noise, which involves biological factors that interfere with accurate reception: illness, fatigue, hearing loss, and so on. Communicators can also encounter psychological noise: forces within that interfere with the ability to understand a message accurately. For instance, a student might become so upset upon learning that she failed a test that she would be unable to understand clearly where she went wrong.

Transactional communication isn't something that we do to others; rather, it is an activity that we do with them. In this sense, person-to-person communication is rather like dancing—at least the kind of dancing we do with partners. Like dancing, communication depends on the involvement of a partner. And like good dancing, successful communication doesn't depend only on the person who takes the lead. A great dancer who forgets to consider and adapt to the skill level of his or her partner can make both people look bad. In communication and dancing, having even two talented partners doesn't guarantee success. When two skilled dancers perform without coordinating their movements, the results feel bad to the dancers and look foolish to an audience. Finally, relational communication—like dancing—is a unique creation that arises out of the way in which the partners interact. The way you dance probably varies from one partner to another. Likewise, the way you communicate almost certainly varies from one partner to another.

The transactional nature of communication shows up dramatically in relationships between parents and their children. We normally think of "good parenting" as a skill that some people possess and others lack. We judge the ability of a mother and father in terms of how well their children turn out. In fact, research suggests that the quality of interaction between parents and children is a two-way affair—that children influence parents just as much as the reverse. For example, children who engage in what social scientists call "problematic behaviour" evoke more high-control responses from their parents than do cooperative children. By contrast, youngsters with mild temperaments are less likely to provoke coercive reactions by their parents than are more aggressive children. Parents with low self-esteem tend to send more messages that weaken the self-esteem of their children, who in turn are likely to act in ways that make the parents feel even worse about themselves. Thus, a mutually reinforcing cycle arises in which parents and children shape one another's feelings and behaviour. In cases like this it's at least difficult and probably impossible to identify who is the "sender" and who is the "receiver" of messages. It's more accurate to acknowledge that parents and children—just like husbands and wives, bosses and employees, teachers and students, or any other people in relationships—act in ways that mutually influence one another.

2.3 Communication Process: SMCR Model

There are many communication models which serve a variety of purposes. They range from single event analyses which can be used to instruct beginners, to complex models which are usually understood only by specialists in the field of communication. We have chosen the Sender- Message-Channel-Receiver (SMCR) Model for this publication. The SMCR model (Figure 2.3) is useful for examining a single communicative event; that is, it can isolate one event out of the ongoing communication process and illustrate the actions which take place.

2.3.1 Sender

The sender (or source) in the SMCR model is the transmitter of the message. There are five factors which influence the sender in any communication he transmits:

i) Communication skills

ii) Attitudes

iii) Knowledge
iv) Position in the social system
v) Culture

These five factors also influence the receiver and will only be summarised here.

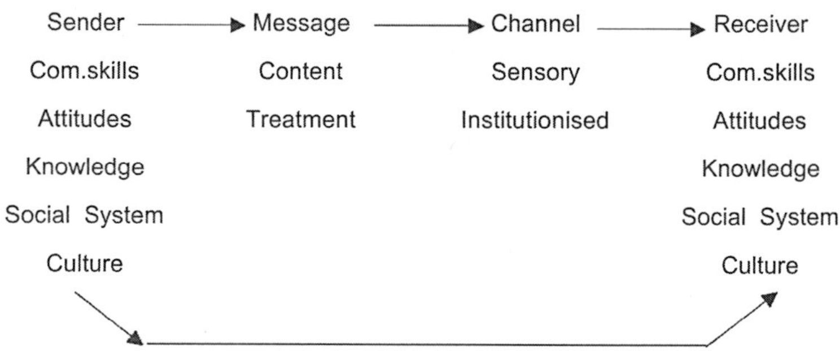

Figure 2.3. SMRC model of communication

2.3.1.1 Communication Skills

There are five verbal communication skills which determine our ability to transmit and receive messages. Two are sending skills: speaking and writing. Two are receiving skills: listening and reading. The fifth is important to both sending and receiving: thought or reasoning. The extent of the development of these skills helps determine our ability to communicate verbally. The effectiveness of our communication is also determined by our ability to make use of non verbal communications skills. A stern look of disapproval from the group leader readily communicates to the group member receiving the look that something he said or did was not well taken.

2.3.1.2 Attitudes

Attitudes, the second factor influencing the sender and receiver, are hard to define. For our purpose we will say that an attitude is a generalised tendency to feel one way or another about something. For instance, you may have a favourable or an unfavourable attitude toward voluntary groups working to solve community problems. If your attitude on this matter is favourable, you may, however, feel that certain problems could be better handled by the city council. Attitudes influence our communication in three ways. Attitudes toward ourselves determine how we conduct ourselves when we transmit messages to others. If we have a favourable self-attitude, the receivers will note our self-confidence. If we have an unfavorable self-attitude, the receiver will observe our uneasiness. However, if our favourable self-attitude is too strong, we tend to become brash and overbearing, and our communication loses much of its effect with the receiver.

Attitude toward subject matter affects our communication by predetermining the way we word our messages about certain subjects. An example would be a community leader with a favorable attitude toward bringing industry into the local area. He is likely to talk about only the good that industry could achieve. He may deliberately neglect to mention the difficulties encountered in trying to recruit new industry or any possible undesirable effects that might result.

Attitude toward the receiver or the receiver's attitude toward the sender is the third attitude item which influences our communication. Our messages are likely to be very different when communicating the same content to someone we like and someone we dislike. We also structure our messages differently when talking to someone in a higher position than ours, in the same position or in a lower position, regardless of whether we like them or not.

2.3.1.3 Knowledge Level

Knowledge level has a bearing on our ability to communicate effectively about a subject. A businessman might feel ill at ease trying to talk with a farmer about hogs, cattle, corn, or beans. The farmer would probably not feel qualified to talk about city slums, urban traffic problems, or city government. However, they may both feel quite comfortable discussing politics.

The position of the sender and the receiver in their respective social systems also affects the nature of the communicative act. Each one of us occupies a position in one or more social systems, such as our family, work groups, church, community, or the organisations to which we belong. We perceive those with whom we communicate as occupying a similar, higher, or lower position in their respective social systems.

2.3.1.4 Culture

Our culture is the fifth influence determining our communication effectiveness. Communication is more effective between persons with similar cultural backgrounds. Culture is relatively independent of social position in many cases. For instance, a voluntary association leader could probably communicate better with the people in his own group, because of their similar cultural background, than he could with a leader in the same organisation located in a different geographic area.

2.3.2 Message

In the SMCR model, the message is what the sender attempts to transmit to his specified receivers. Every message has at least two major aspects: content and treatment.

2.3.2.1 Content

The content of the message includes the assertions, arguments, appeals, and themes which the sender transmits to the receivers. For instance, community leaders may wish to send a message to community organisations appealing for financial support for a new swimming pool. The context of the message may include the results of a survey showing the need for a new swimming pool, the proposed plan for the new pool, the costs involved, and the appeal for financial support.

2.3.2.2 Treatment

The treatment of the message is the arrangement or ordering of the content by the sender. In the above example, the community leaders can arrange the content in many ways. The receiver is likely to be more receptive to the message, however, if the sender talks about the survey illustrating the needs prior to talking about the costs and making the appeal for financial support.

The selection of content and the treatment of the message depend upon our communication skills, attitudes, knowledge level, our position in social systems, and our culture. The selection of content and the treatment of the message we use also depend upon our audience and their communication skills, knowledge, attitudes, social position, and culture. A doctor, for example, would probably select different content and treat the message differently when talking about the same subject to two different audiences, e.g., his fellow doctors and a group of community leaders.

2.3.3 Channel

Social scientists recognise two types of channels:

i) sensory channels based on the five senses of sight, sound, touch, smell, and taste, and
ii) institutionalised means such as face-to-face conversation, printed materials, and the electronic media.

We use the institutionalised means to transmit most of our messages. Each institutionalised medium requires one or more of the sensory channels to carry the message from the sender to the receiver. For instance, when we use face-to-face conversation (an institutionalised medium) we make use of sight (gestures, expressions), sound (voice, other noises), and possibly touch, smell, or taste.

Social scientists have generally found that the receiver's attention is more likely to be gained if the sender uses a combination of institutionalised means using two or more sensory channels. Suppose, for example, someone tells your group that the quality of education in your community is not as good as the public is led to believe. If your group can discuss the problems face-to-face with school administrators during visits to the school (sight and sound) as well as hear about them through institutionalised means, such as television and newspapers, they are more likely to pay attention to the message.

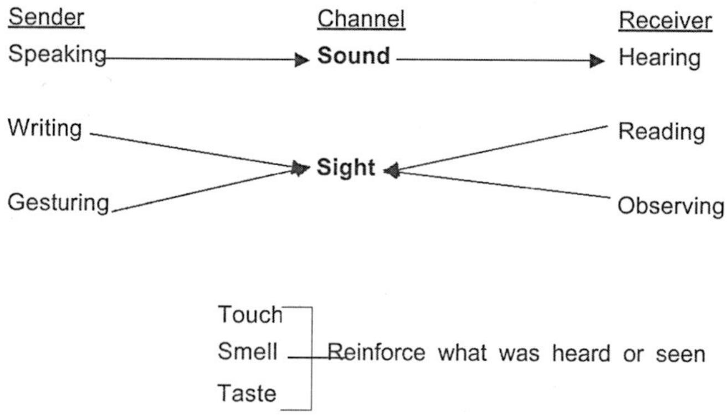

Figure 2.4. Sensory channels

When applying the multi-channel concept to real situations, you need to consider the three basic institutionalised means and a minimum of two of the sensory channels, specifically sight and sound. Face-to-face conversation has the greatest potential for getting the receiver's attention. It should be the primary institutionalised means used by leaders in sending messages to their group members. However, leaders should supplement face-to-face conversation with other institutionalised means and sensory channels in their continuing effort to gain the attention of their group members.

2.3.4 Receivers

The receiver in the SMCR model must attend to, interpret, and respond to the transmitted message. The goal of communication is reached when the receiver accepts the sender's message. Attention and comprehension are the means the receiver uses attain the goal of acceptance of the message.

2.3.4.1 Attention

Attention is the process by which the receiver tunes in on a message and listens to it, watches it, reads it. The sender must consider his receiver and treat the message in such a way that the receiver's attention is more easily gained and retained.

2.3.4.2 Comprehension

Comprehension implies understanding of the message by the receiver. Here again, the sender must consider his intended receiver and use message content and treatment that will enable the receiver understand the message.

2.3.4.3 Acceptance

Once the receiver has attended to the message and comprehended or understood the content, his next task is to accept the message on at least one of three levels: the cognitive, that is, the receiver accepts the message content as true; the affective, the receiver believes that the message is not only true but good; overt action, where the receiver believes the message is true, believes it is good, takes the appropriate action.

The sender can do much in deciding on his content and treatment of the message to gain the receiver's attention and comprehension. However, he has little control over the receiver's acceptance of the message. One consideration required at this point is to note that receivers are more inclined to accept message contents which agree with their previous attitudes. The sender has a less difficult task if his message agrees with the receiver's attitudes. If the receiver disagrees with the sender's message, acceptance is less likely.

2.3.5 Feedback

Feedback is the sender's way of determining the effectiveness of his message. During feedback the direction of the communication process is reversed. When providing feedback, the original receiver goes through the same process as did the original sender and the same factors influence him as they did the sender.

The receiver may use the same channel for feedback as the sender used for the original message; this is usually the case in face-to-face conversation. Or the receiver may take a different channel, as might be the case when you as a leader transmit a message to your group requesting action on a matter and a group acts or does not act in the way you asked. The group's actions have then become the feedback. Another example might be the increased sales of a product due to radio and television advertising. The purchase of the product by the public provides feedback to the manufacturer on the effectiveness of the communicated message.

In face-to-face conversation feedback is more easily perceived. The sender can tell if the receivers are paying attention when he speaks to them. If a receiver falls asleep or looks at other things in the surrounding environment, the sender realises that he does not have the receiver's attention.

If the sender sees furrowed brows or questioning facial expressions in his receivers, he knows that they did not comprehend his message. However, the overt action taken by the receiver is the feedback that the sender uses to determine the amount of influence he has had with the receiver.

Feedback measures influence. We know that democratic leadership involves influencing others. When a group has been successful in raising money for a community project, they can rightfully feel that they were influential. If the group had failed in their effort to raise the money, one of the reasons could be that they were not influential in the community. If your group takes the action you want them to take, you have been influential; if it does not, then you were not influential.

Feedback provides a method of eliminating miscommunication. It is most effective in face-to-face conversation where feedback is instantaneous. If a group leader asks one of the members for some ideas on projects for the next year and the member suggests having travel films, the leader knows immediately that miscommunication has occurred. The group member suggested programme ideas and not project ideas. The feedback would be effective if the leader were to immediately clarify the difference between programmes and projects. Had the situation not been face-to-face, the group member might still be thinking of travel films for next year's project.

2.4 The Two-Step Flow of COmmunication

We will now look at another communication process, the two-step flow. This process occurs when messages are relayed through a third person from the sender to the receiver.

As shown in Figure 2.5, the sender, A, selects messages from the available information he wishes to transmit to C, the receiver. Both the sender and the receiver may be either individuals or groups.

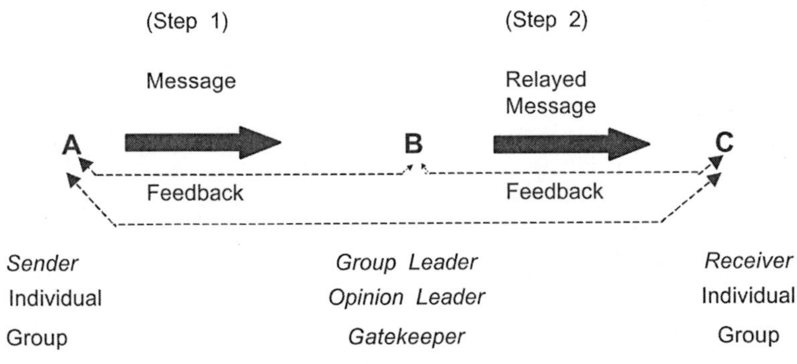

Figure 2.5. The two-step flow of communication

For instance, A might be the national or state president of a voluntary association which has local clubs in numerous communities. In achieving the goals of the association, the national or state president will likely need to communicate to the members, C, in the different local clubs.

Since the national or state president is unlikely to communicate directly with each individual member of the association, we need a third person, B, to relay the messages from the sender to the receiver. B is often referred to as the opinion leader, the group leader, or the gatekeeper. The local group leader (possibly the president or secretary of the local club) selects information from A's messages and transmits it on to C, the receivers or local club members. Thus, we have two-step flow; from A to B and from B to C. The two-step flow can work just as well in the opposite direction.

B is the key to success of the twostep flow. We know that no two people have exactly the same meaning for a message. It is up to B, however, to insure that A's message, when relayed to C, is as close as possible to what A actually said. Otherwise, C will not comprehend the message in the way that A wanted. For this reason, A should require feedback from B to see if B understood correctly, and B should require feedback from C to see if C understood correctly what was relayed to him. If possible, A should try, from time to time, to get direct feedback from C to see if B is relaying the messages properly.

Your group can practice communication improvement by setting up a two-step situation. Have one member be A and transmit a message to another member who is B. The message should be written down as a check on accuracy. B will then transmit the message to C who is played by a third group member. Both B and C provide feedback to A who determines how accurately the message was relayed. Through practice sessions such as these, your group members can develop the habit of providing feedback to indicate the proximity of meanings and also develop skills in relaying messages. Both feedback and message relay are important to successful group communication.

2.5 Factors Influencing the Communication Process

Three things about the sender of a message affect the receptability of his message by the receiver. They are:

i) credibility
ii) objectivity
iii) expertness

These three aspects of the sender are inter-related in their effect on the receiver. The receiver, in order to believe the message or respond in the way the sender wants him to, must perceive the sender as credible, objective, and expert in the area. If your service club wanted to study community juvenile delinquency and its cure, whom would you bring in as guest speakers?

The police chief, county sheriff, probation officer, or welfare director, would be credible sources on the extent of delinquency in your area. A person whose windows were broken several times by vandals might well be credible, but he is not likely to be objective, nor will he be an expert.

When inviting a speaker who could give advice on cures for delinquency, a probation officer or someone from the state training school would be most likely perceived as credible, objective, and expert. However, if the probation officer or training school staff member claimed that their methods for curing delinquency were best, they would lose their objectivity. If the receivers perceived this, the messages would not be accepted as easily as they would if the sender were objective.

If the sender tells us what we want to hear, he will have little difficulty getting us to accept the message. However, many times the sender has to tell us something we do not want to hear. When this happens, he must be credible (someone the audience will perceive as trustworthy), objective (one who looks at all sides of the problem before making an impartial decision), an expert (one who is qualified to comment on the problem in question).

2.6 Patterns of Communication

Figure 2.6 show the communication patterns most frequently used. The large dot represents the sender or the leader, while the smaller dots indicate the receivers or other group members.

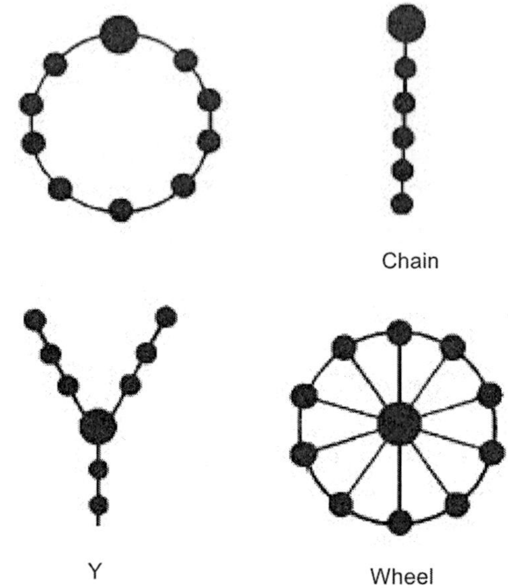

Figure 2.6. Communication patterns

Each of the four patterns presents one basic and serious communications problem. That is, no group member communicates directly with every other group member. Three of the patterns do not allow each member to communicate directly with the leader.

In the circle, the group member communicates only with the persons next to him. A message from the leader is likely to be changed considerably by the time it completes the circle and gets back to him.

With *the chain*, we have the same problem as in the circle. The last man may get a different message than that which the leader transmitted. An even worse problem here is that the sender gets no feedback; he doesn't know how much the message is distorted.

The *Y* is a further complication of the chain. It has all the communication problems of the circle and the chain and the additional one of having three separate groups who can communicate only through the leader.

The *wheel* is the best of the four. The leader can communicate directly with each group member. However, all of the group members cannot communicate with each other. This pattern can be used in all groups that are small enough to allow direct communication between the leader and each member. Larger groups are almost forced to use the other patterns or modifications of them.

Although the goal of our communication is to get the receiver to take some appropriate action, we need to have feedback from group members in ways other than overt action. We may, for instance, want to insure that the meaning was understood or get an opinion from the receiver on the message content without him taking any overt action at the present time.

Several methods can be used to get such feedback. Among the methods are evaluation sheets, verbal reports from audience, listening teams, question cards, or reports and questions from individual members. If a group is small enough that each member can communicate with every other member, they have an ideal situation. Communication will be very informal and the sender's goal of acceptance of the transmitted message is more likely to be achieved. This modified wheel pattern diagrams such a communicative process.

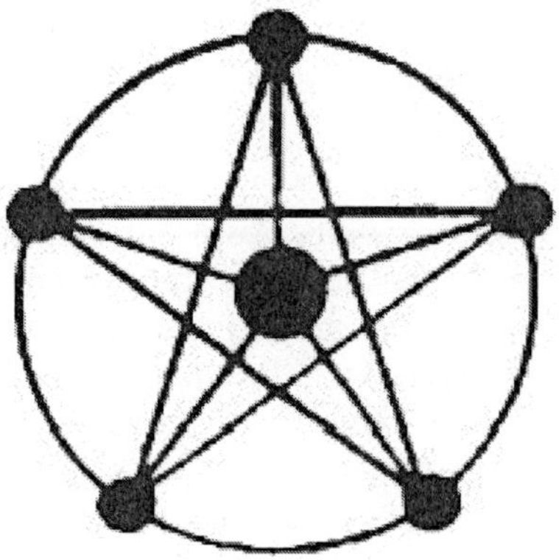

Figure 2.7. Modified wheel pattern

2.7 Principles of Communication Process

2.7.1 Communication is Circular

Since the sender and receiver encode and decode simultaneously through feedback, communication is a circular, on-going process. First one person speaks, then the second person responds, then the first, and back and forth in a simultaneous process. At any given moment, everyone involved in the interaction can be both a sender and receiver of messages, encoding one message while decoding another.

2.7.2 Communication is Based on Our Perception

Perception is an individual's way of understanding reality. Perception depends on a variety of influences including: memory, attention, and selectivity. You cannot pay attention to all the stimuli reaching your senses. No one can. If you are listening to a professor give a lecture, the actual message coming from the professor (including vocal aspects, words, gestures, facial expression, and use of the overhead, for example) competes with other stimuli in the room (the person yawning next to you, the thoughts about what you did last night, and more).

An infinite number of internal and external messages are coming at us at any given time. What we decide to pay attention to (selective attention) and how we process those messages (based on our experiences and selective memory) influence the messages we receive (or create from the selected stimuli).

Since, each of us perceives, remembers, and understands differently, the outcomes of the communication process are unique to the people and situations involved. Hence, truly effective communication is extremely difficult. You cannot talk directly with two people and constantly monitor their perceptual process during the conversation. The process is too complex. The more people who enter the situation, the more complex the process becomes. With a larger group, we have the perceptions of more people to take into account. On the other hand, we lose much information about individuals because they are farther away and provide less feedback. An effective public speaker will recognise the influence of various aspects of the communication process and use every technique possible to enhance effectiveness.

2.7.3 Communication is Irreversible

Communication is not something we can take back. Think of a time when you had a disagreement with someone you love. Perhaps you said something that hurt the person. Afterwards, you might have apologised and said, "Forget it, I didn't really mean it." Even if you "didn't mean it," you cannot erase the memory and effects of your words and actions. In the case of a fight, it may haunt the relationship for a long time. If you stand up and speak in a staff meeting—and you later decide you said something stupid—you can not wish away the effects caused by your remarks. Instead, you must build on the past rather than ignore it. Think of what happens when a person tells an ethnic joke to start a speech, then later discovers the audience is offended. The speaker may apologise, but the perception of the audience members may not change. Since communication is circular, is based on our perception, and is irreversible, all communication must build on previous interaction.

2.8 Levels of Communication

The communication process can occur on multiple levels: intrapersonal, interpersonal, group, public, and mass mediated.

i) *Intrapersonal communication* refers to the communication you have with yourself. Your thoughts, your self-talk, your recognition of your own feelings and attitudes.

ii) *Interpersonal communication* or dyadic communication, is that which occurs between two people. Brief exchanges between strangers, conversations between friends, ongoing discussions with a significant other all fall into this category.

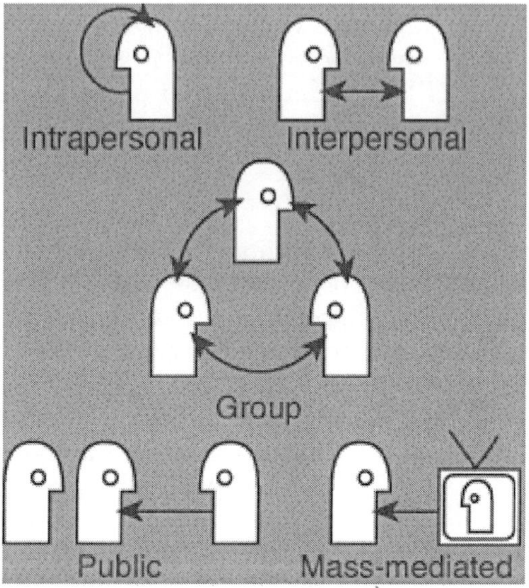

Figure 2.8. Levels of Communication

iii) Group communication usually concerns three or more people who interact and influence one another in the pursuit of a common interest. A study group, an athletic team, and families are usually small groups.

iv) Public communication is one person communicating face to face with an audience. The size of the audience may vary, but the interaction between speaker and audience is more limited than in the previous levels of communication.

v) Mass-mediated communication, or mass communication for short, is the communication which takes place over some form of technology because the audience is so large that they cannot be grouped together in one place. Newspapers, television, and the internet are all examples of mass communication. A speaker does not have direct access to the audience and the audience's feedback is delayed.

All five of these levels share a common process: a source attempting to influence a receiver through the creation of appropriate messages. Although each level has some unique forces affecting the outcome of communication, you will be able to apply the skills and principles of public speaking to other levels of communication as well.

Selected References

Beal, George M., et al. "Communication Impact," Rural Sociology Report No. 41. Department of Sociology and Anthropology, Iowa State University, Ames, Iowa. 1967.

Berlow, D. K., *The Process of Communication: An Introduction to Theory and Practice*, New York: Holt, Rinehart, and Winston, 1960.

Ellis, Donald G. Crafting Society: Ethnicity, Class, and Communication Theory. Mahwah, New Jersey, 1999.

Farace, R. V., Monge, P. R., Russell, H.M., *Communicating and Organizing*, Reading, MA: Addison-Wesley, 1977.

Laswell, H.D., "The Structure and Function of Communication in Society", in L. Bryson (ed.), *The Communication of Ideas,* New York: Harper, 1948.

Leeds-Hurwitz, Wendy, *Communication in Everyday Life: A Social Interpretation*, Norwood, New Jersey, 1989.

Mattelart, Armand, *The Invention of Communication*, Translated by Susan Emanuel, Minneapolis, 1996.

McCroskey, J.C., *An Introduction to Rhetorical Communication.* Englewood Cliffs, NJ: Prentice-Hall, 1968.

McLuhan, Marshall, *Understanding Media: The Extensions of Man*, New York, 1964.

McQuail, Denis, *Mass Communication Theory: An Introduction*, London, 1994.

Peters, John Durham, *Speaking into the Air: A History of the Idea of Communication*, Chicago, 1999.

Rogers, Everett M., *A History of Communication Study: A Biographical Approach*, New York, 1994.

Roloff , M. E. , Miller, G. R., (eds.), *Interpersonal Processes: New Directions in Communication Research*, Newbury Park, CA: Sage, 1987.

Rothenbuhler, Eric W., *Ritual Communication: From Everyday Conversation to Mediated Ceremony*, Thousand Oaks, California, 1998.

Schiller, Dan., *Theorizing Communication: A History*, New York, 1996.

Taylor, Talbot J., *Mutual Misunderstanding: Scepticism and the Theorizing of Language and Interpretation*, Durham, North Carolina, 1992.

Watt, J. H., Van Lear, C. A., (eds.), *Dynamic Patterns in Communication Processes*, Thousand Oaks, CA: Sage, 1996.

Watt, J., A. VanLear (eds.), *Cycles and Dynamic Processes in Communication Processes*, Newbury Park, CA: Sage, 1996.

Westley, Bruce H. and Malcolm S. MacLean Jr."A Conceptual Model for Communications Research," *in Dimensions in Communication*. James H. Campbell and Hal W. Helper-(eds.). Belmont, Calif: Wadsworth Publishing Co., 1965.

3

Sociology of Communication

"A man is as alive as he can communicate," L. Ron Hubbard wrote. Communication skills are essential in any sphere of human interaction. In fact, when all is said and done, on whatever level, communication is the sole activity all people share. The benefits of effective communication are too numerous to list, for they enhance all aspects of life from the personal to the professional.

3.1 Communication Needs of the Society

3.1.1 Physical Needs

Communication is so important that its presence or absence affects physical health. In extreme cases communication can even become a matter of life or death. The link between communication and physical well-being is applicable in all areas of life. Researchers have identified a wide range of threats that can result from a lack of close relationships. For instance:

i) A lack of social relationships jeopardises coronary health to a degree that rivals cigarette smoking, high blood pressure, blood lipids, obesity, and lack of physical activity.

ii) Socially isolated people are four times more susceptible to the common cold than those who have active social networks. Social isolates are two to three times more likely to die prematurely than are those with strong social ties. The type of relationship doesn't seem to matter: Marriage, friendship, religious ties, and community ties all seem to increase longevity

iii) Divorced men die from heart disease, cancer, and strokes at double the rate of married men. Three times as many die from hypertension; five times as many commit suicide; seven times as many die from cirrhosis of the liver; and ten times as many die from tuberculosis.

iv) The rate of all types of cancer is as much as five times higher for divorced men and women, compared to their married counterparts.

v) The likelihood of death increases when a close relative dies.

vi) People who are defensive suffer from higher blood pressure compared to those more willing to acknowledge their possible limitations.

Not everyone needs the same amount of contact, and the quality of communication is almost certainly as important as the quantity. The important point is that personal communication is essential for our well-being.

3.1.2 Identity Needs

Communication does more than enable us to survive. It is the way indeed, the only way we learn who we are. Our sense of identity comes from the way we interact with other people. Deprived of communication with others, we would have no sense of ourselves. In his book *Bridges Not Walls,* John Stewart dramatically illustrates this fact by citing the case of the famous 'Wild Boy of Aveyron', who spent his early childhood without any apparent human contact. The boy was discovered in January 1800 digging for vegetables in a French village garden. He showed no behaviours that one would expect in a social human. The boy could not speak but rather uttered only weird cries. More significant than this lack of social skills was his lack of any identity as a human being. As author Roger Shattuck put it, "The boy had no human sense of being in the world. He had no sense of himself as a person related to other persons." Only with the influence of a loving "mother" did the boy begin to behave and, we can imagine, think of himself as a human. Like the boy of Aveyron, each of us enters the world with little or no sense of identity. We gain an idea of who we are from the way others define us. The messages we receive in early childhood are the strongest, but the influence of others continues throughout life.

3.1.3 Social Needs

Besides helping to define who we are, communication provides a vital link with others. Researchers and theorists have identified a whole range of social needs that we satisfy by communicating. These include pleasure, affection, companionship, escape, relaxation, and control. Needs like these arise in virtually every relationship with friends, fellow workers, family members, lovers, spouses, and even strangers. And communication is the primary way we satisfy our social needs. In fact, some social scientists have argued that communication is the principal way by which relationships are created. Research suggests a strong link between effective interpersonal communication and happiness. In one study of over 200 college students, the happiest 10 per cent described themselves as having a rich social life.

A variety of evidence suggests that many people aren't very successful at managing their interpersonal relationships. For example, one study revealed that one-quarter of the more than 4,000 adults surveyed knew more about their dogs than they did about their neighbours' backgrounds. People believe that communication problems "very frequently" cause a marriage or a relationship to end more than money, relatives or in-laws, sex, previous relationships, or children.

3.1.4 Practical Goals

Since relationships with others are so vital, some theorists have gone as far as to argue that communication is the primary goal of human existence. Anthropologist Walter Goldschmidt terms the drive for meeting social needs the "human career". If you pause now and make a mental list of your own relationships, you'll probably see that, no matter how successful your relationships at home, with friends, at school, and at work, there is plenty of room for improvement in your everyday life. The information that follows will help you improve the way you communicate with the people who matter most to you.

Besides satisfying social needs and shaping our identity, communication is the most widely used approach to satisfying what communication scholars call instrumental goals: getting others to behave in ways we want. Some instrumental goal are quite basic: Communication is the tool that lets you tell the hair stylist to take just a little of the sides and lets you negotiate household duties. Other instrumental goals are more important. Career success is the prime example. Communication skills —the ability to speak and listen effectively—are the top factors in helping college graduates find jobs in an increasingly competitive workplace, ranking higher than technical competence, work experience, and specific degree earned. Good communication on the job is just as important.

Economist James Flanigan explains:

> Communication skills will fetch premium pay. The person who talks on the phone to mutual fund investors will have to be even more knowledge able, efficient, and personable than the bank teller of old. Competition for such jobs won't be based on pay alone but on skills.

This means that good personal skills aren't just a social nicety: They can mean the difference between success and failure on the job.

Psychologist Abraham Maslow suggested that the physical, identity, social, and practical needs we have been discussing fall into five hierarchical categories, each of which must be satisfied before we concern ourselves with the less fundamental needs. The most basic of these needs are physical: sufficient air, water, food, and rest, and the ability to reproduce as a species.

The second of Maslow's needs is safety: protection from threats to our well-being. Beyond physical and safety needs are the social needs we have mentioned already. Beyond these, Maslow suggests, each of us has self-esteem needs: the desire to believe that we are worthwhile, valuable people. The final category of needs described by Maslow is self-actualisation: the desire to develop our potential to the maximum, to become the best person we can be. As you read on, think about the ways in which communication is often necessary to satisfy each level of need.

3.2 Communication, Self and Society

Communication is one of the most interesting aspects of human life. In the words of Kenneth Boulding: "The speaker has some structure that is perceived in the form of images in the mind and no doubt coded in some energy and matter structures in the brain. This structure is translated to structures in the nerves that run down to the vocal cords, which translate it into air waves, which are partly matter, partly energy. These air waves hit the eardrum of the listener and are translated into patterns of nerve impulses, mostly electrical. These pass into the brain of the listener and are translated there into images that are unlikely to be identical to the images in the mind of the speaker but, if the conversation is successful, will be very similar to them. These images will produce a change in the structures in the mind of the listener, who then becomes the speaker, and the whole process is reversed, ending in the mind of the original speaker, who then may react."

3.2.1 Self

Communication always involves at least two entities: one to transmit the message, and one to receive it. The fundamental Shannon/Weaver model of communication includes a transmitter who creates and transmits a message and a receiver who notices and interprets the message. At first, it seems that there will be little difficulty in applying this model to two people who are communicating. However, further thought will demonstrate a need to look more closely at what is meant by the terms "transmitter" and "receiver." In human communication the interaction between these two turns out to be far more complex than was first imagined. When humans speak, they speak in a language. But we also know from our own experience that this language is not adequate to express every thought that we might have. This leads to the imagination of a division between our awareness of ourselves and the speech by which we express this awareness to others.

The study of human communication must consider the process by which inner thoughts, emotions, beliefs and other self-awarenesses are translated into language prior to being spoken. Similarly, once thoughts have been coded into language, they must be converted into sounds that others can hear. Humans accomplish this by expelling the air in the lungs through the larynx to make sounds which are modifed via the mouth and tongue to produce speech. The Shannon/Weaver Model suggests that these translating and converting steps are common to all communication. But unlike non-human transmitters, the human is self-aware. He or she knows "what's on my mind" and often speaks with the intention of making the private, inner world available to others. This notion of intention, or communication for planned effect, is not common to all communicators and is not contained within the Shannon/Weaver Model.

The reception of a human message is similarly complex. Human perceptions are never "turned off" — the ears, for example, hear every sound that comes within range, whether these sounds are messages or not. In fact, much of what is perceived by the senses must be categorised as noise. Thus, if humans are to communicate with one another, they must be able to separate an incoming message from the noise that surrounds it. It is not surprising, then, to find that the study of listening is as important as the study of speaking. Once the sounds of the message have been distinguished from the noise, they must be translated into statements of language. Although this seems as if it might be simply the reverse of the process the transmitter went through in creating the message, it not clear that this is the case. In fact, this process is not well understood. Finally, as might be expected, the language statements that the receiver's mind has derived from the incoming message must be interpreted or merged into his or her existing thoughts, emotions, beliefs and ideas. It is clear that acts of speech and hearing use language codes to connect human minds, and although there are many ways of communicating that do not use language, its study provides important insight into the process of human communication.

3.2.2 Feedback

Communication between humans would seem to fit the Shannon/Weaver Model quite well. Figure 3.1. summarises the model.

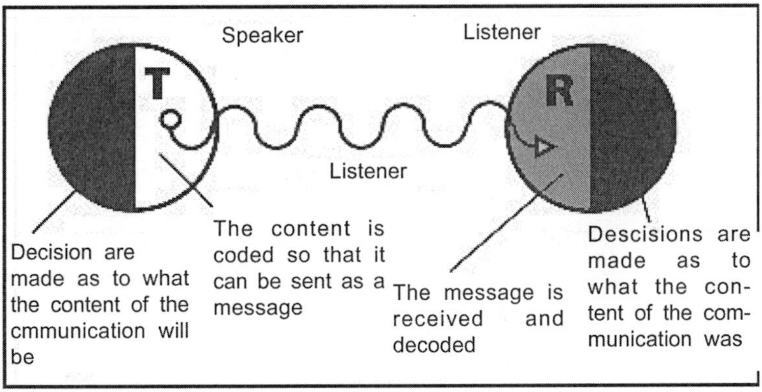

Figure 3.1.Shannon/Weaver model

However, observation of actual human communication finds behaviour that do not appear in this model. For example, when people communicate, the receiver often reacts to a message by generating an immediate return message of her or his own. To show this response, often called feedback, it is necessary to extend the model. Since "feedback" is as much a valid signal as was the original message, the terms "transmitter" and "receiver" are seen to be quite arbitrary. Both individuals transmit and receive messages, and they may both be doing this at the same time.

In non-human communication this is interesting but not particularly troublesome. Such communication is relatively simple, and feedback usually represents an expected return message. For example, the typical home heating system uses feedback to control the temperature. The thermostat monitors the temperature of the air and sends an "on" message if it becomes too cool or an "off" message if it becomes too warm. The heater monitors the electrical channel from the thermostat and turns the heating unit on or off accordingly. In the last example the number and kinds of feedback messages were strictly limited. However, because human communication is intentional, the human receiver is likely to change his or her mind upon the reception of a message. This means that the feedback message may involve something totally new to the former transmitter who consequently may change her or his mind before responding with even more feedback. As this communication flows back and forth, it quickly becomes very complicated and difficult to predict.

People tend to gather in groups, that they engage in communication almost constantly within these groups, and that they communicate on many channels simultaneously. This means that a message may involve any of a number of media: sound waves for speech, light waves for gestures or "body language", even particles of "stuff" for smell. Furthermore, people seem to have the ability to "tune out" perceptions that they deem unimportant, and to "tune in" to messages that matter to them.

3.2.3 Society

One of the things that people have in common is that they spend quite a bit of time communicating with one another. But on closer look, it turns out that all people don't communicate equally well with all others. In fact, scholars are able to distinguish specific groups of people who tend to communicate among themselves much more often than with members of other groups. Furthermore, each of the groups tends to develop its own unique set of languages, values, and beliefs. Such groups are termed "societies". Clearly, the study of human communication must occur within the context of human societies, and by taking this point of view, scholars have discovered that communication helps to establish the way of life of the people in each society, and in particular:

i) each society is distinguished by its own unique characteristics; that is, each society has a way of life that is different from all other societies,
ii) a society involves cooperation on the part of its members,
iii) societies remain in existence over a long periods of time.

Societies are distinguishable from one another in various ways. For example, Japanese society is usually seen as highly communal while American society is usually seen as highly individualistic. Americans see both French and Japanese societies as materialistic, while Chinese society is usually seen as much less so. The French are seen as characteristically focused on food, fashion, and art ; the British on commerce and industry ; the Hindu on spirituality ; and so on. This implies that certain ideas, values, traditions and the like are shared by the members of one society but not others, or that some are more important in some societies than they are in others. We call these shared elements the culture of a society.

Of course these cultural characteristics do not necessarily apply to individuals within the society. Certainly there are communal Americans, materialistic Chinese and industrious French. It is important to see that when we take the societal point of view, we are not speaking of individuals but of the collective way of life of the group. Within a society communication acts to strengthen certain characteristics and lessen others.

Communication among societies is difficult because the very differences that make the societies distinct — languages, customs, meanings — make the connection between sender and receiver difficult to establish. We definitely believe that past societies such as the Roman, or

Mayan, or Assyrian existed for long periods of time. Similarly, some current societies, such as the Chinese, or the Hindu, are believed to have existed for many centuries. This implies that the culture of a society is maintained through the participation of its members, and in some way preserved over the centuries. For a society to survive, its members must cooperate in this participation. A society whose members are in conflict will eventually change into a different society or disappear entirely.

3.2.3.1 Sub-groups of Societies

Societies often contain many smaller groups, some of which may contain even smaller groups, and so on. Communication takes on different aspects within these different groups. Here are some examples of such "sub-groups":

i) A family may be loosely defined as a group whose members live together, or have lived together, and who are closely connected through personal communication. Notice that, as with most definitions of groups, this one is problematical. Family, in this case, might include a single father and his children, a group of college roommates, a gay couple, or a professional baseball team. It also would imply that single individuals living alone are not families in and of themselves.

ii) A socioeconomic class is a group whose members are connected by their common occupational or economic status. For example, "blue-collar workers" identifies the group of people who work for an hourly wage, as opposed to "white-collar workers," who work for a yearly salary. Similarly, "the poor" identifies a group whose members have a very low level of wealth, while "the rich" identifies a group whose members have a very high level of wealth, and "the middle-class" identifies a group whose members are neither rich nor poor.

i) An organisation is a group whose members gather together periodically in the pursuit of some particular goal or task. A business is a form of organisation, as is a club, a political party or a volleyball team. Smaller groups within organisations include such as divisions, departments, offices, and work-groups. A jargon is an example of a kind of specialised language that often develops within organisations to promote communication.

i) An ethnic group is a group of individuals connected by a common cultural heritage. Thus we might study communication within the Afro-American, the Italian, the Asian, or the Hispanic community.

i) A community is a group of people connected by virtue of their living in the same geographic area or, increasingly in our age of electronic communication, by means of a loose association with a common interest.

If we study a particular subgroup, we will find that it, too, contains subgroups. For example, a family may contain such as parents, children, grandparents, and distant relatives. Each of these subgroups will possess certain cultural characteristics and patterns of communication. A bit of thought will show that if scholars continued to break groups into subgroups, they eventually would find themselves studying communication among individuals — and thus would have come full circle.

Although human communication may be studied in terms of groups, the groups are composed of individuals. Similarly, although human communication may be studied in terms of individuals, the individuals live together in groups.

3.3 Communication and Social Interactions

Despite the extraordinary complexity of social life in all contemporary societies, social relations are not random. If you look carefully, you will see that your life and virtually everyone's life has certain patterns of social interaction that are repeated over and over again. It is called as 'social structure'—the ordered relationships and patterned expectations that guide social interaction—and it is fundamental to life in all societies.

3.3.1 Social Status

Once social structure was restored, people assumed their social statuses and roles and went about the routine social interactions of their everyday lives. We often use the word status to refer to high social standing or prestige. Sociologists define status as a socially defined position in a social structure. A status is not an individual possession, but rather a relationship to others. For example, the status of mother is socially meaningful only in relationship to the statuses of child or father. Statuses define a multitude of other relationships as well, including those of father-son, doctor-patient, teacher-student, and shopper-merchant. These and other statuses affect the expectations and behaviours of others, a person's social identities, and even one's sense of self.

Statuses, which may be ranked high or low, determine where a person fits in society. Moreover, every person occupies a variety of statuses and each status has an appropriate social context. Sociologists call all of the statuses a person has at a given time that person's status set. The statuses that people occupy change not only according to social context, but over the life course as well. Usually a person's statuses are more or less consistent, but occasionally a person occupies two or more statuses that society deems contradictory. This is called status inconsistency.

Every society limits access to statuses. Ascribed statuses are statuses assigned to individuals without reference to their abilities or efforts, such as age, gender, race, ethnicity, and family background. Although these statuses greatly influence how a person is defined, they allow the individual few options or choices. Some societies allocate a great many statuses on the basis of ascription. For example, in the traditional Indian caste system, family background largely determined one's occupation, marriage choice, neighbourhood, political affiliation, and most statuses a person could claim during life. By contrast, modern industrial societies favour more competitive access to social positions. Achieved statuses are statuses secured through effort and ability. In all societies, a person's ascribed statuses strongly influence those statuses he or she might achieve. For example, gender, age, and race have either restricted or boosted a person's opportunities of gaining entry to a college, country club, job, or the position of President of the United States during most of the twentieth century.

A particular status in an individual's status set tends to dominate the thinking of others. This status is called a master status, a status that dominates all other statuses. It largely defines who that person is and his or her limitations and opportunities. Sometimes a person's master status is revealed by self-definition. Most people in college describe themselves as students, and the master status of most adult Americans is typically their occupation. Occupation is so important that many years after retirement, people continue to define themselves and others in terms of their former occupations-ex-professor, ex-nurse, or ex-auto worker. Likewise, students often identify themselves by their academic major-which identifies their future occupation. Since rather strong expectations are attached to a person's master status, they may have either positive or negative consequences.

No matter what other statuses they may occupy, people with the status of ex-convict are usually labelled ex-convicts—ex-convict painters, ex-convict fathers, and ex-convict neighbours—and this master status denies them many opportunities. This is not always the case, however. Increasingly, in contemporary industrial societies deviant identities, such as "former substance abuser", are being transformed into 'professional ex-s', who capitalise on a deviant past by transforming it from a liability to an occupational asset.

3.3.2 Roles in Society

A role is a set of expectations, rights, and duties that are attached to a particular status. Some sociologists use the metaphor of the theater to describe how roles influence social life. Like actors on a stage, all of us play roles in our daily lives-sons, friends, pizza deliverers, students, sorority sisters, and a multitude of other roles. Attached to each role is a script that tells us how we should behave toward others and how they should act toward us. But, as noted earlier, social life is far more complex than any stage, and in most roles people are allowed considerable latitude in how they interpret their "scripts". Without roles, human social life would be almost impossible, for roles guide our interactions in virtually every social situation. For example, during a cross-country trip we depend on many people-gas station attendants, toll booth operators, fast-food clerks, and so on.

Roles simplify the process of interaction because we do not have to base our actions on the unique personality of each individual with whom we interact. Rather, we respond to their roles, and they respond to ours. For example, in the role of traveller, when we arrive at a toll booth we have a duty to give the attendant the proper toll, and he or she is obligated to receive it and allow us to proceed.

Although expectations are attached to roles, the role performance, or how each occupant of a status fulfils his or her role, may vary widely. One reason is that people's emotional commitment to and identification with roles may vary. A college athlete, for example, may never miss tennis or basketball practice but cuts classes regularly because he or she considers the student role to be of minor importance. Another reason role performance varies is that role expectations are usually flexible enough for individual interpretation. Some roles allow a narrow range of individual expression. By contrast, artists are expected to be creative and as a result are given great latitude in how they behave. This too is restrictive, however, in that artists must be creative to be judged fully competent in the role.

Some roles are entered into or discarded with little effort or commitment. At other times, in cases of role distance, people play a role but remain detached from it to avoid any negative aspects of the role. Erving Goffman used the example of adults riding a merry-go-round with their children to describe role distance. According to Goffman, because their adult role might be threatened if they appeared to enjoy the ride, adults typically express their detachment by exaggerating the performance of merry go-round rider, or by acting bored and disinterested. Role embracement occurs when a person's sense of identity is partially influenced by a role. Sometimes role merger occurs when a role becomes central to a person's identity and the person literally becomes the role he or she is playing.

People usually try to fulfil their roles as they understand them, but role performances also are influenced by the fact that multiple roles are attached to almost every status, which sociologists call a role set. The role set of a student includes rights and duties toward professors, classmates, roommates, friends, parents, employers, and many others in reciprocal roles. In everyday interaction, we play many roles simultaneously. Sometimes we move from role to role with relative ease. Not all roles are logically consistent.

In cases of role strain, there are contradictory expectations and demands attached to a single role, which is quite common in everyday life. The student role offers a good example, for it includes numerous expectations that pull students in opposite directions. Professors expect students to study, but when friends visit they expect students to put away their books and talk or go out for fun. Role conflict occurs when a person cannot fulfil the roles of one status without violating those of another. Television dramas probably could not exist without role conflicts—such as the cop show favourite where a police officer responds to a burglary only to discover that the thief is a child, sibling, or close friend.

Role strain, conflict, and the choices they demand are important forces in social change. In everyday interaction people must tiptoe through a minefield of role conflicts and strains and make choices they may or may not wish to make. That people play their roles so well, and adhere so strongly to them despite the costs, tells us much about the power and necessity of roles. They provide the vital framework of social interaction that links individuals to others in reciprocal roles, patterned relationships, and social networks.

3.3.3 Social Networks

Social networks include our families, friends, and neighbours, as well as all other people and groups with whom we have ongoing relationships. People often create and maintain social networks for functional reasons, such as advancing their careers, for social support, and to promote a host of other interests and needs. Social networks do not have clear boundaries, and their members may or may not interact on a regular basis. Moreover, people in social networks do not always have a sense that they belong together, nor do they necessarily have common aims and goals, as do members of a group.

Social networks are a vital part of social structure and are extremely important in our everyday lives. Social networks radiate out from individuals and groups, and through them groups, organisations, and nations are bound together. Social networks also provide linkages between one individual and another, and then through other people's social networks to still others, until, in theory, people everywhere are linked together. Every person's social network is unique. The social networks of husbands and wives differ, as do those of brothers and sisters. For example, a husband's social network might include family members, neighbours, people in his car pool, co-workers, and members of his bowling league. A wife's network overlaps with her husband's to some extent; she and her husband share ties with some family members, neighbours, and friends. But her network may also include members of her car pool, her co-workers, and friends and acquaintances with whom she alone maintains a relationship.

Each person's social network also includes two kinds of relationships. One kind, which is characterised by strong ties, is a relationship that is intimate, enduring, and defined by people of special importance. A person typically has strong ties to family members, some neighbours, and a small circle of intimate friends. People in this kind of network usually exert considerable influence on each other; they share information and resources and usually can be counted on if needed. In effect, they are a person's primary social support system and provide "our security and sense of well-being, and even our health". A person's network also includes weak ties to distant kin, co-workers, acquaintances, and even people who have only interacted through cyberspace on the

Internet. While they are more tenuous and impersonal, they provide the individual with many contacts beyond family and friends that offer a wide range of information and services which would not be available otherwise.

Social networks are of critical importance in most societies. Contrary to popular thought, social networks are just as important to city dwellers as they are to rural folks. While urbanites are likely to have fewer family members in their social networks, they are nevertheless just as likely to use networks for procuring goods and services and finding jobs. It is through social networks that information, knowledge, and resources are shared among individuals and groups. For example, many companies prefer these networks in hiring, and pay bonuses to employees for recruiting friends and acquaintances, believing social networks produce savings in screening costs. In both small-scale and complex societies, social networks can be very useful for such things as getting a promotion, mobilising political support, gaining entry to a club, getting a date, or finding a marriage partner.

Personal networks are influenced by gender, race, social class, and a variety of other social factors that can serve to expand or limit one's access to information, resources, and power. In many societies networks composed exclusively of men who are members of dominant class, racial, and ethnic backgrounds routinely exclude women and minorities from becoming members of their clubs and associations, thereby denying them access to information and other resources. Informal social networks of social connection are becoming an increasingly important means through which corporate decision makers maintain and reproduce their power and influence not only nationally but globally.

3.3.4 Social Institutions

All societies create social institutions—relatively enduring clusters of values, norms, social statuses, roles, and groups that address fundamental social needs. Sociologists generally identify five major social institutions that exist in every society: family, education, religion, government, and the economy. These institutions along with the mass media and technomedia serve as powerful social forces that shape and alter our social structure and impact social interaction in our everyday lives.

3.3.5 Patterns of Social Interaction

Social roles, groups, institutions, and other social forces have such powerful influence on human behaviour. Yet it is abundantly clear that while people often conform to social expectations, in everyday social interaction we also interpret the rules to suit ourselves, create and manipulate meaningful symbols, present ourselves to others in a variety of ways, and are constantly interpreting and redefining the meaning of our actions. These processes are what guide and provide meaning to the social interaction in our everyday lives. Social interaction is the building block of the entire social order.

Among individuals, groups, organisations, and societies there are five fundamental patterns of social interaction: exchange, cooperation, competition, conflict, and coercion. Robert Nisbet described these elements as the "molecular cement" that binds people, groups, and societies together.

i) *Exchange*. Exchange is perhaps the most basic form of social interaction. Social exchange theorists maintain that our interactions with others are guided by the "profit motive",that is, we seek to maximise rewards and minimise costs. Social exchange is based on the norm of reciprocity—that we help and not harm those who have helped us. This norm establishes the expectation that gifts, recognition, love, and other favours will be returned. In the course of a day, people exchange smiles, waves, and other simple courtesies. Exchanges of this kind are most often taken for granted—at least until people fail to meet our expectations. The norm of reciprocity, of course, has a negative side, which includes the expectation that hostilities, threats, social slights, and other acts meant to harm will be reciprocated. Exchange theorists believe that people, groups, organisations, and nations keep a running account of what they are owed and what they owe others. Top priority is given to exchange relationships with business partners, political allies, friends, kin, or lovers who provide the greatest benefits at the lowest costs. Since people have an interest in searching for the most favourable cost-benefit ratios in their dealings with others, relationships are forever shifting. Nevertheless, exchanges and ties of mutual obligation are a vital social glue.

ii) *Cooperation*. Cooperation is a pattern of interaction in which individuals, groups, and societies work together to achieve shared goals. Cooperation is fundamental to human survival; without it social life would be impossible. Cooperation sustains routine, face-to-face encounters. It is also necessary if people are to make love, raise children, protect themselves, and make a living. Some societies place greater emphasis on cooperation than others.

iii) *Competition*. Competition is much like cooperation, in that both individuals and groups strive to achieve a shared goal. It differs from cooperation, however, in that in competition, instead of joining with others to achieve valued goals, people or groups contest for them, recognising that society's prizes are in limited supply and only one person or group can attain them. Competitive relationships are especially common to capitalist economies and pervade almost all aspects of people's lives.

iv) *Conflict*. Conflict is a pattern of interaction in which people or groups struggle to achieve a commonly prized object or goal. Conflict is especially common when competitors violate rules and seek to gain their objective by any means available. Robert Nisbet wrote, "There is no group or relationship, however small and intimate, in which conflict does not occasionally occur." We most often consider conflict to be opposed to human interests, harmful to the social order, and something to be avoided or resolved as quickly as possible. Yet, as conflict theorists emphasise, conflict has a positive side. It may enhance social solidarity, for nothing reduces conflicts and strains within a relationship better than an external threat observed, it also may serve as a vehicle for social change in which stagnant beliefs and values are dissolved, old tyrannies loosened, and individuals released to achieve new and higher goals.

v) *Coercion.* When people or groups are compelled to interact with each other, coercion is the glue that binds them together. Coercion is the actualisation of the threat of force that those with power sometimes use to achieve their objectives. Coercion involves an individual or group that dominates another, the superordinate, and a person or group that is dominated, the subordinate. There cannot be one without the other for the behaviour of one is conditioned by the other.

These patterns of social interaction are neither distinctive nor mutually exclusive. In everyday life, there is a fine line between competition and conflict, coercion and exchange, and the same is true concerning other patterns of social interaction.

3.3.6 Social Perception

In everyday life, we both give off and receive cues about the kinds of persons we are. We do this in almost every situation: when we enter a class, during a stroll across campus, while shopping at the mall, or when trying to flag down a taxi. How we perceive others and how we are perceived by them depend on such symbolic elements as physical appearance, clothing, gestures, tone of voice, facial expressions, posture, and other elements that reveal our various statuses, attitudes, and expectations.

Social perception depends in part on our impressions of other people's personal characteristics, such as whether they are attractive or ugly, good or bad, strong or weak. At the beginning of an encounter, people appear to devote considerable energy to discovering with whom they are dealing. Once people feel they have enough information, their attention to this assessment wanes, and early impressions continue to dominate their thinking and behaviour. Our initial impressions of others also depend on our perceptions of people's social identities. When we encounter others, we mentally make a checklist of their various statuses, such as gender, age, and race, as well as search for clues to their less obvious identities. We scan clothing, hair style, body posture, and hand and eye behaviours for clues to occupational identity, social class, group membership, and other social statuses. Since we cannot know everything about everyone we meet, we cut corners by fitting people into ready-made categories.

We use a variety of stereotypes in everyday life, which are static and oversimplified ideas about a group or social category, that strongly influence our expectations and behaviours. In our society, there are stereotypes of women, men, jocks, the elderly, racial and ethnic minorities, college students, and countless other groups and social categories. When people are identified as belonging to a particular category, we assume they possess particular traits, and we act accordingly. Thus many people believe that redheads should be approached with caution, for they have hot tempers and can "explode at any time". By the same measure, negative stereotypes influence our interactions with racial and ethnic groups.

3.3.7 Social Acts

Social acts are behaviours influenced or shaped by the presence of others and are of much and importance in every day life. When people enter our presence, we alter our behaviour based on their expectations and demands, or at least on what we think they will consider appropriate. Social acts include countless daily behaviours that are usually taken for granted—such behaviours as walking across campus, shopping at a mall, or merely standing in a crowded elevator.

3.3.8 Personal Space

Each of us surrounds ourselves with an invisible "bubble" that constitutes what we consider our personal space, an area around our body that we reserve for ourselves, intimate acquaintances, and close friends. On occasion we must allow others to "invade" this personal space, for example, when a doctor examines us, or perhaps when we are standing on line or in a crowded elevator. These situations often make us uncomfortable, however, and may call for "defensive strategies" such as folding our arms across our chest, placing an obstacle between us and the other person, or at the very least, avoiding eye contact and verbal communication.

Famous Anthropologist Edward Hall discovered that people tend to surround themselves not with one, but with four "invisible bubbles" and identified four different zones of comfort regarding social interaction:

i) *Intimate distance.* For most people this distance extends from the body outward approximately 18 inches. Generally we protect this space fiercely and allow it to be penetrated only by loved ones, very close friends, and our family pets. In the course of our daily interactions, this intimate zone is generally reserved for hugging, kissing, lovemaking, or comforting. Occasionally, medical professionals such as doctors, nurses, and dentists must invade this intimate space, sometimes making us feel rather uncomfortable. When strangers invade this space, we are likely to defend the space and our bodies by either retreating to a safer and more comfortable distance or by striking out in defence. Criminologists and law enforcement officials, for example, know that deaths by stabbing and strangulation are more likely to have been committed by intimates, family members, or friends than total strangers, because of the nature of intimacy involved in the crime.

ii) *Personal distance.* This zone tends to extend from approximately 18 inches from the body out to about four or five feet. While not reserved for intimates, we tend to feel most comfortable allowing friends and acquaintances within this space for any length of time. Generally when we are being introduced to people for the first time, we like to maintain somewhere between two to four feet between our bodies and theirs, not coincidentally the most comfortable distance for two people to shake hands. Again, criminologists and police figure that if a person is shot from this distance that the perpetrator was probably a friend or family member.

iii) *Social distance.* A distance of four or five feet out to approximately 12 feet is commonly used for impersonal and formal interactions. This is a common distance used in job interviews, for example. It also is the distance that podiums are usually set from the front row to separate speakers and audience, and if you observe the professor in your classroom, probably about the distance from which he or she lectures or leads class discussions. Shootings from this distance are as likely to have been committed by casual acquaintances or total strangers as friends or family members.

iv) P*ublic distance.* This distance, beyond 12 feet, is open to just about anybody and rarely do we feel threatened when somebody is 12 or more feet away from us. We can walk past total strangers, acknowledging them only with a glance or a nod, or ignoring them altogether if we choose to do so. Secret Service agents and bodyguards like to keep this much distance between dignitaries and the general public. Killings that take place from this distance often involve total strangers, as in the case of drive-by shootings, or random sniper shootings.

These "comfort zones" identified by Hall vary greatly from one culture to another and within cultures when people of different age, race, sex, and social class categories interact. Middle Easterners, for example, have much smaller distance requirements for casual interaction and men often embrace or kiss on the cheek when introduced for the first time-something that makes American men very uncomfortable. Despite living in a very densely populated country, the Japanese often maintain a larger social space when interacting with strangers. When two Japanese men are introduced, they bow toward one another, an act that requires a distance of about six feet to prevent bumping heads. In the United States, women are generally far more comfortable touching, hugging, or kissing one another than are men, and women generally will allow other women within their intimate distance, something a man rarely allows from another man, even if they are blood related. Also, not all men are comfortable with the same amount of personal and social distance.

The difference in attitudes toward personal space between the sexes can cause some awkward situations. For example, if a woman touches a man, he often misreads this gesture as a sexual overture because she has invaded his intimate space; hence, he considers it an intimate gesture-something she may not have intended at all. Similarly, older people often feel comfortable touching younger people, but children often feel uncomfortable approaching adults they do not know. While members of the lower socioeconomic classes often hug one another, embrace upon meeting, and feel comfortable in close proximity, members of the upper class usually maintain a "proper" distance between themselves and others, especially when interacting with members of lower social classes.

All of these examples involve non-verbal communication—the body movements, gestures, and facial expressions that we use to communicate with others. Smiles, nods, winks, eye contact, hand gestures, and other forms of non-verbal communication can be just as important, if not more so, than words in shaping our interactions with others. They are especially important in helping social actors to define social situations and give meaning to everyday interactions.

A critical element of everyday social interaction involves creating a definition of the situation, the idea that when people define situations as real they become real in their consequences. Not everybody defines situations in the same way. So, a class that is fun and exciting to some is dull and boring to others, and vice versa. Also, because we are constantly defining and redefining social situations in ways that are meaningful to us, we always run the risk of misinterpreting other people's actions, especially their non-verbal forms of communications. Did that girl just wink at me, or does she have something in her eye? Did that person just hold up their index finger toward me, or was it the middle finger? Does holding up two fingers signify victory, peace, or simply the number two? Certainly, the meanings imputed to these actions and gestures become critical in shaping the meaning of our present and future interactions with others. How we define social situations becomes an important part of our presentation of ourselves to others and how we attempt to manage their impressions of us. In that sense, to paraphrase Shakespeare, life becomes much like a drama, with each of us performing various roles on the stage of life.

3.3.9 Presentation of Self

Much of our day-to day interaction constitutes a performance—one that is judged by others and, as a result, has tremendous impact on how we are viewed by others and how we view ourselves. Erving Goffman introduced the theoretical framework of dramaturgical analysis, which uses the analogy of the theater to analyse social behaviour as a way of understanding these social performances. Dramaturgical analysis focuses on the ways we present ourselves to others and our attempts to manage their impressions of us in a favourable light. In everyday life, some interactions are simple and direct and people's behaviours are fairly predictable. Casual greetings are a good example. Most other face-to-face interactions, however, require more of participants, and people's responses may be highly variable.

According to symbolic interactionists, who study how symbols, language, and gestures shape social behaviour, we do not respond directly to individuals, events, acts, and objects, but to our images of them. As Herbert Blumer wrote, in social interaction the key to a person's response is how he or she organises, defines, and interprets another's behaviours. William Swann noted that people's identities and self-views are not like bowling balls that are unaffected by either people or objects they encounter in their travels. For people, the exact opposite is true we are acutely sensitive to those with whom we share ongoing relationships. This may explain the remarkable consistency of "self" over time—even over a lifetime. People usually cling to their selfviews because dramatic changes would disrupt relationships with those we deem important—in some cases, even relationships with others that may sustain negative selfviews and behaviours.

3.3.10 Impression Management

Many everyday interactions appear as if they were scripted minidramas, in which people encounter one another, assess each other's personal and social characteristics, assume identities, and behave in appropriate ways. Given the complexity of most social situations and the fact that spontaneity and surprise are integral features of virtually all social interactions, however, improvisation is usually required. Using the analogy of the theatre, dramaturgy analyses social interaction as though participants were actors in an ongoing drama. Dramaturgy, however, emphasises that in real life "actors" passively accept neither the definition of the situation nor the identities granted by others. Instead, people take an active part in social interaction, manipulating it to their perceived advantage. Erving Goffman called this impression management, ways that people use revelation and concealment to make a favourable impression on others.

Dramaturgists note that people not only have an interest in presenting their best "selves" to others but also tacitly agree to support each other's performances and help each other maintain face. Teamwork requires that people regularly overlook or ignore poor performances (a professor who stutters), embarrassing acts (a growling stomach), and deceits (excuses for being late). Also, we may sometimes be called on to do remedial work or help out by agreeing with others, even though we may totally disagree with their definition of the situation. Why we do these things should be obvious. When a "bad actor's" performance is called into question, the entire social interaction may be threatened.

Few cultures are more aware of this fact than the group-oriented Japanese, who recognise that when emotional outbursts occur, those present must realign their behaviours to suit the individual's goals, rather than those of the group. Daniel and Cheryl Albas provide an example of impression management that is very familiar to college students everywhere—when graded exams are returned in class. They called their research report "Aces and Bombers", noting that students who receive A's want to tell others about their success-and they usually do-whereas those who receive D's and F's take great pains to cover up their failure.

The self that we present in one social situation may be totally inappropriate in another. This discrepancy is illustrated in a series of experiments conducted by Harold Garfinkel who introduced ethnomethodology, which literally means people's methods, or is more generally described as a way of analysing the "taken-for-granted" aspects that give meaning to social interaction. Ethnomethodologists contend that much of what transpires when we interact with others relies on unspoken and commonly understood assumptions about the meanings of our words and actions.

To illustrate the taken-for-granted aspects of everyday interaction, Garfinkel had his students act as though they were boarders when they returned home from college during a visit, instead of behaving as sons or daughters. Pretending to be strangers in their own homes, the experiments tended to last only a few minutes because parents could not comprehend why their children were behaving so courteously and formally, and so "out of character". In some cases, tempers flared, and parental responses included, "What's the matter? Are you sick? Are you out of your mind or are you just stupid?" In today's world the presentation of self, impression management, and the taken for-granted aspects of interaction now involve interacting through cyberspace. The advent of the technomedia has dramatically affected social interaction in our everyday lives.

3.3.11 Role of Mass Media in Social Interactions

Mass media have had tremendous influence in shaping social interaction in our everyday lives. Our social perceptions and stereotypes have been largely shaped by portrayals of institutions and various categories of people on television. Today, perhaps no genre of television programming is more popular than the so-called "reality shows". Virtually every night of the week at least one, if not all, of the major networks, and several cable stations offer some type of "reality" programming. Programme participants live together, date, have sex, argue, fight, and in some cases compete for prizes of over a million dollars. Viewers "interact" with the people on these programmes by helping to select their mates or determining whether they remain in the competition or are "voted off" the show.

For many people around the world, participants in these programmes vicariously become friends, enemies, partners, and adversaries. Social attitudes, values, beliefs, norms, and stereotypes are simultaneously reinforced, challenged, questioned, redefined, and shattered. From a sociological perspective, however, the question looms as to whose reality is this? What lasting impact do these programmes have on our values, attitudes, beliefs, and norms? To what extent is the so-called reality displayed in these programmes shaped and altered by television producers, directors, film editors, and corporate sponsors? More important, how do these programmes affect our social interactions with others in our everyday lives? And remember, television is but one form of the ever increasing technomedia that influence our day-to-day interactions with others.

The technomedia, especially the internet, have expanded our daily social interactions from personal face-to-face encounters to the realm of cyberspace and interaction in virtual communities. Online shopping allows people to browse and shop from the comfort of their own homes without the need to interact with sales people or other customers. E-mail, chat rooms, and other forms of communication through cyberspace have made letter writing almost a lost art, and despite the widespread use of cellular phones, with widespread computer access, even the telephone is losing its importance as a means of communication. Moreover, on the World Wide Web people can be virtually anybody they want. Thus, influential variables and potential barriers to social interaction, such as age, race, ethnicity, sex, gender, social class, and others are at least temporarily suspended as people interact with one another through cyberspace.

3.3.12 Sociological Approaches to Social Interaction

3.3.12.1 Structural Functionalist Approach

According to functionalists, for society to exist, whether it is a colony of ants, a pack of dogs, a swarm of bees, or a human society, it must have a structure-patterned and recurrent relationships among group members. Much of social life is repetitive and enduring. A university, for example, is stable because it is structured. It has a president, vice-presidents, department heads, and specialists in many areas, and all have fairly clear ideas about their rights and duties relative to other members of the campus community. People are hired and fired, some retire and others die, yet the university endures. To some, this suggests that social structures, whether families, schools, or sororities, are relatively rigid and changeless structures.

Functionalists take a similar approach to social institutions: institutions are basic to the proper functioning of contemporary societies. Therefore, institutions provide the framework for social interaction in our everyday lives. Of all social institutions, the family is perhaps the most important. It regulates sexual activity and it produces new members and socialises and cares for them. In some societies families also transmit cultural knowledge, but in modern societies the educational institution fulfils the basic need of training each new generation. The economic institution produces and distributes goods and services, the political institution provides order and defence, and the religious institution fulfils the social need for meaning, social solidarity, and control. Religion (and the family) provided for the health of people in small-scale societies, but in modern industrial societies the medical institution, which includes a relatively stable cluster of norms and values, medical specialists, administrators, insurance companies, and other groups and organisations, maintains people's health.

To functionalists, institutions are a society's blueprint for solving basic needs, and any particular institutional structure channels experience along certain lines; it prohibits certain possibilities, tolerates or ignores others, and encourages still others. To say that a social arrangement is "institutionalised" means it is deeply embedded in the fabric of a group or society and is surrounded by customary beliefs, values, and norms. Institutions provide solutions to what are defined as long-term problems, and as such they are comfortable and familiar. Institutions provide the illusion of order and stability that is necessary if people are to have and rear children, plan, build, and invest in the future.

3.3.12.2 Conflict perspective

Conflict theorists disagree with this line of reasoning, noting that it is a fiction that institutional arrangements benefit all individuals and society as a whole. Instead, institutional arrangements grant a disproportionate share of wealth, power, and privilege to certain individuals and classes, and it is they who seek to maintain the status quo by defining particular institutional arrangements—whether slavery, feudalism, or the capitalist system—as vitally important to "society".

According to conflict theorists, society is structured but emphasise that roles, statuses, and institutions do not exist for the good of "society." Instead, they are used by superordinates to exploit and dominate subordinates as well as to maintain and perpetuate elite wealth, power, and privilege. Conflict theorists agree with functionalists on one point, however; once institutional patterns develop into a coherent system, their "common sense" logic may come to pervade all social institutions and make them highly resistant to change. Moreover, linkages among institutional complexes reinforce conservative tendencies.

Conflict theorists argue that it is impossible to understand human behaviour without reference to social stratification, for people's positions in the social hierarchy influence virtually everything they think and do. From the conflict perspective, roles such as teacher and business owner have advantages and in various ways are used to exploit those in linked roles-student and worker. Social networks and institutions operate in much the same way. In each case, those at higher levels in the social hierarchy use their wealth, power, and influence to dominate and exploit those at lower levels-whether locally, nationally, or globally.

Conflict theorists also tend to view social interaction from a macro level, but they focus on the last three patterns discussed earlier: competition, conflict, and coercion. From the conflict perspective, the unequal distribution of power and economic resources shape not only institutional configurations, but influence our day-to-day, face-to-face interactions with one another. From this viewpoint, social classes as well as individuals enter interactions with different vested interests and different goals. In this "dog-eat-dog" view of the world, the strong and powerful use daily interaction to dominate those who are weaker and less powerful. In contrast to the functionalist view, from this perspective, survival of the individual, society, and the species resides not in cooperation but in intense competition, with the "fittest" becoming the ultimate winner.

3.3.12.3 Symbolic Interactionist Approach

Symbolic interactionists contend that all of social life—including social institutions-are in a constant state of flux. This is because people continually define and redefine relationships, and even those social arrangements that appear to be deeply embedded in social structure change. For example, religious institutions are undergoing radical changes as more women enter divinity schools, especially elite schools that play a major role in shaping public opinion. Interactionists contend that there is more flexibility in roles and relationships and much greater possibility for change than either functionalists or conflict theorists would allow. Interactionists stress that human social structure is built of collections of people who interact with one another according to expectations rather than certainties. This results in a constant reordering of society as people in interaction define and redefine social relationships and expectations change.

Personal space, non-verbal communication, definition of the situation, dramaturgical analysis, presentation of self, impression management, and ethnomethodology are all important elements of the symbolic interactionist perspective. Interactionists primarily view social structure and social institutions as mutually agreed-upon fabrications of social interaction. The seeming permanence of these institutions and their impact on our daily lives relies on us, as social actors, continuing to define them as stable and important.

3.3.13 Social Interactions in the Age of Technomedia

We live in an age of communication. Communication is the problem and the opportunity addressed by a great deal of technology design and development. But because communication is an interpersonal and a social phenomenon, technology issues must be approached with a particular appreciation of human and social factors. The organisation of societies today requires effective global communication between diverse and far-flung social and cultural systems. Only through technical mediation are we able to maintain the flows of commerce and information required by the worldwide interdependence.

Technologies of communication become the means of production, or production format, of communication. Their use in communication is not transparent. In fact, technologies introduce new contingencies and context into communication. Analysis of communication and interaction in society today needs to account for the transformative effects of mediation. Technologies are rational by design, and in use, they rationalise human activity. Human communication and interaction, however, are neither rational nor designed. The difference between the technical and the human shows up in technology at what we call the "interface".

Social interface issues generally involve ambiguities of communication, intent, outcome and so on. These ambiguities result from technology's mediation of practices in which individuals are normally able to address and resolve ambiguities as they come up. It's at the social interface where the distinction between communication's content and participants' relationships becomes an issue, because the technology that's good for transmitting content may not be good for reproducing relationships.

The implicit purpose of communication is to motivate a listener to do, or understand, something communicated. Thus the use of technology extends and limits the very power of communication. It extends our ability to access and connect, but limits our ability to communicate and bind. Repercussions can be seen at all levels of society, from individual and interpersonal to macro-social. To function, technologies must map to human action just as humans must grasp and relate through technology. The greater the transparency of one domain to the other, and the greater the transitivity of actions from one through the other, the more effective their interface.

From the perspective of the network, we function as nodes through which communication flows. In short, we are transitive to the net's communication flows, and our participation is as important to it as it is to us. All experience is situated in time and place. But communications technologies lift communication and interaction from the here and now that grounds face-to-face interaction. This dislocation of temporality from its situatedness in the world is one of the fundamental operations of mediation. Indeed, communications technologies are as much about time and temporality as they are about distance and space. Synchronous media permit direct communication in real time. Asynchronous media permit communication only through use of a recording medium, and not in real time. Both intervene in the temporality of our relations.

Since communications media enable us to stretch our relationships across time and space, they inform and even produce our proximity to one another. These proximities involve rhythms of interaction, activity coordination, ways of communicating, and ways of offering or protecting our availability to each other. They put us into a kind of virtual immediacy with respect to our access and presence to each other. We become virtually equidistant to one another.

Proximity, commonly measured as a physical field in which persons are distributed in space, also unfolds temporally, as duration. We can think of proximity as a distribution of relations in a spatial sense, and an intensification in a temporal sense. Unlike physical proximity, whose distances are extensive, or spatial, the distances that characterise temporal proximity are intensive. They can be described as having qualities of speed, duration, acceleration, rhythm, and synchronisation. To this end, a critical part of our inquiry into the impact of communication technology rests on the assumption that we, as individuals, sense and pursue some level of synchrony in our interactions with one another. Technology becomes a means of production for interpersonal communication and interaction because it enables communication regardless of spatial distances. Connective technologies radically transform our presence and presence availability to others in relational and temporal terms.

Language occupies a privileged position in the co-production of inter-subjective experiences. When people speak, their proximity in physical terms becomes a proximity in relational terms also. This is because speech not only serves as a means of expression: speech produces effects that bind us. These effects are described by sociologists and linguists as the product of a special case of language use called speech acts. Speech act theory offers descriptions of the ways in which speaking is doing and speech is action. The actions may only "occur" as mutual understanding reached by those in conversation, and produce no material consequence; or they may accompany physical activity also.

It is through linguistic exchange that people reproduce the normative basis of society. In other words, society is reproduced and maintained through speech-based performances. These performances, though coloured by individual style of expression and delivery, embed the normative claims "belonging" to a society at a given time. Actors unwittingly embed these claims in their own use of language as speech.

Speech act theory further argues that these performances bind actors to one another through their mutual understanding of the claims embedded in their exchanges. To accept the premises of speech act theory, in other words, is to view society as a system of meanings that have claims upon individuals, but which is only maintained through their use of language. It would seem that a view of communication in which the binding of actors to one another is a linguistic phenomenon, and the effect of which is to reproduce society and nothing less, would place the mediation of communication in a position of critical importance.

The consequences of mediation are many, but among them are some of direct significance for a communication-oriented view of society. First is that speech act theory and its related theoretical perspectives tend to assume face-to-face interaction and performance. This opens up several lines of concern.

First, is the bracketing of physical co-presence, which means the elimination of access to visual and physical cues, or what are described as "facework". Mediation eliminates the physicality of interaction and thus the countless non-linguistic gestural cues we provide through facework, body language, intonation, and so on—what are also called "paralinguistic markers".

Second, is the loss of physical context. "Situated" (co-present) interactions provide actors with access to contextual cues and meanings belonging to location. Our interactions are informed by where we are (physically) and how that place is coded (culturally). By reflecting the expectations that characterise a place, we help to maintain it.

Third, is the integration of space and time. All human experience unfolds in a here and now. But the "here" that characterises mediated interactions has neither place nor visibility. The virtuality of interaction through technology indeed creates a new kind of experience, but not as a form of "cyberspace". Rather than look for spatial dimensions in virtual interaction, we will argue that it's concepts of temporality and time that help us to understand this transformation.

Our use of technology for communication transforms not only our interactions, but also their role in reproducing and maintaining relationships that persist through space and time. Then, the bracketing of the physical and co-present performance of linguistically-embedded interaction by technologies of communication mediates: (i) the facework of interaction, (ii) the contextuality of situation, (iii) and the intrinsic relationship of action to time and place. Our inquiry into mediation of communication will take the shape of an investigation of the transformative effects of mediation, and for several reasons. These run from the micro to the macro, or from the impact technology has on the user and his or her immediate experience of communicating through technology, or primary effects, to the macro, or what we might call the secondary effects of mediation.

In so far as communication unfolds through social practices, the transformations resulting from our use of technology as a production format ultimately become embedded in new social practices. Where there is a new ambiguity around a person's intentions, say as a consequence of talking over e-mail, there are or will be conventions that help to reduce that ambiguity. Our dependence on the possibility of communicating anytime, anyplace, is not going away. However, its impact on our experience and pursuit of relationships, and their ability to contribute to reproducing society, trust, and social commitments is enormous. This effort is an attempt to map some of the theoretical and critical territory covered by this new and emerging "age of communication".

We have developed a dependence on technologies for the execution and coordination of distributed and yet tightly-integrated activities. This historical fact has produced a new human reality: our experience of time, and our relation to temporalities, is becoming increasingly unanchored from face-to-face interaction. Our bodies and our direct physical experience no longer produce all of our realities. Nor is our physical presence any longer the condition of the speed with which we encounter real and inter-subjective realities. Rather, technologies and systems increasingly define the limits of speed, information, access, and the demands they place on us. It could be said that we are a culture increasingly defined by the machine connections and media rhythms in competitions with the long-since eroded traditional connections and rhythms of local community and institutionalised traditions.

The very nature of interaction changes when it is mediated by communication technology. Bracketing of face-to-face cues and gestures shifts attention and awareness of the other to the production of communication instead. We recede from the shared rhythm of interaction to tap on keys, multi-task, or otherwise fragment our attention and awareness. Emotions are often screened out by technologies. And our deep and internal sense of timing, so crucial to the successful performance of face-to-face interactions, is displaced by the asynchronous back and forth of messaging technologies. On an interpersonal level, we find it difficult to achieve a sense of being in synch.

Communication technologies undo the regularity of time and temporality that characterises a life built on personal habits and social routines. Temporal regularity in the human experience has a place; habits and routines do not automatically equate to tedium or dull repetition. What looks like repetition is still unique and spontaneous human experience, and every repetition or habit is different from the last. Technologies, on the other hand, produce a recurring sameness. The operations and functions codified in the form and service of technology reproduce the same abstracted operation with each repetition. The lived spontaneity of repeating social tradition is displaced by the cold functional repetition of the operation.

Culture develops attention deficit disorder. Immediacy and access, and the constant flow of communication and information, demand that we attend to whatever is nearest and most urgent. We lose a thread of continuity to the dashed line of distraction. Attention deficit disorder is not a lack of attention, but a lack of internal continuity and an excess of contingency. We pay attention, but in spurts that contribute little to a healthy and grounded sense of self.

The widespread adoption of technologies of communication has displaced the causality normally found in a social chain of action. Technologies operate by a logic of "one event upon the other". Where our social activities involve recognisable conventions (and ordering) of "one event after the other," technologies introduce a radical dislocation of sequence and cultural logic. The sequence and procedure is initiated by and maintained according to technical terms, where the logic seeks efficiency over understanding. The logic of procedure, or temporal arrangement, by which technology engages us is a logic of non-social contingency and temporality.

The process underneath interpersonal and social activities is implicit and transparent. Technology makes process explicit. Consequently, we tend to spend increasing amounts of attention and effort on the explicit operation of functions, operations, and steps by which we make technologies work. This shifts our participation from tending to the care of our social partners to "interacting" with technical conditions.

The culture of technology externalises us. We dedicate more of ourselves to identifying with extensions, those being extended subjective powers and abilities, or objective technologies and mediated practices. An ever-greater amount of our mental and emotional life becomes occupied with matters of technique, method, material contingency, mediated image, and so on. The shift of attention from the state of face-to-face interactions to the state of technical processes results in a tendency towards efficiency, regulation, and control. Even our ideas of what constitutes successful interaction may change: from qualities like emotionally healthy, clear, supportive, and understanding, to interaction effectiveness, efficiency, and task completion. Work practices shift from concern with inter-subjective process to technical process first. But ultimately, even interpersonal communication may suffer the same kind of translation.

The cultural shift towards technology and technical process in communication and social interaction may produce a shift in how we see ourselves and in how we produce our identities. The interdependencies among communication technologies and social practices would suggest that we produce our identities increasingly through our integration into mediated social networks—be those friends, family, work, etc. Our sense of self and well-being may become interested in identity forms that are resolved without face-to-face encounters: online visibility, popularity, connectedness, "virtual presence", etc.

Participation in communication networks encourages us to be transitive to the steady stream and flow of communication moving through networked participants. Being connected means more than simply being online, or being plugged in. It means being in the loop and serving as a transitive node in the network. We are encouraged less to "speak" than to "repeat", less to converse and more to pass along. The importance of knowing what's going on in an interaction shifts to issues created by the introduction of technology: who's on, what's the mood and energy, who's paying attention to whom, etc. Those aspects of an interaction that are easily gleaned from performance and face-to-face interaction become explicit concerns when technology brackets them out. Participants, often unwittingly, attend to matters of production rather than to each other.

Selected References

Barrett, E., NetLibrary Inc., *Sociomedia, Multimedia, Hypermedia, and the Social Construction of Knowledge*, Boulder, Colo.: NetLibrary Inc. 1999.

Baym et al., "Social Interactions Across Media", *New Media Society*.2004; 6: 299-318.

Burgoon Michael, et.al., *Human Communication,* Sage Publications, London, New Delhi, 1994.

Carey, James. W., *Communication as Culture: Essays on Media and Society*. Winchester, Massachusetts, 1989.

Daiute, C., Damon, W., *The Development of Literacy through Social Interaction*, San Francisco: Jossey-Bass, 1993.

Penalosa, F., *An Introduction to the Sociology of Language*, Rowley, MA: Newbury House, 1981.

Peters. D., *Speaking into the Air: A History of the Idea of Communication*, Chicago and London, University of Chicago Press, 1999.

Ruben, B. D., Stewart, L. P., *Communication and Human Behavior,* Boston, Allyn and Bacon, 1998.

Taylor, O. L., (ed.), *Nature of Communication Disorders in Culturally and Linguistically Diverse Populations*. San Diego, CA: College Hill Press, 1986.

Watzlawick, P., Beavin, J., & Jackson, D. (1967). *Pragmatics of Human Communication.* NY: Norton.

Wilmot, W. W., *Relational Communication,* New York, McGraw-Hill, 1995.

Wood, J. T., *Relational Communication: Continuity and Change in Personal Relationships,* Belmont, CA: Wadsworth, 1995.

4

Forms of Communication

4.1 Interpersonal Communication

Interpersonal communication refers to communication with another person. This kind of communication is subdivided into dyadic communication, public communication, and small-group communication.

Interpersonal communication encompasses:

i) Speech
ii) Non-verbal communication
iii) Unconscious communication
iv) summarising
v) paraphrasing

Having good interpersonal communication skills support such processes as:

i) selling
ii) counselling
iii) coaching
iv) mentoring and co-mentoring, which is mentoring in groups
v) conflict resolution

Interpersonal communication is the subject of a number of disciplines in the field of psychology, notably transactional analysis. It can be affected by a communication disorder or by arrogance, shyness, etc.

4.1.1 Defining Interpersonal Communication

4.1.1.1 Contextual View

One way of defining interpersonal communication is to compare it to other forms of communication. In so doing, we would examine how many people are involved, how physically close they are to one another, how many sensory channels are used, and the feedback provided. Interpersonal communication differs from other forms of communication in that there are few participants involved, the interactants are in close physical proximity to each other, there are many sensory channels used, and feedback is immediate. An important point to note about the contextual definition is that it does not take into account the relationship between the interactants.

4.1.1.2 Developmental View

We have many different relationships with people. Some researchers say that our definition of interpersonal communication must account for these differences. These researchers say that interacting with a sales clerk in a store is different than the relationship we have with our friends and family members. Thus, some researchers have proposed an alternative way of defining interpersonal communication. This is called the developmental view. From this view, interpersonal communication is defined as communication that occurs between people who have known each other for some time. Importantly, these people view each other as unique individuals, not as people who are simply acting out social situations.

4.1.2 Functions of Intepersonal Communication

Interpersonal communication is important because of the functions its achieves. Whenever we engage in communication with another person, we seek to gain information about them. We also give off information through a wide variety of verbal and non-verbal cues. The various functions of interpersonal communication are described below.

4.1.2.1 Gaining Information

One reason we engage in interpersonal communication is so that we can gain knowledge about another individual. Social Penetration Theory says that we attempt to gain information about others so that we can interact with them more effectively. We can better predict how they will think, feel, and act if we know who they are. We gain this information passively, by observing them; actively, by having others engage them; or interactively, by engaging them ourselves. Self-disclosure is often used to get information from another person.

4.1.2.2 Building a Context of Understanding

We also engage in interpersonal communication to help us better understand what someone says in a given context. The words we say can mean very different things depending on how they are said or in what context. *Content messages* refer to the surface level meaning of a message. *Relationship messages* refer to how a message is said. The two are sent simultaneously, but each affects the meaning assigned to the communication. Interpersonal communication helps us understand each other better.

4.1.2.3 Establishing Identity

Another reason we engage in interpersonal communication is to establish an identity. The roles we play in our relationships help us establish identity. So too does the face, the public self-image we present to others. Both roles and face are constructed based on how we interact with others.

4.1.2.4 Interpersonal needs

Finally, we engage in interpersonal communication because we need to express and receive interpersonal needs. William

Schutz has identified three such needs: inclusion, control, and affection.

i) Inclusion is the need to establish identity with others.

ii) Control is the need to exercise leadership and prove one's abilities. Groups provide outlets for this need. Some individuals do not want to be a leader. For them, groups provide the necessary control over aspects of their lives.

iii) Affection is the need to develop relationships with people. Groups are an excellent way to make friends and establish relationships.

4.1.2 Relationship Development

Researchers have studied relationships to understand how they develop. One of the most popular models for understanding relationship development is Mark Knapp's Relational Stages Model. Knapp's model works well to describe many types of relationships: romantic couples, friends, busines partners, roommates, etc. Other models have also been discussed. For instance, Stephen Duck's Relationship Filtering Model is another way of looking at how relationships begin. Read about these models and then complete an interactive activity and short quiz to test your knowledge.

4.1.3.1 Knapp's Relationship Escalation Model

Initiation	This stage is very short, sometimes as short as 10-15 seconds. In this stage, interactants are concerned with making favorable impressions on each other. They may use standard greetings or observe each other's appearance or mannerisms.
Experimenting	In the next stage, individuals ask questions of each other in order to gain information about them and decide if they wish to continue the relationship. "Many relationships progress no further than this point".

Intensifying — Self-disclosure becomes more common in the intensifying stage. The relationship becomes less formal, the interactants begin to see each other as individuals, and statements are made about the level of commitment each has to the relationship.

Integrating — The individuals become a pair in the integrating stage. They begin to do things together and, importantly, others come to see them as a pair. A shared relational identity starts to form in this stage.

Bonding — During the bonding stage, a formal, sometimes legal, announcement of the relationship is made. Examples include a marriage, "best friend" ritual, or business partnership agreement. Few relationships reach this level.

4.1.3.2 Duck's Relationship Filtering Model

Sociological/ Incidental cues — Duck's model is a set of filters through which we make choices about the level of relationship we wish to pursue with others. The first filter, socioligical/incidental cues, describes the constraints placed on our meeting people due to where we live or work. In other words, given our sociological location, there are some people we see a lot of and others we never meet.

Preinteraction cues — Information we gain about people before we even interact with them leads us to exclude or include individuals with whom we wish to have a relationship. For instance, the appearance of some individuals will cause you to avoid or approach them.

Interaction cues — As we begin to interact with others, we make judgements about whether to include or exclude them from possible relationships.

Cognitive cues	At the deepest level, we make judgements about people based on their personality and the degree to which we think it will match ours. As others reach this level, we consider them "best friends".

4.1.3.3 Knapp's Relationship Termination Model

Differentiating	In this stage, partners begin to stress the "me" instead of the "we". In other words, the individuals begin to assert their independence. They may develop different hobbies or activities. The relationship may continue to dissolve, or this stage may be a warning sign that the couple needs to address their relationship status.
Circumscribing	Communication between the couple diminishes during this stage. They tend to avoid certain topics of discussion. Outwardly, the couple appears normal. At this stage, attempts can be made to discuss the relationship and return it to a positive state.
Stagnating	During the stagnating stage, the individuals avoid discussing the relationship because they think they know what the other will say. Others begin to take notice that something is wrong.
Avoiding	The pair begins to physically separate themselves during the avoiding stage. The individuals try to reduce the opportunities for discussion.
Terminating	This is the final stage of the relationship. Termination may come naturally, such as at the end of the semester when roommates move out, or arbitrarily, through divorce. Termination of the relationship can occur positively or negatively.

4.1.4 Self Disclosure

Self-disclosure is seen as a useful strategy for sharing information with others. By sharing information, we become more intimate with other people and our interpersonal relationship is strengthened. Read about self-disclosure and then complete the interactive activity and take a short quiz to test your understanding of the concept.

Self-disclosure is not simply providing information to another person. Instead, scholars define self-disclosure as sharing information with others that they would not normally know or discover. Self-disclosure involves risk and vulnerability on the part of the person sharing the information.

4.1.4.1 The Johari Window

A useful way of viewing self-disclosure is the Johari window. The concept of Johari window was invented by Joseph Luft and Harry Ingham, who combined their first names to create the name. The Johari window model focuses on the balance of interpersonal communication. It is a way of showing how much information you know about yourself and how much others know about you. It divides interpersonal relationship between people into four quadrants based on two dimensions: whether information is or is not known by each of the two parties.

The window contains four panes, as shown below.

	Known to self	Unknown to self
Known to others	*Open Pane* known to self and others	*Blind Pane* blind to self, seen by others
Unknown to others	*Hidden Pane* open to self, hidden from others	*Unknown Pane* unknown to self and others

Figure 4.1. The Johari Window

The *Open Pane* includes information such as hair colour, occupation, and physical appearance.

The *Blind Pane* includes information that others can see in you, but you cannot see in your self. You might think you are poor leader, but others think you exhibit strong leadership skills.

The *Hidden Pane* contains information you wish to keep private, such as dreams or ambitions.

The *Unknown Pane* includes everything that you and others do not know about yourself. You may have hidden talents, for example, that you have not explored. Through self-disclosure, we open and close panes so that we may become more intimate with others.

4.1.4.2 Functions

Self-disclosure performs several functions. It is a way of gaining information about another person. We want to be able to predict the thoughts and actions of people we know. Self-disclosure is one way to learn about how another person thinks and feels. Once one person engages in self-disclosure, it is implied that the other person will also disclose personal information. This is known as the norm of reciprocity. Mutual disclosure deepens trust in the relationships and helps both people understand each other more. You also come to feel better about yourself and your relationship when the other person accepts what you tell them.

4.1.4.3 Risks

While there are several advantages to self-disclosure, there are also risks. One risk is that the person will not respond favourably to the information. Self-disclosure does not automatically lead to favourable impressions. Another risk is that the other person will gain power in the relationship because of the information they possess. Finally, too much self-disclosure or self-disclosure that comes too early in a relationship can damage the relationship. Thus, while self-disclosure is useful, it can also be damaging to a relationship.

4.1.5 Relational Patterns

As relationships progress, patterns of interactions take shape that we may not recognise. Some of these patterns are described below.

4.1.5.1 Rigid Role Relations

There are two basic types of behaviours in relationships: dominance and submissiveness. Dominance is often referred to as one-up, while submissiveness, one-down. In some relationships, the two are complementary—one individual is one-up, the other one-down—and the relationship is rewarding. Other relationships are symmetrical, where both parties are one-up or both are one-down. Problems can result when individuals feel trapped by their role as the dominant or submissive member of the relationship. Flexibility can help both partners enjoy the relationship.

4.1.5.2 Disconfirmations

Whenever we communicate with someone else, we open ourselves up for rejection. The other individual can accept what we say or reject what we say. Researcher Evelyn Sieburg has identified seven "disconfirming" responses that reject the other individual.

i) *Impervious*: Failing to acknowledge the other person.
ii) *Interrupting*: Cutting the other's message short.
iii) *Irrelevant*: Giving a response that is unrelated to what the other has said.
iv) *Tangential*: Briefly responding to the other's message.
v) *Impersonal*: Responding by using formal, jargon-laden language.
vi) *Incoherent*: Responding with a rambling, difficult to understand message.
vii) *Incongruous*: Giving contradictory verbal and non-verbal messages.

4.1.5.3 Spirals

A third type of relational pattern is a spiral. "In a spiral, one partner's behaviour intensifies that of the other". Spirals can be progressive, in which one partner's behaviour leads to increasing levels of satisfaction for the other. Spirals can also be regressive, where one partner's communication leads to increasing dissatisfaction. Stopping regressive spirals from getting out of control depends on the open communication between the two individuals.

4.1.5.4 Dependencies and Counter-dependencies

A final type of relational pattern is dependencies and counterdependencies. In a dependency relationship, one individual sees himself or herself relying on another person for something. Soon, he or she agrees with whatever the other says or does. In a counter-dependency, one individual sees himself or herself as not being dependent on the other. Thus, he or she disagrees with the other quite frequently.

4.1.6 Interpersonal Conflict

Conflict is a part of most every interpersonal relationship. Managing conflict, then, is important if the relationship is to be long-lasting and rewarding. Conflict has been defined as "an expressed struggle between at least two interdependent parties who perceive incompatible goals, scarce resources, and interference from the other party in achieving their goals." Important concepts in this definition include "expressed struggle", which means the two sides must communicate about the problem for there to be conflict. Another important idea is that conflict often involves perceptions. The two sides may only perceive that their goals, resources, and interference is incompatible with each other's.

4.1.6.1 Problems in Conflict Management

Researchers have identified several problems that typically arise in conflict situations. First, the parties will simply avoid the conflict. This can be damaging, because it can lead to greater problems in the future. It is usually best that the individuals discuss their differences. Second, individuals involved in conflict may blame the other individual. Often, individuals go beyond the specific behaviour in question and blame the character of the person. When people use words such as, "He's such a slob," they are engaging in blame the other behaviour. A final problem that is often encountered in conflict management is adopting a win-lose mentality. Focusing on each individual's goals/outcomes will help avoid using a win-lose strategy.

4.1.6.2 Defensive Climate

The climate in which conflict is managed is important. Dyads should avoid a defensive climate, which is characterised by these qualities:

i) *Evaluation*: judging and criticising other group members.
ii) *Control*: imposing the will of one group member on the others.
iii) *Strategy*: using hidden agendas.
iv) *Neutrality*: demonstrating indifference and lack of commitment.
v) *Superiority*: expressing dominance.
vi) *Certainty*: being rigid in one's willingness to listen to others.

4.1.6.3 Supportive Climate

Instead, individuals should foster a supportive climate, marked by these traits:

i) *Description*: presenting ideas or opinions.
ii) *Problem orientation*: focusing attention on the task.
iii) *Spontaneity*: communicating openly and honestly.
iv) *Empathy*: understanding another person's thoughts.
v) *Equality*: asking for opinions.

vi) *Provisionalism*: expressing a willingness to listen other the ideas of others.

A few final tips can help insure that conflict is successfully managed:

i) *Conflict can be constructive*. Recognise that conflict can strengthen your relationships.

ii) *Be prepared*. Plan how you will communicate about conflict in order to create a supportive climate.

iii) *Be involved*. Do not withdraw from the conflict or avoid conflict situations.

iv) *Withhold quick retorts*. Be careful about what you say and how you say it.

v) *Review*. Summarise what you have discussed and make plans to continue the discussion if time permits immediate resolution.

4.2 Intrapersonal Communication

Intrapersonal communication is communication that a person has with him or herself.

Although some might take the position that no communication is needed if only one party is involved, we communicate with ourselves all the time.

Intrapersonal communication can encompass:

i) Sense-making, e.g., interpreting maps, texts, signs, and symbols

ii) Interpreting non-verbal communication, e.g., gestures, eye contact

iii) Communication between body parts;, e.g., "My stomach is telling me it's time for lunch."

iv) Speaking aloud ("talking to oneself"), reading aloud, repeating what one hears; the additional activities of speaking and hearing (in the third case of hearing again) what one thinks, reads or hears may increase concentration and retention.

v) Writing (by hand, or with a wordprocessor, etc.) one's thoughts or observations: the additional activities, on top of thinking, of writing and reading back may again increase self-understanding and concentration. It aids ordering one's thoughts; in addition it produces a record that can be used later again. Copying text to aid memorising also falls in this category.

vi) Making gestures while thinking: the additional activity, on top of thinking, of body motions, may again increase concentration, assist in problem solving, and assist memory.

vii) Day-dreaming

viii) Nocturnal dreaming

In the field of communication studies there is a widely held belief in intrapersonal communication as a unique process of message exchange and information transformation within the individual. Of all the commonly acknowledged forms of communication—interpersonal, small-group, organisational, non-verbal and mass communication—intrapersonal communication is the youngest and least developed notion, and the one about which the least has been published. For all that, however, it is regularly mentioned and defended in the literature as an important component in the spectrum of communication types. Indeed, one of the strongest claims made repeatedly is that intrapersonal communication is the basis and foundation of all other forms of communication. Quite simply, intrapersonal communication has become an accepted model in communication theory, especially in the areas of speech and interpersonal communication.

Recently, questions have been raised about difficulties just in trying to define intrapersonal communication. For the most part, however, it remains an uncontested model. Its theorists assume that intrapersonal communication, either as a reality or as a powerful model, comprises a range of functions, and that it augments our understanding of both what communication is and what it means to be a human being. Many intrapersonal communication theorists refer to the work of psychologists and neurophysiologists to reinforce their point that intrapersonal communication comprises a number of intrapersonal processes. At first glance, that kind of referencing seems to lend scientific credence to Iac, but some weighty assumptions have been made.

In most cases the scientific authorities alluded to are usually not talking about a form of communication, but, more conservatively, about inner processing in general: cognitive, perceptual and motivational episodes. To call these psychophysiological processes 'communication' is to exercise a transformation that exceeds the interests and insights of the allegedly supporting authorities.

Now, an essential requirement in the life of any theory is those reflective moments in which its adherents adjudicate competing interpretations and respond unflinchingly to challenges directed against the model itself. Just as the phenomenon of mass communication has been exposed to a declension of competing interpretations in the course of efforts to understand what it is, how it works and what kinds of effects it generates, there is a corresponding need for the same kind of interpretative exercises vis-a-vis intrapersonal communication.

4.2.1 Operations and Properties

The literature makes a surprising number of claims about intrapersonal communication. Many of these claims identify functions, events or operations such as inner dialogue, reasoning or the processing of information. Other claims have more to do with the characteristics or properties of intrapersonal communication. For example, some believe that intrapersonal communication is the foundation of all communication, and that it is an important source of self-knowledge. Accordingly, as a first step in understanding what intrapersonal communication is supposed to be, it is important to provide a catalogue of these operations and characteristics. In the inventory that follows, both functions and properties commonly attributed to intrapersonal communication have been identified and assembled into numbered classes. These classifications do not pretend to be complete, but they are representative.

4.2.1.1 Operations

i) *Talking to oneself*, the process of communicating with(in) oneself, of inner speech, or a self-contained communication system within the person is often mentione.

ii) *An internal dialogue* or interchange of meanings between parts of the person, such as consciousness and the unconscious, or between the "I"—that "part of ourselves that is fundamentally idiosyncratic and personal"—and the "Me"—that "part of ourselves that is social product" is also mentioned. A related operation is the transfer of messages between the brain and an individual's other parts.

iii) *A process whereby a person transacts with the environment* or adapts to the environment; a process of manipulating cues (stimuli) impinging upon us from without or even from within is attributed to intrapersonal communication.

iv) *Perception* is another operation, a process whereby the individual receives, stores, and retrieves information or symbolic abstractions.

v) *An interactive process whereby the "raw data" of perception are endowed with meaning* or transformed into information of a more conceptual nature has been described. Budd and Ruben term this epistemic sublimation variously as "the metabolism of information", "conversion", "extraction", and "inference" in order to underscore the more abstract level of the resultant information. intrapersonal communication, they write, supplies the individual with a "conceptual surrogate for environment data".

vi) *Data processing* functions are described as well. Given the functions recorded in (iv) and (v) above, it is not surprising that some authors choose to think of intrapersonal communication in metaphorical terms as a "data processing centre". Where that metaphor is not explicitly invoked, the recurrent use of the data and information-processing idioms encourages that and other sorts of biomechanical interpretations.

vii) *Feedback* is sometimes identified, but more often than not is only implicit in some of the operations identified in (iii)-(vi) above.

viii) Though individual accounts may stress this or that aspect, the literature attributes a wide assortment of mentalistic operations to intrapersonal communication—that is, a range of epistemic functions that do not seem to be reducible to purely material changes or elements. These include the following:

a) the assignment of meaning to, or interpretations of, perceptions, events and experiences

b) thinking and understanding

c) problem solving, conflict resolution, applied thinking, evaluation, planning, decision making

d) memory

e) introspection; awareness, self-consciousness and self-knowledge; reflection; metacognition

f) dreaming;

g) imaging;

h) feeling;

i) intrapersonal communication comprises or is allied to a number of dispositions and emotional states that, in turn, affect overt behavior and speech. These inner states range anywhere from willingness to communicate to unconsciousness and mindlessness.

ix) In a move that is highly reminiscent of Immanuel Kant's intuition of time, Bruneau suggests that intrapersonal communication is that whereby we experience time in all its modalities. intrapersonal communication, he writes, is "basically and essentially temporalities concerning internal time dimensions, cycles, periods, rhythms and kinds of sequential phenomena."

x) *intrapersonal communication crops up as an easily recognisable synonym in the literature of persuasion.* More precisely, "self-persuasion" is taken to be an internal process involving the production and intransitive movement of messages within the individual.

4.2.1.2 Properties

i) *Intrapersonal communication is exclusively a neurophysiological activity*, and it can be "defined" through experimental procedures in purely neurophysiological terms. It is something that is "mainly a concern of the psychologist and neurologist". Roberts states that "all of the communication within the individual is physiological." Some argue, with less desire for precision, that intrapersonal communication can be viewed as a mental process, a physical state, and as a biological-psychological system.

ii) *Intrapersonal communication is virtually a continuous process in our waking state.*

iii) *From the earliest days of this theory, the relationship of intrapersonal communication to language and symbols has been problematic* Though Budd and Ruben raise the possibility that "language may not be a requirement for Intrapersonal Communication", the consensus among most is that language (or some form of encoding/decoding) plays a "decisive role" and an "important part".

iv) *Intrapersonal communication is essential both to the reality of, and to our understanding of, all communication.* Intrapersonal communication is the basis or foundation of all communication Barker and Edwards are not alone when they say that interpersonal communication cannot occur without intrapersonal communication going on simultaneously. Littlejohn says that it is "so pervasive that it cuts across all other contexts, making it a universal theme." Larson enthusiastically universalises the significance and import of self-persuasion in a manner which parallels the claims made for intrapersonal communication: "In one sense", he writes, "all persuasion is self-persuasion—we are rarely persuaded unless we participate in the process"

v) *Intrapersonal communication, or knowledge of intrapersonal communication adds to our knowledge of ourselves and to our understanding of the process of communication with others.* It is a source of personal development and self-discovery, of self-understanding, of our view of ourselves—both as a part of and apart from our environment,

vi) *Intrapersonal communication has therapeutic value.* By developing this level of communication, we can promote inner harmony, the union of body and soul; we can regain health and stability, and improve physical functioning.

vii) *Intrapersonal communication has a valid role in empirical research.* It is something that can be studied through empirical methods.

4.2.2 Weaknesses of Intrapersonal Communication

This section identifies a number of weaknesses in the intrapersonal communication construct. Target of these evaluations and criticisms is not the reality of our inner operations, nor indeed the causal and conditioning role they might play in the business of communicating with others. Rather, the focus of this critique is the uncritical extension of communication terminology and metaphors to the facts of our inner life space. It is one thing to say that communication behaviour is rooted in intrapersonal events or processes, or that it has an important psycho-physiological dimension.

4.2.2.1 Ambiguity

There is a profound ambiguity at the core of the phrase "intrapersonal communication processes". Depending upon how we bracket its phrase constituents, it is possible to come up with two different interpretations. Intrapersonal communication processes is the weaker reading which may simply denote the inner behavioural aspects or foundations of communication in general without positing any distinctive communication type. This interpretation is not controversial since no one would seriously question the reality of the inner physico-psychological basis of communicative behaviour. Even though they appear in the general context of a unique communication type, a few articles seem to content themselves with this interpretation. On the other hand, intrapersonal communication processes is a much stronger reading: linguistically and semantically, it says that distinctive micro-messages or communication units circulate within each of us. This latter interpretation is the majority view among intrapersonal communication theorists and the object of this critique.

In any case, what we have here is more than just a piece of linguistic ambivalence. Due to of this ambiguity it is difficult to know whether the referent of intrapersonal communication theorising is a unique mode of human exchange—Blake and Haroldsen call it a "distinct concept"—or whether "intrapersonal communication" is little more than a misleading label for the psychophysical dimension of all human communication. Without precision in its opening terms, we can scarcely expect clarity in the ensuing speculations.

It is uncertain whether the terms intrapersonal communication and intrapersonal communication processes signify one overarching theory, several theories, or, less ambitiously, one or more pretheoretical postulates. Intrapersonal communication theorists often seem to speak as if intrapersonal communication has a solid theoretical status, but it may be closer to the intent of most to view intrapersonal communication as a pretheoretical construct. None the less, it is difficult to know whether the manifold accounts of intrapersonal communication operations and properties are posited as neutral descriptions, definitions, or explanations. As neutral descriptions they might simply stand as components of an abstract theory without any ontological commitment to the reality of intrapersonal communication. Many accounts, those which invoke cross-disciplinary research and empirical grounding, present themselves as explanations that genuinely augment our understanding of human nature.

4.2.2.2 Counter-intuitivity

If only initially, the theory of intrapersonal communication seems to be counter-intuitive, and it violates customary usage. In both ordinary language and communication theory, the term communication typically denotes the exchange or sharing of messages between and among persons, something situated within a community. That is, communication is typically regarded as a molar social phenomenon. In contrast to this normal acceptance, intrapersonal communication posits a message transfer within the individual. This means that the intrapersonal communication model is in sharp conflict with paradigm models of communication.

Now, the concept of communication is admittedly polymorphous, but both in theoretical discussion as well as in everyday discourse it characteristically entails a core of three features:

i) a community of at least two persons

ii) a message, construed as something meaningful or informative

iii) a sharing, transfer, or exchange of that message

iv) a system of symbols whereby the message is structured

v) a degree of consciousness or awareness

vi) an element of purpose or intent, and/or an element of choice either of which serves to distinguish communication as a human activity from mere mechanical impact or physical transfer.

For the sake of convenience and brevity, this enumeration does not include such standard features as noise, feedback, medium or channel, and effects—let alone the welter of more refined notions such as rules, proxemics, redundancy, and so on. Notwithstanding these omissions, however, the six enumerated features, especially the first three, are theoretical requirements which spell out minimal conditions for communicative performance and theory building. They are necessary conditions either mentioned, embedded, or implied in any theoretical discussion of communication ranging from mass communication to non-verbal and interpersonal communication. However, the various claims made about intrapersonal communication are seriously compromised by the fact that these core features are not clearly instantiated; and when they are invoked, they figure only in a highly metaphorical and tenuous fashion. The tenuousness of these moves can be illustrated by attending more closely to intrapersonal communication's reliance upon (a) the language of personhood, (b) its appeal to the concept of message, and (c) its inherent dependency upon the notion of private language.

4.2.2.3 Persons Unknown

For one thing, the person within whom intrapersonal communication is said to take place is not a community, but a single self. Some descriptions seem to respect partially that constraint by depicting intrapersonal communication as something that goes on within the single person or individual or "within the life space of one organism". In other accounts, it could be said that the indivisibility of the self is implied and protected by vesting plurality not in any parts or divisions of the person, but in reflexive verb forms and pronouns: "talking to oneself", "self-persuasion", "privately interpreting to oneself". In either case, the point is that any real community of persons is not apparent. The duality, so necessary for communication, seems to be nothing more than grammatical.

4.2.2.4 Message as Cipher

What is said and left unsaid about the message component compounds the uncertainty of intrapersonal communication. The term message is frequently used in the literature, but just as often other synonyms are used, such as dialogue, inner speech, meaning, information. In most cases the message element is described as a process in language which is intended to underscore its dynamism. Now, while most accounts ascribe a highly semantic and epistemic nature to the message process, its symbolic status remains indefinite. Descriptions such as "inner speech" and "talking to oneself" suggest that intrapersonal communication is a fully language-mediated experience cast primarily in propositional form. Phrases such as "encoding-decoding process" and "symbolic abstractions" indicate that some form of symbolism is at work, though not necessarily a linguistic one.

There is a certain irony within this confusion. Language is not simply a conduit by which meanings are exported and imported between senders and receivers. On the contrary, language theory over the last few decades, and in a variety of disciplines, has done much to show that language itself plays a central and constitutive role in the formation of meaning. intrapersonal communication threatens to become unintelligible in direct proportion to the distance placed between it and the structure of symbols and language.

Until something is done to clarify or reduce the element of symbolic indeterminacy in intrapersonal communication, it is virtually impossible to decide in what sense its "message" is to be interpreted as really being a message. That uncertainty is compounded when we try to relate the alleged message element to some of the purely affective processes attributed to intrapersonal communication: feelings, emotional states, and dispositions such as unwillingness. These processes are clearly experiential, but many would hesitate to ascribe symbolised message structures to these affective states.

4.2.2.5 Radical Privacy of Language

This symbolic and linguistic indeterminacy should not be surprising because of an unremovable barrier between intrapersonal communication and its theorists: By definition, the message is unavailable for public examination. "Message" in its normal, non-metaphorical sense, means a symbolically structured text that, in principle at least, is accessible to more than one person. But the message of intrapersonal communication is so private and indeterminate that not only agreement but even disagreement about its symbolic or nonsymbolic status is ruled out of order. "Talking to oneself" might seem to escape that blanket constraint, but to the extent that it is verbalised or externalised, it thereby seems to disqualify itself as an inner, self-contained exchange. Besides, Barnlund seems to voice a consensus found in intrapersonal communication discussions when he writes that "it is desirable to restrict 'intrapersonal communication' to the manipulation of cues within an individual that occurs in the absence of other people".

The situation here is not unlike the issue of private language that has exercised the attention of philosophers in the last few decades, and so it may be instructive to look at what Wittgenstein had to say. In the *Philosophical Investigations,* Wittgenstein raises the question of the possibility of a radically private language or notational system put together by an individual in order to record and describe inner experiences only, such as pain.

Wittgenstein's aphoristic reflections are relevant to the issue of intrapersonal communication's message factor. Those accounts of intrapersonal communication that posit or imply a privately generated symbolism, or that make intrapersonal communication itself an originating condition or defining element for other levels of communication, veer into the same kind of tenuousness diagnosed by Wittgenstein. On the other hand, if intrapersonal communication is taken to mean talking to oneself in words and phrases borrowed from another language already learned, then its so-called privacy or intrapersonal nature is seriously compromised. Such verbal behaviour, it can be argued, is simply truncated conversation, a derivative practice that does not take place unless one already knows a publicly shared language. About this kind of behaviour one can say, without significant theoretical loss or penalty to communication theory in general, that there is indeed a type of nondirected, non-communicative thinking and verbalising that does nothing more than imitate some features of dialogue. To call it intrapersonal communication, however, is to make it into something much more than it has to be.

4.2.2.6 Non-specificity

The difficulties involved in trying to see how community, personhood and message do or do not apply to intrapersonal communication are facets of much more comprehensive defects in the model,namely, its non-specificity and general aura of indeterminacy.

Consider the proliferation of operations attributed to intrapersonal communication. Pearson and Nelson, for instance, write that:

> intrapersonal communication is not restricted to "talking to ourselves"; it also includes such activities as internal problem solving, resolution of internal conflict, planning for the future, emotional catharsis, evaluations of ourselves and others, and the relationships between ourselves and others.

Roberts et al. confidently pose an even greater totality in their definition of intrapersonal communication as all of the physiological and psychological processing of messages that happens within individuals at conscious and nonconscious levels as they attempt to understand themselves and their environment. Some might see the above definition as either harmonising with or conveniently summarising the catalog of functions commonly attributed to intrapersonal communication. However, by virtue of its very comprehensiveness it becomes indistinguishable from a tautology.

With an eye to such metatheoretical issues as the definability of intrapersonal communication, more specific criticisms can be framed. For example, the identification of intrapersonal communication or its message with an assortment of mentalistic and/or neurophysiological operations seems forced and hasty. No one would deny that any number of cognitive processes are somehow involved in communication behaviour, but the descriptions of intrapersonal communication for the most part unguardedly set up an identity between the definiendum and one or more of these operations. The move is premature because it rules out the possibility of other kinds of relationships.

Indeed, given its epistemic scope, there seems to be little difference between intrapersonal communication and the philosophical concept of mind or, more comprehensively, the Greco-medieval concept of soul and its system of interactive sensory and intellectual powers.

There is conflicting testimony as to whether or not intrapersonal communication is linguistically or symbolically structured. Additional pairs of conflicting interpretations accentuate the overall indeterminacy of the intrapersonal communication model. For one thing, it remains unclear from the literature whether intrapersonal communication is a biomechanical agency explainable without residue in terms of neurophysiology, or one that should be thought of in non-physicalist or mentalistic terms. Some allow that intrapersonal communication can be viewed as a mental process, a physical state, and a biological-psychological system. That sort of generous allowance, however, seems to do more to identify the confusion than to dispel it.

Second, it is equally unclear whether intrapersonal communication should be thought of as atomic or particulate information, or as being a more discursive mode of cognition. Descriptions that underscore stimuli, raw data, storage, retrieval and reacting with the environment seem to imply that it works at the level of discrete bits of information. Other accounts picture intrapersonal communication as functioning at a more abstract level in which propositional and inferential forms of knowledge predominate: talking to oneself, inner dialogue, thinking; problem solving, planning and evaluation. In either case, nonspecificity is compounded by the welter of qualitatively different functions attributed to intrapersonal communication.

Third, we have no way of knowing whether intrapersonal communication should be construed as free or chosen behavior or whether, as merely physiological motions, it should be treated as something involuntary in which purpose and intention play no role. Descriptions that stress or incorporate the neurophysiological and the continuous data-processing aspects of intrapersonal communication do much to minimise the element of personal agency in human communication. When it emphasises the biomechanical processes, intrapersonal communication signalises a retreat from the concept of human action by reducing communication or its genesis to a series of physical episodes. That sort of reductionism, though not uncommon, does something to erode the specificity of human communication.

4.2.2.7 Circularity

The logical impropriety of intrapersonal communication is evident in repeated claims that it is the basis and foundation of all other forms of communication. It is also said that all communication is to some extent intrapersonal communication. Consistent with these claims are the added claims that intrapersonal communication contributes significantly to our understanding of all forms of communication as well as to our own self-knowledge.

There appears to be an embarrassing circularity here. Communication is a molar phenomenon which we first encounter and come to know through its public forms: interpersonal, group and mass communication, body language. Intrapersonal communication, on the other hand, is a later theoretical construct elaborated in the identical terms and metaphors already in use to explain these public forms: message, sender, receiver, dialogue, speech, talking, feedback, coding and decoding, and, of course, "communication" itself. Yet in the very same breath, theorists insist that intrapersonal communication is the basis of these other forms of communication from which it has just borrowed its principal concepts and vocabulary.

4.3 Group Communication

Most researchers define a group as having at least three and no more than 12 or 15 members. A group needs to have at least three members, otherwise it would simply be a dyad. With three members, coalitions can be formed and some kind of organisation is present. Too large of a group (more than 12 or 15 members) inhibits the group members' ability to communicate with everyone else in the group.

A group's members must be able to communicate freely and openly with all of the other members of the group. Groups will develop norms about discussion and group members will develop roles which will affect the group's interaction.

A group must have a common purpose or goal and they must work together to achieve that goal. The goal brings the group together and holds it together through conflict and tension.

People join groups for a variety of reasons. Some group members are motivated by task concerns and others are motivated by interpersonal attraction to other group members. Some reasons of why do people join a group are outined below:

i) *Group synergy* : Group synergy refers to the idea that two heads (or more) are better than one. You may have also heard the phrase, "The whole is greater than the sum of its parts," which also refers to group synergy. Put simply, groups are often capable of producing higher quality work and better decisions that can an individual working alone.

ii) *Support and commitment:* A group may be more willing to take on a large project than would an individual. In addition to its increased ability to perform work, the group can provide encouragement and support to its members while working on a big project.

iii) *Interpersonal needs*: Individuals often join a group to meet their interpersonal needs. William Schutz has identified three such needs: inclusion, control, and affection.

   a) *Inclusion* is the need to establish identity with others.

b) *Control* is the need to exercise leadership and prove one's abilities. Groups provide outlets for this need. Some individuals do not want to be a leader. For them, groups provide the necessary control over aspects of their lives.

c) *Affection* is the need to develop relationships with people. Groups are an excellent way to make friends and establish relationships.

4.3.1 Types of Small Groups

Groups form to accomplish some objective. The objective may be to complete some kind of task or it may be to promote the interpersonal relationships between the group members. Many groups, however, fulfill both of these functions. Some more information about the various types of groups are given below:

4.3.1.1 Social Groups

While all groups will have both social and task dimensions, some groups are predominantly social in their orientation. Examples of these groups would be families and social clubs. These groups provide for our safety and solidarity needs and they help us develop self-esteem.

4.3.1.2 Work Groups

Work groups function to complete a particular task. In a work group, the task dimension is emphasised. The group members pool their expertise to accomplish the task. Examples of this would be workplaces, campus organisations, or juries. There are several types of work groups, based on the work of Ivan Steiner:

i) *Additive work group*: All group members perform the same activity and pool their results at the end. An example of this would be gathering signatures for a petition drive.

ii) *Conjunctive work group*: Group members perform different, but related, tasks that allow for the completion of a goal. Every group member must complete their task in order for the group task to be completed. An example of this would be an assembly line, in which each worker performs tasks that together build a completed car.

iii) *Disjunctive task*: Members meet to determine the best alternative for a problem or issue. There are two types of disjunctive tasks:

iv) *Judgment task*: Group members must choose one correct answer from all alternatives.

v) *Decision-making task*: Group members must choose the best alternative from a set of options. There is no one correct answer for a decision-making group.

4.3.1.2 Contrived or Emergent Groups

Some groups form spontaneously, such as a group of friends. Other groups are contrived, that is, they are formed for a specific purpose. Organised clubs, social groups, or committees are contrived groups.

4.3.2 Small Group Development

Researchers have studied groups to understand how they develop. Several different models have been suggested, but they all tend to follow a similar progression. Listed below are three of the most common models.

Table 4.1. Linear models of group development

Tubbs's theory	Fisher's model	Tuckman's model
1. Orientation	1. Orientation	1. Forming
2. Conflict	2. Conflict	2. Storming
3. Consensus	3. Emergence	3. Norming
4. Closure	4. Reinforcement	4. Performing
		5. Adjourning

4.3.2.1 Tubbs's Theory

i) *Orientation:* In this stage, group members get to know each other, they start to talk about the problem, and they examine the limitations and opportunities of the project.

ii) *Conflict:* Conflict is a necessary part of a group's development. Conflict allows the group to evaluate ideas and it helps the group avoid conformity and groupthink.

iv) *Consensus:* Conflict ends in the consensus stage, when group members compromise, select ideas, and agree on alternatives.

v) *Closure:* In this stage, the final result is announced and group members reaffirm their support of the decision.

4.3.2.2 Fisher's Model

i) *Orientation*: During the orientation phase, Fisher says group members get to know each other and they experience primary tension, the awkward feeling people have before communication rules and expectations are established. Groups should take time to learn about each other and feel comfortable communicating around new people.

ii) *Conflict:* The conflict phase is marked by secondary tension, or tension surrounding the task at hand. Group members will disagree with each other and debate ideas. Remember that conflict is good, because it helps the group achieve positive results.

iii) *Emergence*: In the emergence phase, says Fisher, the outcome of the group's task and its social structure become apparent.

iv) *Reinforcement*: In this stage, group members bolster their final decision by using supportive verbal and non-verbal communication.

4.3.2.3 Tuckman's Model

i) *Forming*: In the forming stage, group members learn about each other and the task at hand.

ii) *Storming*: As group members become more comfortable with each other, they will engage each other in arguments and vie for status in the group. These activities mark the storming phase.

iii) *Norming*: During the norming stage, group members establish implicit or explicit rules about how they will achieve their goal. They address the types of communication that will or will not help with the task.

iv) *Performing*: In the performing stage, groups reach a conclusion and implement the conclusion.

v) *Adjourning*: As the group project ends, the group disbands in the adjournment phase.

4.3.2.4 Poole's Model

Marshall Scott Poole and his colleagues have found that group development is often more complicated than the three previous models indicate. He has argued that groups jump back and forth between three tracks: task, topic, and relation. The three tracks can be compared to the intertwined strands of a rope.

i) *Task track*: The task track concerns the process by which the group accomplishes its goals.

ii) *Topic track* : The topic track concerns the specific item the group is discussing at the time.

iii) *Relation track*: The relation track deals with the interpersonal relationships between the group members. At times, the group may stop its work on the task and work instead on its relationships. When the group reaches consensus on all three tracks at once, it can proceed in a more unified manner as the three previous models illustrate.

iv) *Breakpoints*: Breakpoints occur when a group switches from one track to another. Shifts in the conversation, adjournment, or postponement are examples of breakpoints.

4.3.3 Decisionmaking

Many groups meet to solve problems or make decisions. The detains of how groups can effectively accomplish their task objectives are discussed below.

i) *Standard agenda:* Developed by John Dewey, reflective thinking involves a careful, systematic approach to a problem. Groups who use reflective thinking to make their decisions make use of a six-step guide called the standard agenda.

   a) *Problem identification.* What is the problem? What is wrong with the current situation?

   b) *Problem analysis.* View the current situation as a balance between restraining forces and helping forces. What are the forces in play in your group's situation?

   c) *Criteria selection.* What are the goals of the final decision?

   d) *Solution generation.* Generate as many solutions as possible. Avoid groupthink by listing many solutions.

   e) *Solution evaluation and selection.* Measure each solution against the criteria from step three.

   f) *Solution implementation.* Enact the chosen solution.

ii) *Brainstorming:* Another option for decisionmaking is brainstorming. When brainstorming, group members are encouraged to generate as many ideas about a particular topic as they can. For instance, group members may use brainstorming to generate as many solutions as they can in step four of the standard agenda. Group members should be encouraged to say anything that comes to mind when brainstorming. Every idea is written down and judgments about ideas are saved until later, when the group returns to all of the ideas and selects those that are most useful.

iii) *Nominal group technique*: Nominal group technique is a group decision-making tool used when the group must rank order a set of options. In order to use the nominal group technique, group members work individually to list all alternatives to a problem or issue. Sometimes, nominal group technique is used after a brainstorming session is held. Then, the group facilitator asks each group member to individually rank all of the options from lowest to highest priority. Finally, the facilitator computes an average score for each idea. the lowest score is the highest priority for the group.

iv) *The final decision*: There are many ways that a group can make a final decision, decide on a solution, or come to agreement. Some of the most popular ways of making the decision include:

a) *Consensus*: The group members all agree on the final decision through discussion and debate.

a) *Compromise*: Through discussion and readjustment of the final plan, group members come to agreement by giving up some of their demands

a) *Majority vote*: The decision is based on the opinion of the majority of its members.

a) *Decision by leader*: The group gives the final decision to its leader.

a) *Arbitration*: An external body or person makes a decision for the group.

4.3.4 Groupthink

Groupthink is a concept that was identified by Irving Janis that refers to faulty decision-making in a group. Groups experiencing groupthink do not consider all alternatives and they desire unanimity at the expense of quality decisions. The details of groupthink are discussed below:

i) *Conditions*: Groupthink occurs when groups are highly cohesive and when they are under considerable pressure to make a quality decision.

ii) *Negative outcomes*: Some negative outcomes of groupthink include:

a) Examining few alternatives
b) Not being critical of each other's ideas
c) Not examining early alternatives
d) Not seeking expert opinion
e) Being highly selective in gathering information
f) Not having contingency plans

iv) *Symptoms*: Some symptoms of groupthink are:

a) Having an illusion of invulnerability
b) Rationalising poor decisions
c) Believing in the group's morality
d) Sharing stereotypes which guide the decision
e) Exercising direct pressure on others
f) Not expressing your true feelings
g) Maintaining an illusion of unanimity
h) Using mindguards to protect the group from negative information

v) *Solutions*: Some solutions include:

a) Using a policy-forming group which reports to the larger group
b) Having leaders remain impartial
c) Using different policy groups for different tasks
d) Dividing into groups and then discuss differences
e) Discussing within sub-groups and then report back
f) Using outside experts
g) Using a devil's advocate to question all the group's ideas

h) Holding a "second-chance meeting" to offer one last opportunity to choose another course of action

4.3.5 Leadership

Leadership is concerned with control and power in a group. Leadership can be aimed at either maintaining the interpersonal relationships in the group or prodding the group to achieve its task. Groups will sometimes have two leaders: one for the social dimension and one for the task dimension. There are also three main perspectives on leadership. First, some researchers believe some people are born with traits that will make them a good leader. A second perspective is that the group's leader selects an appropriate leadership style for the given task. A third way of understaning leadership says that to some degree, leaders are born with traits that make them good leaders, but that they also learn how to become a leader and use strategies appropriate to a given situation. Different approches of group leadership are discussed below.

i) *"Good leaders are born"*: This approach says that people are born with traits that make them effective leaders. The challenge for the group is to find a person with these traits.

ii) *One-best-style*: This approach says that in a given situation, one particular style of leadership is most effective. There are four main styles:

   a) *Autocratic*: Leader uses his or her authority to make decisions.

   b) *Democratic*: Authority is shared and all group members help make decisions.

   c) *Laissez-faire*: A "hands-off" style in which the leader allows the group to make its own decisions.

   d) *Abdacratic*: No one in the group exercises leadership. This style, says researchers, leads to group disintegration and is followed by autocratic leadership.

iii) *Contextual approach*: This approach says that leaders are to some degree born with leadership traits, but that the situation, personalities of other group members, pressures on the group, and group norms also determine leadership.

4.3.6 Roles in Groups

Every member of a group plays a certain role within that group. Some roles relate to the task aspect of the group, while others promote social interaction. A third set of roles are self-centered and can be destructive for the group. Read about the roles group members play and then complete the activity.

4.3.6.1 Task-oriented Roles

Researchers Benne and Sheats identified several roles which relate to the completion of the group's task:

i) *Initiator-contributor:* Generates new ideas.

ii) *Information-seeker:* Asks for information about the task.

iii) *Opinion-seeker:* Asks for the input from the group about its values.

iv) *Information-giver:* Offers facts or generalisation to the group.

v) *Opinion-giver:* States his or her beliefs about a group issue.

vi) *Elaborator:* Explains ideas within the group, offers examples to clarify ideas.

vii) *Coordinator:* Shows the relationships between ideas.

viii) *Orienter:* Shifts the direction of the group's discussion.

ix) *Evaluator-critic:* Measures group's actions against some objective standard.

x) *Energiser:* Stimulates the group to a higher level of activity.

xi) *Procedural-technician:* Performs logistical functions for the group.

xii) *Recorder:* Keeps a record of group actions.

4.3.6.2 Social Roles

Groups also have members who play certain social roles:

i) *Encourager*: Praises the ideas of others.

ii) *Harmoniser*: Mediates differences between group members.

iii) *Compromiser*: Moves group to another position that is favored by all group members.

iv) *Gatekeeper/expediter*: Keeps communication channels open.

v) *Standard setter*: Suggests standards or criteria for the group to achieve.

vi) *Group observer*: Keeps records of group activities and uses this information to offer feedback to the group.

vii) *Follower*: Goes along with the group and accepts the group's ideas.

4.3.6.3 Individualistic Roles

These roles place the group member above the group and are destructive to the group.

i) *Aggressor:* Attacks other group members, deflates the status of others, and other aggressive behaviour.

ii) *Blocker:* Resists movement by the group.

iii) *Recognition seeker*: Calls attention to himself or herself.

iv) *Self-confessor:* Seeks to disclose nongroup related feelings or opinions.

v) *Dominator*: Asserts control over the group by manipulating the other group members.

vi) *Help seeker*: Tries to gain the sympathy of the group.

vii) *Special interest pleader*: Uses stereotypes to assert his or her own prejudices.

4.3.7 Conflict in Groups

Conflict can be good for a group if it is managed appopriately. By airing differences, group members can produce quality decisions and satisfying interpersonal relationships.

4.3.7.1 Managing Conflict

The first step in managing conflict is to identify the conflict.

i) Do the group members know that a conflict exists?

ii) Are the group members arguing over competing goals?

iii) Are scarce resources at stake?

iv) Are the group members dependent on each other to solve the conflict?

There are five styles for managing conflict. They are:

i) *Competitive*: high in assertiveness, low in cooperativeness. Competitive people want to win the conflict.

ii) *Accommodative*: low in assertiveness and high in cooperativeness. These group members are easy going and willing to follow the group.

iii) *Avoiding*: low in assertiveness, low in cooperativeness. Avoiding people are detached and indifferent to conflict.

iv) *Collaborative*: high assertiveness, high in cooperativeness. These group members are active and productive problem solvers.

v) *Compromising*: moderate in assertiveness, moderate in cooperativeness. Compromisers are willing to "give and take" to resolve conflict.

4.3.7.2 Defensive Climate

The climate in which conflict is managed is important. Groups should avoid a defensive climate, which is characterised by these qualities:

i) *Evaluation*: judging and criticising other group members.

ii) *Control*: imposing the will of one group member on the others.

iii) *Strategy*: using hidden agendas.

iv) *Neutrality*: demonstrating indifference and lack of commitment.

v) *Superiority*: expressing dominance.

vi) *Certainty*: being rigid in one's willingness to listen to others.

4.3.7.3 Supportive Climate

Instead, groups should foster a supportive climate, marked by these traits:

i) *Description*: presenting ideas or opinions.

ii) *Problem orientation*: focusing attention on the task

iii) *Spontaneity*: communicating openly and honestly

iv) *Empathy*: understanding another person's thoughts

v) *Equality*: asking for opinions.

vi) *Provisionalism*: expressing a willingness to listen other the ideas of others.

4.3.8 Mediated Groups

As technology becomes more accessible, groups will hold more of their meetings either online or via video or telephone connections. Mediated groups take several forms:

i) *Teleconferences* in which the group members talk via the telephone.

i) *Videoconferences* in which a video and audio connection allows the group members to communicate with each other.

i) *Computer-mediated discussions* such as Listservs, chat, or Usenet, in which the group members communicate via email.

There are several advantages to mediated groups. First, they are usually inexpensive to operate. Instead of travelling long distances to meet, groups can meet over the telephone or via email. In addition, when using email or telephones, the group does not have to meet as a whole. It can carry on its business over time and without everyone being present.

There are also some disadvantages to mediated groups. When communicating via the telephone or by email, it is difficult to judge other group members' non-verbal expressions. Also, the technology can be a difficult adjustment. Finally, the social aspects of the group are downplayed when the group does not meet face to face.

4.3.9 Group Meetings

Meetings are often dreaded by group members because they lack focus and appear to be unproductive. However, group meetings can be a great asset if they are planned properly and administered effectively.

4.3.9.1 Preparation

i) Give appropriate notice to those involved.

ii) Identify a purpose for the meeting.

iii) Include only people who are relevant to the discussion.

iv) Distribute an agenda before the meeting. Include the following items:

   a) Call to order

   b) Approval of previous minutes and treasurer's report

   c) Unfinished business (specify)

   d) New business (specify)
   e) Announcements
   f) Adjournment

v) Establish start, stop, and break times.
vi) Set deadlines for follow-up actions.

4.3.9.2 During the Meeting

i) Start promptly and end on time.
ii) Use Robert's Rules of Order
iii) Assign someone to take notes and write the minutes.
iv) Use an appropriate discussion model
   a) Standard agenda
   b) Nominal Group Technique

4.3.9.3 Behaviour to avoid

i) Hold unnecessary meetings.
ii) Invite everyone
iii) Let people dominate the discussion
iv) Allow discussion to wander from the topic
v) Fail to act on decisions made.

4.4 Mass Communication

Mass communication is the term used to describe the academic study of various means by which individuals and entities can relay information to large segments of the population all at once through mass media. Almost every university that has a journalism programme also offer a distinct programme —often from the same department— of studies in mass communication, which includes the technical aspects production of newspapers, radio programmes, television shows, and films. Unlike journalism and related fields like public relations and advertising, the study of mass communication focuses less on the message that is delivered, and more on the means by which this delivery occurs. In today's world the internet is playing a vital role in delivering news and information to remote places where traditional delivery means do not serve. The discipline also differs from media studies, which focuses on the effects that mass media have on the population.

4.4.1 Defining Mass Communication

The term 'mass communication' is a term used in a variety of ways which, despite the potential for confusion, are usually clear from the context. These include (i) reference to the activities of the mass media as a group, (ii) the use of criteria of a concept, 'massiveness', to distinguish among media and their activities, and (iii) the construction of questions about communication as applied to the activities of the mass media. Significantly only the third of these uses does not take the actual process of communication for granted.

'Mass communication' is often used loosely to refer to the distribution of entertainment, arts, information, and messages by television, radio, newspapers, magazines, movies, recorded music, and associated media. This general use of the term is only appropriate as designating the most commonly shared features of such otherwise disparate phenomena as broadcast television, cable, video playback, theatre projection, recorded song, radio talk, advertising, and the front page, editorial page, sports section, and comics page of the newspaper. In this usage 'mass communication' refers to the activities of the media as a whole and fail to distinguish among specific media, modes of communication, genres of text or artifact, production or reception situations, or any questions of actual communication. The only analytic purpose this use of the term serves is to distinguish mass communication from interpersonal, small-group, and other face-to-face communication situations.

A second use of the term involves the various criteria of massiveness which can be brought to bear in analyses of media and mass communication situations. These criteria may include size and differentiation of audience, anonymity, simultaneity, and the nature of influences among audience members and between the audience and the media.

Live television spectaculars of recent decades may be the epitome of mass communication. These may include such serious events as the funerals of John Paul II, Terrorist Attack on Twin Towers and such entertainment spectaculars as the Olympic games, the Wimbledon, and the Oscar Awards. These transmissions are distributed simultaneously and regardless of individual or group differences to audience members numbering in several tens or even a few hundreds of millions. Outside of their own local groups, these audience members know nothing of each other. They have no real opportunities to influence the television representation of the events or the interpretation of those representations by other audience members.

By contrast the audience for most cable television channels is much smaller and more differentiated from other audience groups. The audience for newspapers, magazines, and movies is less simultaneous, again smaller and more differentiated, and there is the potential for a flow of local influences as people talk about articles and recommend movies. But compared to a letter, phone call, conversation, group discussion, or public lecture all of these media produce communication immensely more massive on every criterion. All of the criteria used in defining mass communication are potentially confused when one is engaged in a specific research project or critical examination.

The most confounding problem is encountered when determining the level of analysis. Should the concern be with a single communication event or with multiple events but a single communication channel? Should the focus be upon multiple channels but a single medium? Does the central question concern a moment in time or an era, a community, nation, or the world? Radio provides an excellent example of the importance of these choices. Before television, network radio was the epitome of mass communication; it was national, live, available and listened to everywhere.

Today it is difficult to think of radio this way because the industry no longer works in the same manner. Commercial radio stations depend on local and regional sources of advertising income. Essentially all radio stations are programmed to attract a special segment of a local or regional audience, and even when programming national entertainment materials such as popular songs, stations emphasise local events, personalities, weather, news, and traffic in their broadcast talk. Radio is an industry characterised by specialised channels each attracting relatively small, relatively differentiated audiences. But, the audience for radio is just as big, undifferentiated, and anonymous as that for television. Is radio today, then, a purveyor of mass communication? It depends on whether the concern is with the industry as a whole or with the programming and audience of a particular station.

Most uses of the term "mass communication" fall into one of these first two categories, either to refer to the activities of the mass media as a whole, or to refer to the massiveness of certain kinds of communication. Both uses have in common that they take issues of communication for granted and instead place emphasis on the massiveness of the distribution system and the audience. Attention is given to what are called the mass media because they are the institutional and technological systems capable of producing mass audiences for mass distributed "communications".

Communication, then, ends up implicitly defined as a kind of object (message, text, artifact) that is reproduced and transported by these media. For some purposes this may be exactly the right definition. But it diminishes our ability to treat communication as a social accomplishment, as something people do rather than as an object that gets moved from one location to another. If communication is something people do, then it may or may not be successful, may or may not be healthy and happy. If communication means "to share" for example rather than "to transmit", then what, if anything, of importance is shared when people watch a television show.

Scholars of mass communication are often more interested in communication as a social accomplishment than they are in the media as mass distribution systems. This interest is based on an intellectual independence from both existing habits of terminology, and most importantly, from media institutions as they exist. The term mass, however it may be defined, is then treated as a qualification on the term communication, however it may be defined. Such intellectual exercises, of course, can work out in a great variety of ways, but a few examples will suffice.

At one extreme, if communication is defined so that interaction between parties is a necessary criterion, as in "communication is symbolic interaction", and mass is defined as an aggregate of non-interacting entities, then mass communication is an oxymoron and an impossibility. At the opposite extreme, if the couplet mass communication is defined as involving any symbolic behaviour addressed "to whom it may concern" then choices of clothing, furniture, and appliance styles, body posture, gestures, and any other publicly observable activity may well count as mass communication. Both of these extremes may seem like mere intellectual games but they are important precisely because their intellectuality frees them of the practical constraints under which we operate in other realms. The contribution of such intellectual games is precisely to stimulate new thinking.

Definitions of mass communication that take communication for granted and focus on the massiveness of the medium are always in danger of implicitly adopting, or certainly failing to question, the taken for granted criteria of evaluation already used in industries. In commercial television, just like any of the other commercial media, what is assumed is that it is a business. The conventions of the industry are to evaluate things in business terms. Today, it is an important to point out that these industries are communicators as well as businesses. As such they can and should be held to communicative standards. The public has a right to ask whether a television show is good for communication, whether an hour of network news would be a successful form of communication, whether there is a communication need for non-commercial, educational children's programming. As the terms of the questions shift, so, of course, may the answers. Becoming aware of such possibilities begins with being sensitive to the definitions of such terms as mass communication.

4.4.2 Evolution of Mass Communication

For much of human history speech and body language were the only available forms of communication. This changed when writing was developed, probably around the year 3000 BC in the area of the world that we now call the Middle East. The most obvious difference between writing and speech is in their media. Whereas speech is carried by sound waves in the air, writing is usually carried by one substance impressed upon another, as, for example, ink on paper. Even in its simplest form, the invention of writing produced significant changes in human communication. The next major change came with the discovery of printed text in Europe in the late 1500s. Whereas written documents could only be produced by individuals, one document at a time, printed documents could be mass produced. The phenomenon that we now call mass communication dates from the invention of print. Some scholars argue that the next great change occurred in or around 1950 with the discovery of the computer. However, while digital data processing certainly has brought changes to our society, we are perhaps too close to the date of its birth to evaluate it clearly.

4.4.3 Text

The fact that writing remains in existence long after it has been created is so remarkable that we give a special name, text, to the visible remains. Humans receive textual messages via their eyes. It has been argued that this visual aspect of text is important in and of itself because it shapes the way human beings pay attention to their environment, and this shapes the way that they think about themselves.

Text-using societies tend to be visually oriented, whereas speech-using societies tend to be aurally oriented. Thus, when scholars initiated the study of text, they discovered that communication not only helps shape individual relationships, but it also plays a role in defining the social environment. Those who study communication disagree as to the exact definition of the term, "text". In its broadest sense text is "that which is perceived by the reader," however, this conceivably could be any data that is taken in by the eye, and to many this seems to be too broad a concept.

4.4.3.1 Text and Meaning

The Shannon/Weaver Model describes communication as a process that includes a transmitter who initiates the communication, a signal that moves through a medium, a receiver who notices the signal, and noise that may alter the signal. In terms of this model, text can be seen as being created by the writer and then moving through time and space until it is encountered by the reader. The medium is light waves, and the signal is formed as light bounces off of the paper and ink and into the reader's eyes. While the text is in transit, noise may act to make it less understandable — the writing may fade, for example, or pages may be torn or missing. This is accurate as far as it goes, but it does little to demonstrate how text relates to meaning. However, it is possible to produce a somewhat different model that is more amenable to the discussion of meaning.

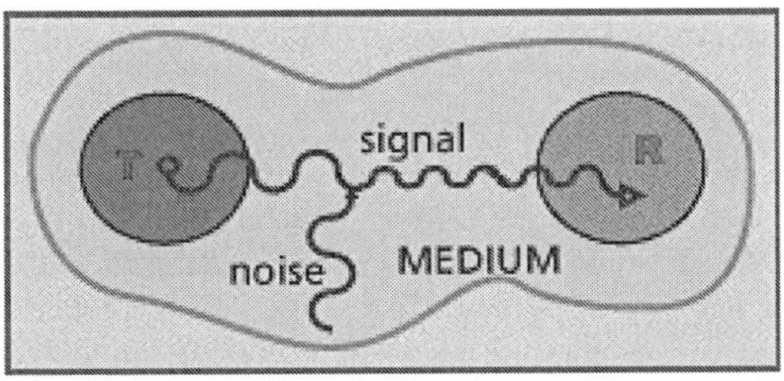

Figure 4.2. Shannon/Weaver model of text

In this model the reader, the writer and the text exist in the world, which is their environment and with which they interact. The reader and the writer interact directly with the text, and indirectly with one another by means of the text, which itself becomes a medium of communication. Thus, reader, writer and text are seen as an interconnected system.

One way to interpret this model is to imagine that the writer, who has thoughts to communicate, expresses them by creating a text. The reader and the writer share a language code, and so when the reader encounters the text, he or she becomes the receiver of the writer's thoughts. But this description leads to a number of perplexing questions. For example:

i) What if the writer is dead? Can a dead individual somehow be said to be communicating with the living?

i) There are many examples of anonymous text? Who, exactly, is the writer in these cases?

i) What if the code is only partially known to the reader, and he or she misunderstands the text? Is communication meaningful if it is based on mistakes and errors?

Attempts to answer these and similar questions have produced four basic approaches to explaining the relationship between text and meaning. Not surprisingly, these conflict with one another. As each is examined in turn, keep in mind this question: Which of these is most responsible for the meaning of a text:

i) writer's intention,

ii) reader's interpretation,

iii) text itself, or

iv) society in which the reader and writer live

Writer's intention: Perhaps the most familiar approach takes the point of view that the writer of the text, who is often called the author, created the text with the intention of communicating meaningfully with the reader. From this point of view, the focus is on what the writer meant to say, and the reader's task is to discern the author's thoughts.

Reader's interpretation: Text is composed of symbols, and the transmission of symbolic messages requires that the sender and receiver share a code by which the sender encodes and the receiver decodes the message. In military orders this code is very narrow — the words "attack" and "withdraw", for example, have very specific meanings — in order to insure that the sender will not be misunderstood.

But the codes used in literature, and the texts of everyday life such as newspapers and magazines, are very broad and ambiguous, with many words having more than one possible meaning.

When the reader encounters such a text, he or she cannot be completely certain as to which of these meanings the writer intended. Further, the reader has led a life which contains different experiences that of the writer. Consequently, the reader is likely to make of the text something other than what the writer might have expected. In fact, those who adopt this approach point out that the reader need have no knowledge of the writer at all. Nor does the reader need to be concerned as to the writer's intentions. When the reader draws a meaning from the text, then that meaning is the reader's and the reader's alone. Anonymous text fits this approach well, but in fact, any text that is read without knowledge of its author lends itself to the *reader-oriented* approach.

Text itself: The *text-centred* approach argues that because the text was brought into the world by a writer who lived in the world, the text must contain essential truths about the world. As these truths are permanently embedded in the text, the reader, who is also living in the world, ought, with sufficient effort, to be able to discern them. This approach is adopted most frequently by those who study sacred texts. These, having been created by a deity, are taken to be composed entirely of truths, and in fact, it is not unusual for such texts to assert this as a primary fact.

If a text is taken in and of itself to contain the truth, then neither the intentions of its human writers nor the interpretations of its readers are relevant. The meaning is in the text, and if two readers disagree, then they must consult the text further in attempting to resolve the disagreement. There is no other authority. A telephone directory is a good example of a text that lends itself to this approach. A book that contains only names and phone numbers, and assuming that there are no errors, contains only the truth. As readers, we consult the book and take what it says as fact.

Text as environment: Although each of the previous approaches works well for some varieties of text, none of them works entirely well for all text. In fact, most of the text that we encounter was written by someone who intended to say something; most readers extract meanings that the writer did not intend; most text contains some truth. Given this, scholars continue to argue as to which of the three approaches is the most effective.

A fourth approach attempts to resolve this dilemma by considering text as part of the human social environment. According to this approach, each author adds to the "communication environment", and each reader takes meanings from it. When considered from this point of view, the text is not separate from the world, but is part of it. Writers and readers, who are also part of the world, participate in the "textual experience".

As an example, consider the text called a "newspaper". Since many writers and editors contribute to each edition, there is no way to identify a single "author". As readers read the paper, they compare what they read to their experience in the world, and they discuss what they read with other readers. The meanings that readers take from the newspapers become the raw material of other texts, including such as the television and radio news of the day, and the next day's newspapers. The text of the newspaper is stored in libraries and other archives where it can be referenced at any time. Thus, the text becomes part of the fabric of the life of a society.

This goes deeper than the simple thought that "everyone reads more or less the same text." Since the codes by which humans communicate are shared by all members of the society, they, too, are part of the communication environment. This means that the texts, the people, the interpretations, and the rules that govern the interpretations are all mutually interactive.

The fourth, or cultural approach points out that these resources are applied in different ways at different times. Sometimes humans express their intention as authors, sometimes they develop unique connotations as readers, sometimes they search for eternal truths. Thus, the common ground of text is found in the two complementary faces of human communication: the society and the self.

4.4.3.2 Data as Text

An even broader definition of the term "text" arises from considering the maxim that "you can't not communicate." An the words of Anthony Wilden:

> Let it be emphasised that the communication of information does not necessarily imply the use of language, nor consciously perceived sending or receiving, nor consciously intended communication, nor consciously noted understanding. As already noted, every act, every pause, every movement in living and social systems is also a message; silence is communication; short of death it is impossible for an organism or a person not to communicate.

Thus, those who accept the existence of the communication environment, are driven to conclude that any source of information might be considered as text. For example, natural phenomena can be "read" — a red sunset tells the watcher that it might rain tomorrow, flocks of geese flying south indicate that winter is near, and so on. In terms of this approach, scholars may view the physical world as a large, complex text which communicates a part of reality to its human readers.

4.4.4 Mass Media

Mass communication media make it possible to deliver messages to millions of people at roughly the same time. The authors of these messages are usually organisations, and the audiences are composed of individuals.

i) *The telephone*: speech without walls.

ii) *The phonograph*: music without walls.

iii) *The photograph*: museum without walls.

iv) *The electric light*: space without walls.

v) *The movie, radio and TV*: classroom without walls.

The development and widespread use of printed text in Europe in the1500s produced a brand new form of communication. For the first time a single message could be duplicated with little error and distributed to thousands of people. First used to propagate religious texts and arguments, this "mass" approach to communication quickly caught on and was soon being used to distribute news, entertainment, and government regulations. From these first primitive pamphlets, the "mass media", as they are often called, have grown to include the *print media* of books, newspapers and magazines, the *electronic media* of television, radio, and audio/video recording, and the *new media* of computers and computer networks. While these media differ in many ways, they all share the characteristics by which scholars define mass communication:

i) Mass communication messages are produced by organisations.

ii) The medium for these messages permits accurate duplication.

iii) The messages are distributed to large audiences at roughly the same time.

Face-to-face communication occurs on many channels, with many opportunities to send and receive messages, and with much complexity in the communication process. Yet, the situation becomes even more complex when the many media organisations with their production and distribution of millions of messages are considered. Media may be received by millions of people, all of whom are also engaged in face-to-face communication. The intersection of these two types of communication makes for a picture that must include all communicators and their interactions with one another.

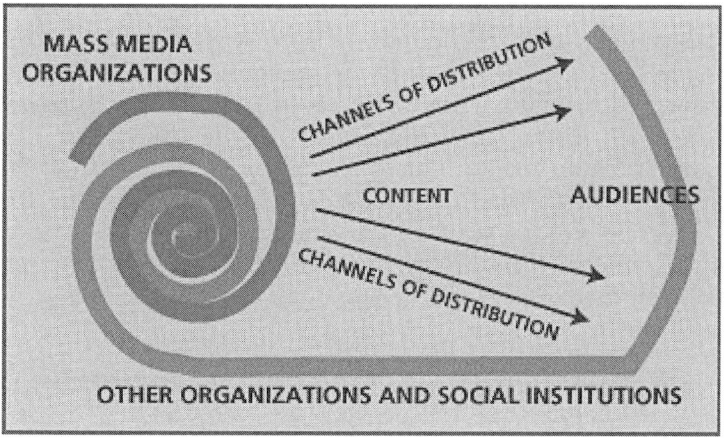

Figure 4.3. Components of mass communication

The individual parts of this model will be described in more detail. The parts include:

i) Channels of distribution
ii) Audiences
iii) Mass media organisations
iv) Other organisations and social institutions
v) Content

4.4.4.1 Distribution Channels

Scholars tend to identify the various mass media by their distribution channels. Books, newspapers, and magazines are often called the "print media", while radio and television are often called the "electronic" or "broadcast" media. Two other electronic channels of distribution are also recognised as very important: "electronic recorded" media which include such as CDs, cassette tapes, video tapes, and the like — these are electronic in nature but are sold and delivered much in the same way as books — and "film" or "movies" which are similar to television but which are delivered in special buildings called "theaters".

Telephones are electronic media, but telephones have not traditionally been included in the "mass media" because telephones are used mainly in person-to-person communication. Similarly, computers, especially large computer networks, have the potential to be used as mass communication media, however, these are so new that their uses are still developing. Although they have no true category as yet, computers are sometimes referred to as the "new" media. The following table illustrates the most common way of organising the distribution channels of the mass media.

Table 4.1. Distribution channels of the mass media.

Print	*Electronic*
Books	Radio
Newspapers	Television
Magazines	Film
Direct mail	Tape and disc recordings

Telephones and computer networks have been omitted because at the present time they are mostly used as person-to-person, rather than mass, media, and some channels that might have been included — posters, flyers, memoranda, filmstrips, slide shows, and video games, for example — have been omitted not because they are unimportant, but because they are not as widely studied as the primary media.

A mass medium's distribution channel "aims" a "flow" of messages in the direction of a particular audience. Some media are best fitted to an audience that consists of individuals, each of whom is more or less alone when the message arrives. Other media are better fitted to an audience that gathers in groups. Books, newspapers, magazines and direct mail are usually read by individuals. Film, on the other hand, is shown in theatres which gather audiences together in fairly large groups. Radio, television, and recordings are often delivered in group settings, but these groups are usually smaller than those who attend the showing of a film, and the three are also often used by individuals.

The relationship between the target audience and the delivery medium are especially important to commercial media organisations because they must compute the cost and effectiveness of their media products. In the case of print media, for example, the price of each book, newspaper or magazine plays a part in a person's decision to join or not join the audience. Although many people like to read books, for example, it was only when inexpensive "paperback" books became available that the audience jumped to its present size. Media organisations that use advertising to offset their costs must pay particular attention to their target audiences because their advertisers are often interested in presenting their ads to particular groups of people. For example, the recent trend in magazine publication has been towards an increase in the number of different magazines each of which appeals to a narrow audience that is desirable to a particular set of advertisers.

4.4.4.2 Access and Availability

In order to receive messages from a particular mass communication medium, an audience member must be able to "connect up" to the reception end of the channel. For example, television is not available to people who do not own television sets; CDs are useless to people who do not own CD players, and so on. The extent to which an potential audience is able to make use of a mass medium is called its availability.

Availability includes more than equipment. Language also plays a role, as does geographic location and economic class. A radio broadcast in Spanish, for example, is only available to those who speak Spanish. Similarly, printed media are only available to those who are able to read, and cable television will not be available to those who cannot afford the monthly fee.

Media access refers to the ability of members of the society to make use of a particular medium to send messages of their own. Print media is relatively more accessible than broadcast media. For example, anyone who can write can, at relatively little expense, print up and distribute a flyer or newsletter. Access to television and radio broadcast channels, however, is tightly regulated by the government. Even when a channel is provided, as with public access cable television, it is much more difficult and expensive to produce video than to produce print.

Newspapers and magazines traditionally provide public access by means of "letters to the editor" or "editorial pages". Television and radio news do not traditionally offer this kind of access. In recent times, however, radio and television shows featuring listener and viewer "call-ins" have become popular, and this provides access to a large number of people.

Access and availability have become increasingly important with the advent of cable television and the new computer networked media. We might argue that our society's decision to require all children to attend school and learn to read has the effect of making the important documents of our society available to them. Similarly, our society's insistence that everyone learn to write and our belief in "freedom of the press" encourages citizens to access the print media.

As the electronic media have begun to replace the print media as the major channels for public information, critics have begun to question whether this societal availability and access will be continued. Government control of the broadcast channels limits access to these media to large corporations, and cable television is available only to those who are able to afford the relatively high cost of connection. These issues are now being widely debated in the United States.

4.4.4.3. Audiences

An audience is a group of people who are receiving or have received a particular mass communication message. In some cases all members of the audience are paying attention to the medium at the same time — as, for example, the television audience that tuned in just after the space shuttle Challenger exploded. In other cases, however, the attention of the audience is spread out over time — the audience for a particular magazine, for example, may consist of people who read copies of the magazine at various times over the period of a month or more. And, in some cases, the attention of the audience may be spread over a very long period of time. The audience for Shakespeare's plays, for example, is very large and hundreds of years in duration.

In the early days of mass communication research, the audience was believed to be very passive and innocent. It was supposed that members of the audience believed whatever they read in the newspapers or heard on the radio. As studies of the relationship between the audience and the mass communication organisations have progressed, the researchers' view of the audience has changed. Nowadays, the audience is believed to be active and sophisticated. That is, the audience chooses the media that it attends to, and the audience is critical of the messages that are delivered to it by the media.

4.4.4.4 Magic Bullet of Media Influence

The earliest theories of mass communication imagined that mass media had very strong effects on their audiences. The Shannon/Weaver model illustrates how these theories saw the media message as a kind of "magic bullet". Sent out by the organisation, the magic bullets "hit" the members of the audience in their "minds" and changed their thoughts.

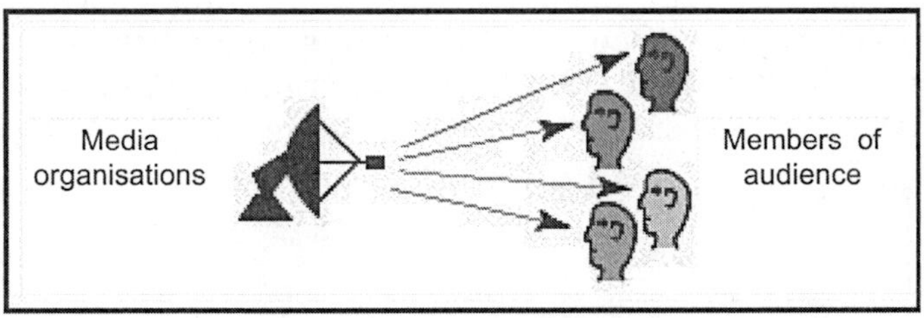

Figure 4.4. Conceptual model of magic bullet theory of media influence

The bullet theory assumed that an audience was passive, waiting for the media to shoot a propaganda message into it, and would roll over in a state of docile surrender when hit, as long as the bullet was sufficiently powerful. Accordingly, researchers did not bother to study the audience. Instead, they analysed the content of the messages, assuming that content was the secret of a successful propaganda bullet. However, the researchers were due for a surprise. The audience obstinately declined to fall under the spell of the messages. Sometimes they reacted in ways that were opposite to the propagandist's intentions, or enjoyed the bombardment without allowing it to change their opinions in the slightest. Once the Magic Bullet Theory was seen to be false, researchers began to propose alternative theories and design experiments to test them out. This led to the creation of new research methods, and to a sizable growth in the study of mass communication.

4.4.4.5 Interpersonal Diffusion

Studies that followed the "Martian Invasion" broadcast began to focus on the fact that members of the audience also engaged in face-to-face communications with family, friends and coworkers. Theorists hypothesised that certain members of the audience, called "opinion leaders", would be more influential than other members. In theory the opinion leaders would make up their minds as to what the media messages meant and then tell their friends and neighbours. Research studies conducted to test this hypothesis did find that certain members of the audience were opinion leaders. However, different members were the opinion leaders on different subjects. Due to of this, it was (and continues to be) very difficult to find a simple explanation for the spread, or diffusion, of the content of media messages through a society.

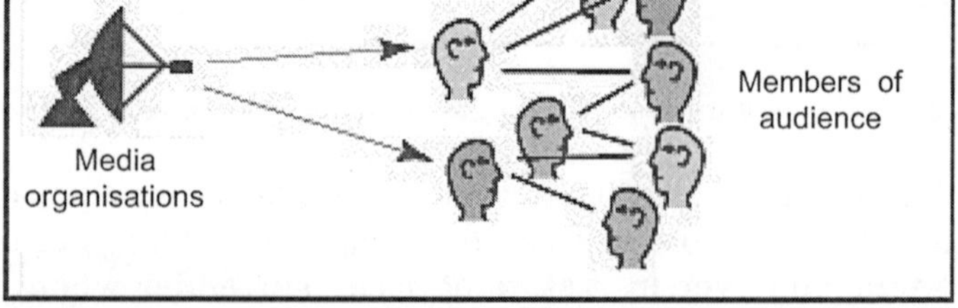

Figure 4.5. Conceptual model of interpersonal diffusion

Another finding that contributed to the difficulty of explaining diffusion came from the study of rumours. Researchers found that the accuracy of a statement spread by word-of-mouth decreases very rapidly as it travels through a population. Thus, it is hard to see how messages sent to opinion leaders via the mass media could be passed on with any accuracy. These studies resulted in the conclusion that face-to-face communication is much more important to the process whereby people form and change their opinions than the content of mass media messages.

4.4.4.6 Uses and Gratifications

One current approach to mass communication studies argues that because mass media products are highly available in American society, its audiences tend to "use" it much as they would use any other product or service. The appearance of this approach marks an important change in the way media researchers think about the audience. Previously, they saw the audience as *passive* — made up of people who simply accepted whatever was put in front of them. In these models the audience was a captive of the media organisations.

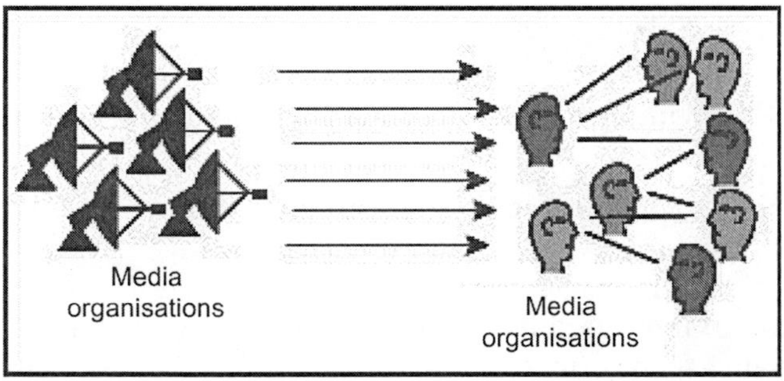

Figure 4.6.Conceptual model of uses and gratifications approach

In the uses and gratifications approach the audience is *active*. Audience members are seen as consumers of a media product, and as with consumers of other goods and services, they shop around, consider alternatives, and make choices.

The earlier approaches assumed that the content of the media must be having some kind of an effect on the audience members, and researchers spent their time trying to locate and measure those effects. However, few substantial effects were ever found, perhaps because the model for the audience was too simplistic.

The uses and gratifications approach seems to provide a richer way of looking at the audience. Instead of asking, "How does the media change our minds?" the uses and gratifications researchers ask "What is the role of media in our lives?"

Here are some examples of the uses to which the media are put:

i) Getting the "news"
ii) Getting information about available products and services
iii) Starting the day in the morning or ending it at night
iv) Establishing common topics to talk about with friends
v) Creating a substitute for having friends
vi) Providing a way to feel connected to other members of the audience
vii) Providing a way to escape from the day's problems and worries
viii) Hearing someone else support our own values and opinions.

In this view media becomes just one of many cultural influences in our environment, and far from the most important.

4.4.5 Media Organisations

In face-to-face communication the participants are easily identified — the same is not true for mass communication. The mass media message is created by a team of people, and it is sometimes difficult to establish exactly who is responsible for what. For example, the author of a book, may produce the initial set of words, but an editor will review and alter those words, designers and graphics specialists will choose type faces, create illustrations and organise the format of the text, production specialists will manufacture the book, and marketing and sales specialists will oversee its distribution. Although it is traditional to assign "authorship" to the person who wrote the original text, all of these people play a part in the communication process.

Electronic media are even more complexly organised. In a television production, for example, there will be one or more scriptwriters, a number of actors, a producer, a director, camera operators and other technical crew, and a host of others. A television show is truly a group project, with no single "author". Yet, to say that mass communication is produced by an organisation is not to say that it is random or "neutral" in terms of the ideas and opinions that are expressed. Readers encounter "liberal" and "conservative" newspapers, for example, or religiously-oriented television programming, or politically-oriented music. Thus, a discussion of mass communication must investigate the nature of the organisations that produce it, and it must also investigate the social, political and economic relationships that might exist among the media organisations and their audiences.

With the recognition of the active audience has come the realisation that the content of the mass media is actually a *product*. No less than soap or breakfast cereal or automobiles, mass communication is produced and distributed for human consumption. This means, of course, that the mass media organisations have something to sell, and that the audiences are their customers. Thus, one approach to the study of mass communication is to focus on the economics of media production.

4.4.5.1 Gatekeeping

The media product passes through many levels of organisational processing on its way to the audience, and at each step in the process, the original data is filtered —

reduced in length, edited for style, censored, and so on. Each step in the process can be thought of as a gate through which the data must pass on its way to the consumer, consequently this situation is known as gatekeeping. Suppose, for example, that a network television news team is sent to the midwestern United States to cover the heavy rains and flooding that are occurring there. The gatekeeping on this story begins with the observation of the event by the news team.

The flood may extend over hundreds of square miles and affect the lives of millions of people, but the team will have time to record only a very small portion of this. Let us say that the team decides to focus on damage being done to the corn crop. This decision filters the available data by including data relating to the corn crop and excluding data relating to other crops and other types of damage.

Within the news organisation many people will contribute to the production of this "story". Editors will select the bits of video to be used in the final presentation; writers will create a script for the commentator to read; graphic artists will create titles, maps, animations and other video enhancements; musicians may create a musical score for the piece and so on. Other editors will decide which evening the story will "run", and where the story will come in the sequence of stories, advertisements, and other material running that night. An anchorperson will introduce the story and various technicians will ensure that it gets "on the air".

During its stay in the flood zone, the news team may have shot hours of video tape, gathered many facts and interviewed many people. Yet the story as broadcast, if it is broadcast at all, will be only minutes in length. And, each gatekeeper will have had an effect on the content and style of the story. Each person will have added to or subtracted from the original data, and in his or her own way each person will have helped to formulate this particular communication product.

4.4.5.2 Agenda Setting

The failure of the "Magic Bullet" theory left mass

communication researchers with a puzzle. On the one hand, studies continued to find little reason to believe that mass communication was able to change people's opinions and beliefs. On the other hand, mass communication plays such a large role in the day-to-day lives of industrial societies that it seemed that it must have *some* kind of large impact on what people think. In recent decades media researchers have been able to demonstrate an indirect, but none the less powerful, connection between what the news media presents and what people think. This connection has been dubbed agenda setting.

In investigating the relationship between the top stories in the news and "what people are talking about", communication researchers found that stories tend to appear in the news somewhat prior to their becoming widely discussed among the public at large. The conclusion we might draw from this is that the media tend to set the "agenda" — the list of items that people will be discussing. Thus, the power of the media may lie not in its ability to sway people's opinions, but rather in its role of determining what issues will be considered important enough to discuss.

Agenda setting connects the constant use of the media in our society with the results of studies that show that most people form their opinions and beliefs based on face-to-face communication with others. It has become a widely accepted theory of mass communication.

4.4.5.3 Content

The term "content" refers to the message that is distributed by the mass media organisation by means of the mass communication channel. In American television, for example, the content includes such as entertainment, advertisements, station-breaks, news, and "infomercials." These categories of content may be further divided. Entertainment, for example, might be divided into "genres" such as situation comedies, detective shows, soap operas, sports, and so on. The content of each medium is subject to analysis and criticism by its readers. "Literary criticism," "film criticism," and "television criticism" are all well established fields of academic study, and some members of mass media organisations make their livings by publishing their critical views.

4.4.5.4 Social Institutions

Typically, mass communication operates as a "one way street" — messages flow from the media organisations to their audiences in a way that allows for very little immediate feedback. However, because those who work in media organisations are themselves a part of the society within which their audiences exist, there is a path by which audience response to mass communication messages can feed back to the producers of the messages. For example, the person who edits a newspaper story may be in the audience of a radio broadcast. The radio technician may be in the television audience. The television producer may read the newspaper. And, all of these people may talk to one another about what they have watched and heard and read. Thus, "mass communication" and "interpersonal communication" seem to merge into one another.

4.5 Non-verbal Communication

Communication is an interactive process whereby people seek to induce some form of change in attitude, belief, or behavior. It is a dynamic and ongoing process whereby people create shared meaning through the sending and receiving of messages via commonly understood codes. It is the process of senders stimulating meaning in the minds of receivers and then having the receivers respond to the message they have received and interpreted (feedback). Although most communication is intentional, intent is not absolutely necessary in order for communication to take place. The receiver of the message often perceives intent, even though the sender had no intention of sending the message received. In short, the sender of the message may not have meant what you thought he or she meant. When you are motivated to get your non-verbal message across to your receiver, you will be much more intentional with your non-verbal behaviours.

Communication is a reciprocal process, creating a norm of reciprocity (or a dyadic effect). This concept says that we should expect those with whom we communicate to respond in a manner similar to our original communication. For example, in non-verbal communication, if you use a positive non-verbal indicator (such as your tone of voice or a smile), you should expect a similar positive response from the person with whom you are communicating.

The non-verbal part of communication is that aspect of the communication process that deals with the transmission and reception of messages that are not a part of the natural language systems. Whether they are spoken or written, words are considered part of verbal communication. Any aspect of communication that does not include words is considered part of the non-verbal code. This does not mean that you do not combine verbal and non-verbal codes to create a message; indeed, much of non-verbal communication occurs in conjunction with verbal communication.

Non-verbal communication may come via the characteristics of the speaker (hairstyle, vocal characteristics, appearance, behavioural displays); it may come via the characteristics of the receiver (obvious boredom, dress, audible sighing); or it may rest in the features of the situation (cold room, institutional cream-coloured walls, burned-out light bulbs). Non-verbal communication often occurs through the interaction of all three of these: the speaker (dress, voice, distance maintained), the receiver (posture, facial expression, distance maintained), and the situation as perceived by the sender and/or receiver (the context, the environment, the time of the interaction).

4.5.1 Defining Non-verbal Communication

Non-verbal communication is complex because it creates communication by use of non-verbal behaviours, either by themselves or combined with words. It may be shared between people (interpersonally) or within a person (intrapersonally). It may be intentional or unintentional. It may also be used without words, or it may take on meaning only when it is used in combination with words.

Before we clarify what non-verbal communication is, we must address some of the considerations just mentioned. In the following paragraphs examines behaviour versus communication, intentionality, signs versus symbols, and how people process non-verbal communication.

Behaviour versus communication: First, let us distinguish between non-verbal behaviour and non-verbal communication. Some scholars do not make this distinction; however, it is an important factor for understanding the scope of non-verbal communication. The perception of cream-coloured walls is part of non-verbal communication.

The walls may be said to "communicate" only because living things—people—perceive and interpret them in certain ways and act accordingly. Only living things behave. In a given context, the size of a room may communicate; you probably feel quite awkward when you have a class of five students in a room designed to hold two hundred. At the same time we say that inanimate objects may communicate, as just defined, human beings might behave without communicating. It is true to say that people cannot not behave; it happens as a natural process of being a living human being. However, that people who are behaving are not necessarily communicating. For communication to occur, a receiver must be present and must interpret (decode) the transmission of symbols (messages). These messages may be either verbal or non-verbal; as long as a receiver has interpreted a message, whether it was sent intentionally or not, communication has taken place.

You can communicate non-verbally with yourself (intrapersonally), which is actually being your own sender and receiver, and in that case, there may be a fine distinction between behaviour and communication. As Dittman points out, a message may be controlled by the person and yet be below the level of consciousness (or subliminal) and not actually perceived. For example, suppose you are driving down the highway. You look around and see that there are no cars approaching. There are no other people around, so you pick your nose. Is this action non-verbal communication or non-verbal behaviour?

In this incident, it is non-verbal communication. Why? It is non-verbal communication because you yourself interpreted the behaviour as a message. You checked around to see if anyone might see you do this action, knowing that it would not be considered socially acceptable; it would be against societal norms to be caught in the act of picking your nose, even if it was by someone you did not know. You were weighing the social consequences of the act; you were having social cognition. Social cognition also includes issues other than weighing consequences, such as decision making, the perceptions of others, and the attribution of characteristics to a specific non-verbal behaviour. We focused on weighing consequences because it is one of the more obvious aspects of social cognition. If you had merely acted and not thought about the act, then that act would have been simply a non-verbal behaviour.

4.5.1.1 Intentionality

In verbal communication, we often think about what we say, although some might argue with that position. In the non-verbal system, however, there is often unintentional transmission of messages. For example, if you have an itch, most often you will scratch it. In the event that you think about it and you deem it inappropriate to scratch that particular part of your body in front of other people, you may make the decision not to scratch that itch. If you do not think about it, you might just reflexively scratch whatever itches. In doing this, you create the difference between intentional behaviours and unintentional ones. The actual decision not to scratch makes the absence of scratching intentional intrapersonal communication. Scratching without thinking and sending a message those who see you scratch that you are crass would be unintentional interpersonal communication.

A good example of this difference is the head scratch. Usually you scratch your head in a general context, and it means nothing. In the early 1980s, however, the Head and Shoulders shampoo advertisers created a new meaning for head scratching-dandruff and all the negative connotations, according to the commercial, of having a "flaky" scalp. In later years, NIX and RID advertisements for ridding hair of head lice and Scalpacin's contemporary advertisements for "Stress Itch" added to the social unacceptability of scratching your head in public. What had been a simple reaction (behaviour) to a felt need may now be interpreted as an intentional (and negative) communication between you and receivers (those who actually see you scratch your head).

The perception of some form of intent is enough for an act to be considered communication. In the head-scratching example, communication did occur, although it may not have been the intended message that was transmitted. Non-verbal communication occurs when a message is decoded (or interpreted) as having some meaning, regardless of the sender's intent. Most verbal communication carries with it a greater amount of intent, but non-verbal communication tends to be more primitive and less controllable than its verbal counterpart.

Researchers believe that intention is necessary for communication to take place. This does not mean that you will not receive and interpret events that were not intended for you as communication; you will. You will also be sent messages that you do not interpret as messages; this is another intentionality issue in and of itself. Suffice it to say that effective communication is often dependent on the intentions of the sender.

Non-verbal communication is rarely as easily understood as verbal communication is. The problem is that whether or not the source intends the message is secondary; as long as the receiver perceives intent, then communication has occurred. Often sources simply behave—they do not consciously think about the ramifications of a specific behaviour—but others perceive that the source has done the behaviour on purpose. It often gets confusing and, more often than not, leads to misunderstanding. There are times, however, when neither the source nor the receiver perceives intent; in this case, the act falls under the category of behavior, not communication.

4.5.1.2 Signs and Symbols

Verbal and non-verbal communication guides directs people through the use of signs and symbols. Verbal communication, because of its symbolic nature, includes a code (language) upon which we must agree if communication is to take place. We must create a socially shared system of agreement—a language in which words take on "meaning". If we are to be understood, then people must comprehend the symbols we use to communicate. The perceived intention of verbal communication creates a need to share with others what we mean when we use words. For example, look up the word "dog" in a dictionary. How many different meanings can be taken from the use of a simple three-letter word? Does meaning differ when "dog" is used as a noun as compared to a verb? Add connotations (or emotional meanings) to the definition of "dog", and you have a whole different issue to add to the topic of the meaning of verbal communication.

Non-verbal communication may be symbolic or non-symbolic. One of the more difficult areas in discussing the distinction between verbal and non-verbal communication is the distinction between signs and symbols. In the verbal code we have a symbol; that is, the word takes the place of something else—the word represents an abstraction, such as beauty, God, wealth, or even dog. The symbolic nature of verbal communication is inherent in language; words are abstractions of actual things that may or may not be seen by the receiver.

A sign, on the other hand, is a natural representation of an event or act. Fever is a sign of one's being ill. A cross on a building is a sign of a church or, if a person wears a cross it is a sign of someone who professes Christianity. "$" is a sign of money and sometimes wealth. Much of what we call non-verbal communication falls under the rubric of a signal, though non-verbal communication is sometimes considered symbolic by receivers.

People expressing emotions do so non-verbally. They may smile, cry, or frown; when they do, we label the non-verbal behaviours with a symbol-happiness, sadness, or displeasure. What we try to do in many cases is to infer meaning from a sign.With the verbal code, which must depend on socially shared meanings, the process of inferring meaning is not usually necessary. When we infer meanings without being sure of what was meant, we can damage communication. The crying may have been a sign of happiness, not sadness at all.

Although the verbal code is quite explicit about what it represents-meaning more precise or specific-non-verbal communication is more implicit, meaning more implied or understood. Mehrabian first distinguished between explicit and implicit communication by noting that "Verbal cues are definable by an explicit dictionary and by rules of syntax, but there are only vague and informal explanations of the significance of non-verbal behaviors."

Non-verbal communication would be much easier to understand if we did have a dictionary and syntactical rules for non-verbal signals. Most non-verbal communication involves expectations on both the senders' and receivers' parts. These expectations become the norm in given situations or relationships, and they generate both appropriate and inappropriate behaviours. Distancing zones (or space usage), appropriate dress, hair length, speech rate, amount of touch, and other non-verbal elements differ by culture and subcultures. They take on normative expectations that people can choose to either maintain or violate. Violations of norms can yield both beneficial and hazardous results.

Although verbal communication is symbolic and must be analysed when it is used—we must think about what we are going to say, or at least wish we had said at times—the non-verbal code is less symbolic and is more normative in nature. We often do not think about what we do non-verbally, yet most of us could name what is acceptable and what is not acceptable in specific situations. Waving hello to one of your good friends with your "upraised middle finger" (the proverbial "flip off") may be perfectly fine, whereas doing the same to your professor, your boss, your clergy, or your parents would probably have some negative consequences.

What is the norm in one context may not necessarily be so in all situations. Since we have expectations, we sometimes assume (often inappropriately) that non-verbal communication is less calculating and a more accurate reflection of our feelings than verbal communication. Exploring non-verbal communication in more detail reveals that the relationship really does not exist in the ways we might imagine.

Condisering the factors discussed in the above paragraphs we can define non-verbal communication as a process of creating meaning in the minds of receivers, whether intentionally or unintentionally, by use of actions other than, or in combination with, words or language. Non-verbal communication includes norms and expectations, usually imposed by society, for the expression of experiences, feelings, and attitudes. In other words, non-verbal communication occurs when some non-verbal subcode (e.g., appearance, touch, space, body movements) creates meaning for a receiver, which can happen on purpose or unintentionally. Non-verbal communication, then, operates in much the same way as verbal communication. It provides us with a means to control our communication, although it takes place in a more subtle, spontaneous, and natural way.

Aspects of non-verbal communication make it possible, however, for receivers to be mistaken in interpreting a message, especially if the receiver perceives that message as having been sent on purpose. A shrug meant to convey "I don't know" may have been interpreted as "I don't care." Non-verbal messages, while containing at least as much information as verbal messages, may lose their specificity of content, for a number of reasons. A non-verbal message by itself may be ambiguous or unclear; in many instances, it needs the verbal message to complete the process of communication.

4.5.2 Approaches to Non-verbal Communication

There are many approaches to the study of non-verbal communication; ours is simply one of many. An approach is often identified by one of three related, but different, factors. The first factor is one's theoretical point of view; the second is one's field of study or discipline; the third is one's methodology for undertaking research.

4.5.2.1 Theoretical Approaches

Many researchers think non-verbal communication is learned. People taking this perspective advocate the nurture approach. Traditionally, anthropologists and sociologists have used the nurture approach. We learn our non-verbal communication norms from sources that nurture our education.

In opposition to this approach is the nature approach, developed by Darwin in *The Expression of the Emotions in Man and Animals*. Darwin assumed that non-verbal behaviour is part of the genetic structure of human beings as well as of other animals. In other words, the nature approach claims that our non-verbal communication skills are part of our heredity, and that they are innate.

A third approach, the functional approach, assumes nothing about genetics or learning behaviour. It focuses instead on the types and functions non-verbal communication performs. Psychologists and communication researchers have emphasised the functional approach. This approach looks more specifically at how we use non-verbal channels to accomplish the function of our communication encounters. While these theoretical approaches reveal something about the nature of non-verbal communication, more can be learned by looking at the disciplines of the researchers.

4.5.2.2 Disciplinary Approaches

Perhaps the oldest discipline to consider the effects of non-verbal communication began in considering delivery in public speaking contexts. The early Greeks and Romans, and Cicero in particular, were the first to analyse delivery as one of the five important components of effective public speaking: invention, organisation, memory, style, and delivery. Management of the voice and of gestures was a focus in the consideration of delivery.

This focus on voice and gesture was known as the elocutionary movement, and it brought about an emphasis on the proper use of voice and gesture, which was prescriptive in nature. It provided specific vocal expressions and gestures based on how people should read or recite words. Steele developed a musical staff analogy, in which he wrote "music" for speeches, poetry, and literature. Austin suggested a similar prescription for gestures. The prescriptive approach may be referred to as the "performance/ elocutionary art" approach to non-verbal communication.

Today, this approach is considered antiquated, and, with the exception of some broadcasting and theatre programmes, it is rarely taught. Since it was primarily a learned systematic approach to using specific non-verbal channels, it may be considered a nurture view. Such a nurture view is held by many social scientists, who feel that the non-verbal code is similar to the verbal code and that all we need to do is to understand the structure of the non-verbal code. These scholars do not accept the notion that non-verbal communication is universal. Just as language differs, they argue, different cultures have different non-verbal coding systems.

Non-verbal messages that are normal in the United States may very well have a completely different meaning in an Asian culture, and quite often may be considered socially unacceptable. There are some universal non-verbal codes, such as a smile, but for the most part, we cannot be sure that all people we encounter understand our non-verbal messages the same way. Within the social and behavioural sciences we find many contemporary non-verbal communication researchers, although most of these researchers claim communication studies as their home discipline.

Those closest to the nature view follow a biological science approach and are best represented by Desmond Morris and Robert Ardrey. They are followed by ethnologists, who compare and contrast human behaviour with that of other animals. Probably best known are Ekman and Friesen, both having closely followed Darwin's beliefs. Psychologists often take different approaches from those of communication theorists. Some, like Mehrabian and Ruesch, take a functional view; others take a more psychological (or nature) view. Morris, for example, was a zoologist by profession, and he took the nature view in some instances. Some social anthropologists, such as Birdwhistell, take a linguistic view.

4.5.2.3 Methodological Approaches

The methods used in the study of communication help us understand the many approaches to studying non-verbal communication. Typically, those who take a nature view observe the similarities in behaviours of humans and other animals. The establishment of territoriality is a good example of this approach; both human beings and animals establish their own territories. Those who take a nurture view observe over a period of time how non-verbal communication occurs in groups. For example, someone might videotape a group, and by viewing the tape again and again, the researcher may discover underlying systems of non-verbal communication (e.g., nodding, blinking, and winking). Functionalists focus upon specific functions of non-verbal communication to determine how they work in specific contexts. For example, this approach may be used to study different greeting behaviours.

4.5.3 Non-verbal Functions

Non-verbal communication does not operate in a vacuum. Non-verbal communication often performs one of several functions in relationship to verbal communication. These functions help us to understand and use communication more effectively. The six imprtant functions for which non-verbal communication is used are the following.

i) *Identification and self-presentation*. We use non-verbal devices to let others know who we are. Those who know us well can identify us by our voices on the telephone. Some people call and say, "Hey, it's me." When we know that voice well, we know who "me" is. We also present ourselves through physical appearance, by facial expression, by vocal tone, by postural stances or sitting, by our olfactory signature (how we smell), by our use or misuse of time, among many other factors. We can tell when other people are "dressed up", when they appear excited, and when they sound depressed.

ii) *Control of the interaction.* We use the non-verbal channel to take the floor so that we can speak; we regulate many interactions by non-verbal channels. Instead of saying, "I have a question," we may raise our hand or show a look of puzzlement. In an interpersonal setting, we are likely to raise our index fingers and lean forward to signal our desire to take the floor. We also let others know when it is their turn to speak by slowing down our rate of speaking and pausing, by leaning back, by using silence, among other tactics. All these non-verbal devices, and others, regulate our interactions.

iii) *Relationship of interactants.* We illustrate to others how well we know a person by how closely we stand or sit to him or her, whether we smile and wink at the person, whether we whisper to him or her. Holding hands illustrates a particular type of relationship. For two teenagers, it may mean, "We're together [for now]." For a father and son, it may mean that the father is taking care of the son. If the son tries to pull away, the hand holding may mean that the father is in charge. Employees may assume a stiffer posture in the presence of their bosses than with their co-workers. If you are "in charge", say, as a parent, you may fold your arms across your chest and tap your foot to show impatience with your child, yet you are not likely to use the same non-verbal behaviours with your boss because the relationship is different.

iv) *Display of cognitive information.* We use non-verbal communication to send specific information to the receiver; consider the use of a hand to communicate. A display of fingers maymean, "Okay." Another display, a hand held up by a road worker,may mean, "Stop!" When you allow someone to pull into the line of traffic in front of you, the same hand signal may mean "Thanks!" Thumbs up may mean "Great!" Obscene signs may be delivered in an angry way or a friendly way. Recall the earlier example where you might "flip off" a good friend just to say hello; not everyone you did that to would take it as a friendly gesture. A specific uniform may tell others "I am a police officer." A stethoscope around one's neck is used to illustrate that one is a health care worker.

v) *Display of affective (emotional) information.* We use non-verbal communication to let others know how we feel. Also, our innate knowledge of non-verbal communication allows us to interpret the emotions of others. When we first meet a person, we establish a "baseline" of his or her emotions. Does the person appear nervous, anxious, stressed? When we meet that person again, we use that first occurrence in evaluating how we think that person feels. The better we know someone, the more accurate we are with our suppositions.

vi) *Display of deception.* We also use non-verbal communication to show others that we feel a certain emotion when we actually do not feel it. We try to detect deception in others through their non-verbal behaviours. We tend to think of excessive pauses and "ahs" as indicators that the other person is lying. As we will discuss those that we have long thought are cues to deception are not good indicators.

These six non-verbal functions provide us with a basic set of tools for the examination of non-verbal communication. Other scholars may provide other functions, but we believe these six meet our criteria for teaching about non-verbal communication. Before we begin to examine these functions, we need to look at the general communication process.

4.5.4 Perception

Most researchers agree that the communication process begins with perceptions. Perceptions are derived from the way we look at things-through (i) sensation and (ii) interpretation. A sensation takes place through one of the five senses: touch, or the tactile sense; sight, or the visual sense; sound, or the aural (hearing) sense; smell, or the olfactory sense; and taste, or the gustatory sense. After a stimulus has been sensed by one or more of our sensory organs, the brain interprets this stimulus, and places it in our "memory bank of perceptions". Through this process of perceiving, the external world becomes a part of what we refer to as knowledge.

4.5.5 Perceptual Filters of Non-verbal communication

In non-verbal communication, knowledge is typically related to how we intend to evaluate the message. Non-verbal communication provides us with a message about the message (metamessage). Non-verbal communication tells us, for example, whether people are being serious, joking, or sarcastic when they say, "I love you." Now you take this same expression, and repeat it in these manners: sincerely, sarcastically, and playfully. Can you tell the difference? This evaluation of the meaning is based on the vocal tone and facial expressions used when the message is sent. There are a number of factors that filter, or influence, our perceptions or interpretations. These filters include the function or purpose of the communication, as well as process structure, age, culture and race, status, and sex and gender. These five perceptual filters are discussed in the following paragraphs.

4.5.5.1 Process Structure

Process structure refers to how the brain processes incoming sensations. Some texts use the term hemispheric differences (more commonly known as left brain/right brain) to refer to processing differences; however, we prefer hemispheric style. The left hemisphere of the brain is responsible for most people's verbal communication. This side of the brain is specialised in an abstract, logical, and analytical way that is best used for the analysis of language. The left is also known as the side of the brain that most often processes the cognitive information you receive. The right hemisphere is specialised for the spatiotemporal, gestalt, emotive forms of communication for which non-verbal communication is best suited. The right is often called the side of the brain that processes more of the affective information as well as more of the creative information received. For many years it was thought that one side of the brain dominated the other. More recently, we have begun to realise that each hemisphere's specialisation includes a small share of the other hemisphere's specialty. This means that some language will be processed in the right hemisphere, which may be done automatically or because it is tied to some emotions. The left hemisphere also processes some non-verbal communication.

It is essential to note that each hemisphere of the brain is specialised to analyse either verbal or non-verbal communication. To explain this difference, we will look at a model suggesting that non-verbal communication is more spontaneous, whereas verbal communication is symbolic. According to Buck, spontaneous communication is related to the right hemisphere, is an automatic reflexive response, and is non propositional in nature.

One final approach to hemispheric processing has been proposed by Stacks. Stacks postulates that the two brain hemispheres differ only in terms of style; that is, each is best suited for either verbal or non-verbal communication. He theorises that each hemisphere contains the process necessary for language, but language processed in the right hemisphere is unconscious or repressed by the left hemisphere. How each hemisphere of the brain operates also helps determine what type of material is being processed.

Verbal communication is more digital, much like a computer's information: it is highly arbitrary, discrete, and found in finite units. Non-verbal communication, however, is more continuous and natural. This this kind of communication can be labelled as analogical, which means that the code material is composed of continuous, infinite, and natural representations of what people observe. A metaphor for the analogical nature of non-verbal code material is the colour spectrum. It consists of a finite number of colours, from white (a combination of all colors) to black (the absence of all colors), but our symbolic representations of the colour spectrum are arbitrary and discrete (e.g., aquamarine, tangerine, lilac, navy blue). In the same way a gesture is continuous and infinite, analysis forces us to "create" a meaning for that gesture. That meaning will be arbitrary and it may change by culture or subculture, from relationship to relationship, from situation to situation. Take, for example, the "okay" symbol—creating a circle with the thumb and forefinger and extending the other three fingers upward. In our culture it means, "okay." In some other cultures the same symbol is an expression of what raising the middle finger in the air is in our culture. Those definitions are arbitrary and are based on the norms of the culture.

Richmond and McCroskey take this processing of information in a similar direction, but the distinctions they note are a little different. Two distinctions they make, among others, are between the linguistic distinction and the continuity distinction showing processing distinctions similar to those of Burgoon and Saine. The linguistic distinction is discussed as relying on language, whereas non-verbal communication does not rely on language. This does not deny, however, that verbal and non-verbal communication do work in conjunction with each other. The continuity distinction looks at verbal communication as discontinuous, meaning that a verbal interaction has a start and a finish.

Non-verbal communication is continuous, meaning it is ongoing and does not need a verbal component to have meaning. Even the absence of non-verbal behaviours can send a message (e.g., the "silent treatment" when you are angry). Finally, we must examine the structure of the two codes. As might be expected, non-verbal communication is much less structured than verbal communication. Many researchers believe that non-verbal communication has no particular set of rules, no grammar, and no syntax. Other non-verbal communication scholars would disagree with that statement, however, and say that we actually do create rules for what is non-verbally acceptable and what is not. The verbal code can be indicative of the past, present, and future, and it can also be expressed in a number of different languages.

Non-verbal communication has no written set of rules (although some are probably understood), grammar, or syntax; it is bound to the present, and is its own natural language. For example, although speakers can talk about speeches they give or will give (about how good or bad they were or will be), they cannot do so non-verbally without first providing a context through verbalising. Consider a smile. What does it reflect? Without some other information, say about the topic being discussed or the situation at hand, we have no idea. Although we may infer many things from that smile, a verbal message is needed to understand what the emotion is.

Non-verbal communication, because of its rather singular need to be in the present, tends to be highly contextual. Different situations or environments produce different non-verbal messages. Your non-verbal communication will likely be different at a funeral than it is at a party, although a funeral in New Orleans might be a different experience from what we normally think of as funereal. The way you act in class or while hanging out with a friend would probably not be proper in a job interview or at work. The context helps us to decide what norms and rules to follow.

4.5.5.2 Age

Age is a primary factor in the communication process. For example, children stand closer to one another when they are younger. People who lose some of their hearing as they age will stand closer to people so they can hear. Adults tend to stand farther away from people. These are norms for our society, and such standards will always be contextually based. Individuals whose sight has weakened may have difficulty observing the gestures and facial expressions of others and so may move closer to others. As people get older, they tend to put more distance between others and themselves. We often see children as "space invaders", and we may have a tendency to avoid getting anywhere near senior citizens, almost as if old age were contagious. We should also point out, however, that these are standards of our culture; other cultures that revere their aged members do not avoid coming in contact with the older generation.

Age may also affect other aspects of non-verbal communication. Physical appearance is one area where age may play a role. Children of preschool age may not yet be aware of clothing trends and may, therefore, be less concerned with their physical appearance than when they grow into their school-age years. As people age into senior citizens, they may become less concerned with appearance again, perhaps becoming more concerned with the people they are than how they appear. It would be stereotypical to make any blanket statements about how age affects appearance because each person will certainly make personal choices based on his or her preferences.

4.5.5.2 Culture and Race

Non-verbal aspects of communication vary widely according to culture and race. In some cultures people stand very close to one another; in others, men kiss one another's beards; some cultures' pace of life very different from others. With the many cultural and racial differences, we may find that dress can be different, as can touch, space, scent, usage of time, gestures, and so forth. In addition, some theoretical differences will greatly affect non-verbal communication between people from different cultures.

We should take note of cultural variables that can influence non-verbal interactions. One specific variable that would influence non-verbal communication is whether a culture uses high-context or low-context communication. High-context communication, according to Gudykunst, is seen where most of the information is either in the physical context or internalised in the coded, explicit, transmitted part of the message. What this means is that high-context communication is more indirect, ambiguous, and far more dependent on the non-verbal code. Low-context communication is seen when the mass of the information is vested in the explicit code. Low-context communication is more direct, precise, clear, and is more dependent on the verbal code for message transmission.

Another cultural variable that researchers should determine when studying non-verbal communication is whether a culture is individualistic or collectivistic in nature. Gudykunst tells us that cultures that are more individualistic are ones where individuals' goals take precedence over the group's goals; they are more likely to promote self-realisation, and they see each person as having a unique set of talents and potential.

In individualistic cultures, people are expected to look after themselves and their immediate family only; the "I" identity takes precedence over the "we" identity. In collectivistic cultures, the group's goals take precedence over individuals' goals, which requires that individuals fit into their groups. Emphasis is placed on collectivity, harmony, and cooperation within the group. In collectivistic cultures "people belong to in-groups or collectivities which are supposed to look after them in exchange for loyalty" to the group; the "we" identity is more important than the "I" identity. These two variables can significantly influence the importance of non-verbal communication. Using dress as an example, we can see that people from more individualistic cultures may dress in unique styles. Someone from a collectivistic culture, wanting to fit in with the group, might dress like others in the same culture.

There are other cultural variables that are also important when studying non-verbal communication. Power distance is one variable that affects the use of non-verbal communication in situations involving interactions between people of different statuses. Some cultures' norms say that people who are more powerful should be in control, and their non-verbal communication behaviors will reflect this. This norm is called high power distance. Most of us know some non-verbal behaviours that are expected of us when we are in a subordinate role, so it is easy to see how this variable could affect non-verbal communication norms and expectations. If you are a subordinate in a high power distance culture, you will assume postures that indicate less power, such as shrinkage of your body, whereas the boss might use an expansive posture. You might not initiate eye contact or touch if you are in a subordinate role in a high power distance culture; that privilege is reserved for the person in the higher status role.

The final cultural variable that would cause communicators to modify their non-verbal communication would be masculinity and femininity. In cultures that are considered more masculine, gender roles are clearly distinct. Men are supposed to be assertive, tough, and focused on material success, whereas women are supposed to be more modest, tender, and concerned with the quality of life. People in highly masculine cultures value things, power, and assertiveness; they emphasise differentiated sex roles, performance, ambition, and independence; they tend to have little contact with members of the opposite sex when growing up, and they tend to see same-sex relationships as more intimate than opposite-sex relationships.

In cultures considered more feminine, gender roles overlap; both men and women are supposed to be modest, tender, and concerned with the quality of life. People in highly feminine cultures value quality of life and nurturance; they value fluid sex roles, service, and interdependence. There is also a "middle of the road" position on this issue—that there are also androgynous cultures, which means that they reject the rigid sex roles often imposed by society. A culture that is androgynous would have characteristics of both masculine and feminine cultures. When deciding how to communicate with people who are culturally or racially different from us, we need to take many things into account.

4.5.5.4 Status

How we interact non-verbally with superiors may differ entirely from how we interact with subordinates. In addition, our non-verbal communication sending and receiving processes vary depending upon whom we are interacting with. We may have relaxed kinesics while interacting with our peers, but when in the presence of our "boss", we become more formal. There are reasons to believe that the purpose for which we use non-verbal communication depends on position of legitimate authority. That is, bosses tend to use non-verbal communication to manipulate and even control, while subordinates use it to comply and show deference (or respect) to a boss's authority.

4.5.5.5 Gender

Sex is the biological determination of male and female and gender is a psychological determination with masculinity at one end and femininity at the other. The midpoint of the continuum would be androgyny, which is having both masculine and feminine psychological traits. In her book *Body Politics: Power, Sex, and Non-verbal Communication*, Henley argues that males are the dominant and domineering sex and that males indicate their dominance through a number of channels, including non-verbal communication. Tannen and Wood wrote that males typically use the communication process as a method of control, which complemented Henley's analysis. At the same time, Tannen suggested that females generally use the communication process to negotiate, and Wood's research on "women's speech" confirms that finding.

Over the last decade, many researchers have studied the differences between male and female communication, and the discipline of non-verbal communication is not a stranger to that research. Henley saw significant differences in non-verbal communication when a male boss dominated a female secretary by using non-verbal communication. A situation with a male boss and a female secretary was typical when Henley undertook her research in the early 1970s. Today, while such a relationship may still be somewhat typical, there are also others that are much different, e.g., a female boss with a female secretary, a male boss with a male secretary, and a female boss with a male secretary.

Most people in positions of authority today are very careful about using any discriminatory non-verbal behaviors based on sex for fear of the consequences. We could hope that these changes came as a result of more non-verbal sensitivity, since that would indicate that more effective communication practices were being learned, but the reality is probably that these changes have come about as a result of subtle coercion by our society. Nevertheless, the outcome is still be positive.

To better understand some of the gender differences found in non-verbal communication, we will briefly explore several factors that previous research has indicated as dominating and deferent behaviours. Using the control of interaction function, we might see that there are several ways to dominate a conversation. It may be done by talking too much, interrupting, changing the topic, and by the use of silence. Each of these methods has been viewed as a dominating mechanism.

Amount of talk. James and Drakich and Wood, among others, have reported that men talk more than women in mixed-sex interactions. Tannen, however, suggests that in public situations, males ask more questions, ask longer questions, and typically ask the first question. Tannen suggests further that males talk more in public and females more in private situations, referring to male talk as "report talk" and female talk as "rapport talk".

Interruptions. There are three types of interruptions: positive, negative, and neutral. Positive interruptions include those where a question is asked for clarification purposes (communication function). Neutral interruptions include those that are "asides" (e.g., "Please pass the butter.") Negative interruptions are often referred to as overlaps, although some overlaps are not considered to be negative. Overlapping, by definition, means that you overlap someone's speech with your own; it is sometimes seen as a sign that you are interested and that you are following the conversation. Let's consider what we know thus far about the amount of talk and regulation of conversation between males and females, and then consider how interruptions are a part of the process of communication. We know that men talk more than women in public situations, asking the first questions, asking more questions, and asking longer questions. With that in mind, let us assess how interruptions add to this:

i) Men interrupt more often.

ii) Interruption is often seen as dominance.

iii) Interruption has also been seen as a signal of interest as opposed to dominance.

iv) Women will interrupt more with questions, men with statements.

v) Interruptions and overlaps are different, according to some theorists.

vi) Overlaps are not gender related.

vii) Seventy-five percent of the time, overlaps are cooperative.

viii) Sometimes overlaps are simply conversational "duets."

ix) Men use interruptions more to control conversation; women use interruptions more to indicate interest and to respond.

x) Menmore often consider interruptions as normal and good-natured, at least within masculine environments, so it carries over into all environmentsm.

Silence. If silence means the lack of interruption, it is interesting that some researchers have found that males use silence as a method to dominate. Silence has long been considered a vocalic subcode factor that communicates much information. Sattel has noted that silence can be used as an instrument of power. While Tannenhas indicated that some males use silence as a "taciturnity of spirit" (meaning being subdued or reserved), there appears to be no research to support males using silence as a manipulative tool. Power is not the only issue in the use of silence. Richmond and McCroskey point out that people use silence to communicate many things. We may use silence to establish interpersonal distance, to put our thoughts together, to show respect for another person, or to modify others' behaviours. Most research in the area of gender differences, however, has not determined that either gender uses silence for one of those functions more than the other gender.

Deference. At the other end of the regulation of interaction spectrum is the concept of deference, meaning that we can expect subordinates to defer to their superiors in terms of conversations and other communication interactions. One of the most significant means of deferring is through non-verbal gesturing. When the boss is "lecturing", a subordinate may be compelled to nod his or her head in agreement. Goffman discussed deferential behaviour at length in his studies of advertising. Goffman found that marketing and advertising specialists had taken advantage of the common stereotypes of gender differences. Goffman found six general types of genderisms in advertisements:

i) males were larger than women in relative size;
ii) women were portrayed as outlining and touching objects more often than men (the feminine touch);
iii) males were portrayed as having the more executive, superior, or active role (function ranking);
iv) the family was often used, but whereas sons were shown as inferior to fathers, mother-daughter combinations generally displayed more equality;
v) females were found to physically lower themselves to males (ritual of subordination); and
vi) women were found to be depicted as withdrawn psychologically from the social situation at large, not oriented to it, and dependent on the goodwill of others.

We might think that these findings have changed in recent years. Although there have been some changes, the majority of advertisements still send the same message.

The mass media apparently reflect the gender roles of our society and also contribute to them. Archer, Kimes, and Barrios noted some factors similar to Goffman's findings. Studying photographs in newspapers and magazines, they observed that more of the bodies of females were shown, whereas pictures of males contained mostly faces. Still other researchers look at election campaigns where there are female and male candidates. Media will often pay attention to what the female candidate is wearing, but the male candidate does not receive the same scrutiny.

An overview of gender differences research reveals that males and females differ in terms of facial expressions (women reveal more emotions); posture and bearing (women are more relaxed and sit differently; men expand more, women use shrinkage behaviours); eye contact (women employ more); gesturing (men use more and are more expansive in their use of gestures; women use more in approval-seeking situations); clothing, grooming, and physical appearance (women put more importance on their appearances, and society places more importance on their appearance); use of space (women are approached much more closely); and touch (men often interpret women's touch as sexual, more so than women do men's touch, women are touched more in same-sex interactions than men are). In terms of vocalics, there are gender differences in sound development (female children start speaking earlier, mothers vocalise more to female children); physiology (males have larger larynxes and longer and thicker vocal cords, more males have speech defects); and pronunciation (more females speak standard American dialect, more males, nonstandard, blue-collar English); pitch (lower pitch for males); volume (males generally speak louder); and vocal typecasting.

An individual's sex can often be determined solely on the basis of the voice. Although there are gender differences in how messages are transmitted, there are also gender-related differences in perceptions of others' non-verbal communication. Vocally, women are generally perceived in terms of sociability, and men are perceived in terms of physical and emotional power. Vocal quality cues are used more in judging women than in judging men. As a general conclusion, we can also state that women are more accurate in their interpretation of non-verbal cues and are more responsive to non-verbal cues than are men.

Understanding differences in power and gender is important to effective communication, especially when dominance in an interaction is considered. Just as with all non-verbal communication, it would be impossible to generalise about entire populations just because some findings indicate that certain behaviors are used by the majority of one group. Such a generalisation would be stereotyping at its worst, and it would not allow for the individuality of human beings. Such general differences, however, can be important and helpful in learning to communicate effectively with others.

Selected References

Argyle, Michael, *Bodily Communication*, Methuen & Co., 1978.

Arnold Jeffrey, *The Big Book on Small Groups*, Downers Grove, Ill., InterVarsity Press, 1992.

Barkai, John L., "Nonverbal Communication from the Other Side: Speaking Body Language", *San Diego Law Review*, p 101-25, Jan, 1990.

Barker, Steve, et al., *Good Things Come in Small Groups*, Downers Grove, Ill.: InterVarsity Press, 1985.

Beebe, Steven A., and John T. Masterson, *Communicating in Small Groups: Principles and Practices*, New York: HarperCollins, 1993.

Blanck, P. D., (ed.), *Interpersonal expectations: Theory, research, applications*, Cambridge University Press. 1994.

Burgoon, J., Stern, L. A. & Dillman, L., *Interpersonal adaptation: Dyadic interaction patterns*, Cambridge University Press, 1995.

DeVito, J. A., *Messages: Building interpersonal communication skills*, NY: Longman, 1999.

Donna Bellafiore, *Interpersonal Conflict and Effective Communication*, DRB Alternatives, Inc., 2004.

Duncan, Barry, *Mass Media and Popular Culture*, Toronto: Harcourt, Brace, Jovanovich, 1988.

Harper, Robert, *Nonverbal Communication*, Wiley, 1980.

Kalbfleisch, P. J., and Cody, M. J., (eds.), *Gender, power, and communication in human relationships*, Lawrence Erblaum and Associates, 1995.

______________, *Interpersonal Communication: Evolving Interpersonal Relationshsips*, Lawrence Erblaum and Associates, 1993.

Knapp, M. L., and Hall, J. A., *Nonverbal communication in human interaction*, Harcourt Brace College Publishers, 1997.

______________ Miller, G. R., and Fudge, K., *Handbook of interpersonal communication,* Thousand Oaks, CA: Sage, 1994.

Leathers, D, *Successful Nonverbal Communication: Principles and Applications*, Allyn & Bacon, 1997.

McQuail, Denis, *Mass Communication Theory: An Introduction,* London: Sage, 1987.

Parenti, Michael, *Inventing Reality: The Politics of the Mass Media,* New York: St. Martin's Press, 1986.

Radcliff, C. J., "Interpersonal communication with library patrons: Physician-patient research models", *RQ, 34* (4), pp. 497-506, Summer, 1995

Rothwell, J. Dan., *In Mixed Company: Small Group Communication*, Philadelphia, Harcourt Brace, 1992.

Schrank, Jeffrey, *Understanding Mass Media*, Toronto, Copp Clark, 1986.

Segerstrale, U., and Molnar, P., (eds.), *Nonverbal Communication: Where Nature Meets Culture*, Lawrence Erblaum and Associates, 1997.

5

Theories of Communication

Communication is a slippery concept, and while we may casually use the word with some frequency, it is difficult to arrive at a precise definition that is agreeable to most of those who consider themselves communication scholars. Communication is so deeply rooted in human behaviours and the structures of society that it is difficult to think of social or behavioural events that are absent communication.

We might say that communication consists of transmitting information from one person to another. In fact, many scholars of communication take this as a working definition, and use Lasswell's maxim ("who says what to whom to what effect") as a means of circumscribing the field of communication. Others suggest that there is a ritual process of communication that cannot be artificially abstracted from a particular historical and social context. As a relatively young field of inquiry, it is probably premature to expect a conceptualisation of communication that is shared among all or most of those who work in the area. Furthermore, communication theory itself is, in many ways, an attempt to describe and explain precisely what communication is.

Indeed, a theory is some form of explanation of a class of observed phenomena. Karl Popper colourfully described theory as "the net which we throw out in order to catch the world—to rationalise, explain, and dominate it." The idea of a theory lies at the heart of any scholarly process, and while those in the social sciences tend to adopt the tests of a good theory from the natural sciences, many who study communication adhere to an idea of theory that is akin to that found in other academic fields. None the less, when evaluating the strength of a theory, the criteria commonly found in the sciences, and derived from the scientific method are often broadly applicable.

5.1 Components of an Effective Theory

What makes a theory "good"? Six criteria might be said to be properties of a strong theory.

5.1.1 Theoretical Scope

How general is the theory? That is, how widely applicable is it? In most cases, a theory that may only be applied within a fairly narrow set of circumstances is not considered as useful as a theory that encompasses a very wide range of communicative interactions. The ideal, of course, is a theory that succinctly explains the nature of human communication as a whole.

5.1.2 Appropriateness

Theories are often evaluated based upon how well their epistemological, ontological, and axiological assumptions relate to the issue or question being explained. If a theory recapitulates its assumptions (if it is tautological), it is not an effective theory.

5.1.3 Heuristic Value

Some theories suggest the ways in which further research may be conducted. By presenting an explanatory model, the theory generates questions or hypotheses that can be operationalised relatively easily. In practical terms, the success of a theory may rest on how readily other researchers may continue to do fruitful work in reaction or support.

5.1.4 Validity

It may seem obvious that for a theory to be good, it must also be valid. Validity refers to the degree to which the theory accurately represents the true state of the world. Are the arguments internally consistent and are its predictions and claims derived logically from its assumptions? Many also require that theories be falsifiable; that is, theories that present predictions that—if they prove to be incorrect—invalidate the theory. The absence of such questions significantly reduces the value of the theory, since a theory that cannot be proven false (perhaps) cannot be shown to be accurate, either.

5.1.5 Parsimony

The law of parsimony dictates that a theory should provide the simplest possible (viable) explanation for a phenomenon. Others suggest that good theory exhibits an aesthetic quality, that a good theory is beautiful or natural. That it leads to an "Aha!" moment in which an explanation feels as if it fits.

5.1.6 Openness

Theories, perhaps paradoxically, should not exist to the absolute exclusion of other theories. Theory should not be dogma: it should encourage and provide both for scepticism and should—to whatever degree possible—be compatible with other accepted theory.

It is important to note that a theory is not "true", or "false", but rather better or worse at explaining the causes of a particular event. Especially within the social sciences, we may find several different theories that each explain a phenomenon in useful ways. There is value in being able to use theories as "lenses" through which you can understand communication, and through which you can understand the world *together* with other scholars.

5.2 Theories and Models

Many suggest that there is no such thing as a successful body of communication theory, but that we have been relatively more successful in generating models of communication. A model, according to a seminal 1952 article by Karl Deutsch ("On Communication Models in the Social Sciences"), is "a structure of symbols and operating rules which is supposed to match a set of relevant points in an existing structure or process." In other words, it is a simplified representation or template of a process that can be used to help understand the nature of communication in a social setting. Such models are necessarily not one-to-one maps of the real world, but they are successful only in so far as they accurately represent the most important elements of the real world, and the dynamics of their relationship to one another.

Deutsch suggests that a model should provide four functions. It should organise a complex system (while being as general as possible), and should provide an heuristic function. Both these functions are similar to those listed above for theories. He goes on to suggest models should be as original as possible, that they should not be obvious enough that they fail to shed light on the existing system. They should also provide some form of measurement of the system that will work analogously within the model and within the actual system being observed.

Models are tools of inquiry in a way that theories may not be. By representing the system being observed, they provide a way of working through the problems of a "real world" system in a more abstract way. As such, they lend themselves to the eventual construction of theory, though it may be that theory of the sort found in the natural sciences is something that cannot be achieved in the social sciences. Unfortunately, while models provide the "what" and the "how", they are not as suited to explaining "why," and therefore are rarely as satisfying as strong theory.

The aim in the natural sciences is to create what, since Hempel at least, has been called covering law. Covering law requires the explicit relationship of a causal condition to an effect within certain bounderies. It has been observed that social relationships are very difficult to capture within the structure of covering law. Perhaps this is because people have the annoying habit of violating "natural laws." Wittgenstein's later work in particular put forward the possibility that rules-based systems may provide a more effective descriptive model of human communication. This may account for the propensity of communication theorists to develop models more often than theory. Rules-based approaches are particularly popular within speech communication, where human interaction is seen to proceed along structural, though not necessarily causal, lines.

A discipline is defined in large part by its theoretical structure. Instead communication, at its present state, might be considered a field of inquiry. Theory is often borrowed from other social sciences, while communication provides few examples of theories that have been exported to other disciplines. What is taught as communication theory at one institution is unlikely to be at all similar to what is taught within other communication schools. This theoretical variegation makes it difficult to come to terms with the field as a whole. That said, there are some common taxonomies that are used to divide up the range of communication research. Two common mappings will be briefly presented here.

Many authors and researchers divide communication by what are sometimes called "contexts" or "levels," but more often represent institutional histories. The study of communication in the US, while occurring within departments of psychology, sociology, linguistics, and anthropology among others, generally developed from schools of rhetoric and schools of journalism. While many of these have become "departments of communication," they often retain their historical roots, adhering largely to theories from speech communication in the former case, and mass media in the latter.

The great divide between speech communication and mass communication is joined by a number of smaller sub-areas of communication research, including intercultural and international communication, small group communication, communication technology, policy and legal studies of communication, telecommunication, and work done under a variety of other labels. Some of these departments take a largely social science perspective, others tend more heavily toward the humanities, and still others are geared more toward production and professional preparation.

These "levels" of communication provide some way of grouping communication theories, but inevitably, there are theories and concepts that leak from one area to another, or that fail to find a home at all. If communication is a cohesive field of study, one would expect to see a cohesive set of theories, or at least a common understanding of the structure of the field, and this appears to still be developing.

Another way of dividing up the communication field emphasises the assumptions that undergird particular theories, models, and approaches. While this tends also to be based on institutional divisions, theories within each of the seven "traditions" of communication theory that Robert Craig suggests tend to reinforce one another, and retain the same ground epistemological and axiological assumptions. His traditions include the rhetorical, semiotic, phenomenological, cybernetic, sociopsychological, and sociocultural traditions. Each of these are, for Craig, clearly defined against the others and remain cohesive approaches to describing communicative behaviour. As a taxonomic aid, these labels help to organise theory by its assumptions, and help researchers to understand the reasons some theories may be incommensurable.

While these two approaches are very commony used, it seems that they decentralise the place of language and machines as communicative technologies. The idea that communication is the primary tool of a species that is defined by its tools remains at the outskirts of communication theory. It is represented somewhat in the Toronto School of communication theory as represented by the work of Innis, McLuhan, and others. It seems that the ways in which individuals and groups use the technologies of communication—and in some cases are used by them—remains central to what communication researchers do, and the ideas that surround this, and in particular the place of persuasion, are constants across both the "traditions" and "levels" of communication theory.

5.3 Theories of Interpersonal Communication

5.3.1 Attribution Theory

F. Heider was the first to propose a psychological theory of attribution, but B. Weiner and colleagues developed a theoretical framework that has become a major research paradigm of social psychology. Heider discussed what he called "naïve" or "common sense" psychology. In his view, people were like amateur scientists, trying to understand other people's behaviour by piecing together information until they arrived at a reasonable explanation or cause.

5.3.1.1 Core Assumptions

Attribution theory is concerned with how individuals interpret events and how this relates to their thinking and behaviour. Attribution theory assumes that people try to determine why people do what they do. A person seeking to understand why another person did something may attribute one or more causes to that behaviour. According to Heider a person can make two attributions:

i) internal attribution, the inference that a person is behaving in a certain way because of something about the person, such as attitude, character or personality.
ii) external attribution, the inference that a person is behaving a certain way because of something about the situation he or she is in.

Our attributions are also significantly driven by our emotional and motivational drives. Blaming other people and avoiding personal recrimination are very real self-serving attributions. We will also make attributions to defend what we perceive as attacks. We will point to injustice in an unfair world. We will even tend to blame victims (of us and of others) for their fate as we seek to distance ourselves from thoughts of suffering the same plight. We will also tend to ascribe less variability to other people than ourselves, seeing ourselves as more multifaceted and less predictable than others. This may well because we can see more of what is inside ourselves (and spend more time doing this).

5.3.1.2 Methods

Various methods have been employed in the measurement and categorisation of attributions. Open-ended methods involve the researcher categorising the oral replies of participants to open-ended questions. Derived score methods require the participant to rate his/her reasons for, for example, a success or failure on five-point scales for different elements (e.g., ability or effort) related to the attribution dimensions. The direct rating method, requires the participant to state his/her reasons for the event and then map those reasons onto items referring to attribution dimensions.

5.3.1.3 Applications

Attribution theory has been used to explain the difference in motivation between high and low achievers. According to attribution theory, high achievers will approach rather than avoid tasks related to succeeding, because they believe success is due to high ability and effort which they are confident of. Failure is thought to be caused by bad luck or a poor exam and is not their fault. Thus, failure doesn't affect their self-esteem but success builds pride and confidence. On the other hand, low achievers avoid success-related chores because they tend to (i) doubt their ability and/or (ii) assume success is related to luck or to "who you know" or to other factors beyond their control. Thus, even when successful, it isn't as rewarding to the low achiever because he/she doesn't feel responsible, it doesn't increase his/her pride and confidence.

5.3.2 ACT* Theory

ACT* is a general theory of cognition developed by John Anderson that focuses on memory processes. ACT* distinguishes among three types of memory structures: declarative, procedural and working memory. Declarative memory takes the form of a semantic net linking propositions, images, and sequences by associations. Procedural memory (also long-term) represents information in the form of productions; each production has a set of conditions and actions based in declarative memory. The nodes of long-term memory all have some degree of activation and working memory is that part of long-term memory that is most highly activated.

5.3.2.1 Core Assumptions

According to ACT*, all knowledge begins as declarative information; procedural knowledge is learned by making inferences from already existing factual knowledge. ACT* supports three fundamental types of learning: generalisation, in which productions become broader in their range of application, discrimination, in which productions become narrow in their range of application, and strengthening, in which some productions are applied more often. New productions are formed by the conjunction or disjunction of existing productions.

5.3.2.2 Application

ACT* can explain a wide variety of memory effects as well as account for higher order skills such as geometry proofs, programming and language learning. ACT* has been the basis for intelligent tutors.

5.3.3 Argumentation Theory

Argumentation exists from way before the nineteenth century, where the Aristotle's logical theory is found first. This indicates that argumentation was an important factor already in society. Until the 1950s, the approach of argumentation was based on rhetoric and logic. In the United States debating and argumentation became an important subject on universities and colleges. Textbooks appeared on 'Principles of Argumentation'.

In the 1960s and 1970s Perelman and Toulmin were the most influential writers on argumentation. Perelman tried to find a description of techniques of argumentation used by people to obtain the approval of others for their opinions. Perelman and Olbrechts-Tyteca called this 'new rhetoric'. Toulmin, the other influential writer developed his theory (starting in 1950's) in order to explain how argumentation occurs in the natural process of an everyday argument. He called his theory 'the uses of argument'. Argumentation theory cannot be seen as the theory for argumentation. Various authors have used the argumentation theory all in a slightly different way; it is not to say which version is the most developed.

5.3.3.1 Core Assumptions

Argumentation is a verbal and social activity of reason aimed at increasing (or decreasing) the acceptability of a controversial standpoint for the listener or reader, by putting forward a constellation of propositions intended to justify (or refute) the standpoint before a rational judge. Argumentation is a verbal activity, most often in an ordinary language. In argumentation people use words and sentences to argue, to state or to deny, etc., Non-verbal communication is accompanied with verbal communication in argumentation and can play an important role. Furthermore, argumentation is a social activity, which in principle is directed to other people. Argumentation is also an activity of reason, when people put forward their arguments in argumentation they place their considerations within the realm of reason. Argumentation is always related to a standpoint. An opinion itself is not enough; arguments are needed when people differ on a standpoint. Finally, the goal of argumentation is to justify one's standpoint or to refute someone else's.

The version of Van Eemeren and Grootendorst of the argumentation theory, the pragma-dialectical theory, is currently most popular. They began to study argumentation as a means of resolving differences of opinion. Argumentation starts with four principles.

i) *Externalisation*: Argumentation needs a standpoint and an opposition to the standpoint. Therefore, argumentation research concentrates on the externalisable commitments rather than the psychological elements of people.

ii) *Socialisation*: Arguments are seen as an expression of people's processes. Crucial is to validate the arguer's position by arguments in a certain way. Two people try to obtain an agreement in argumentation; therefore argumentation is part of a social context rather than an individual context.

iii) *Functionalisation:* Argumentation has the general function of managing the resolution of disagreement. Studying of argumentation should concentrate on the function of argumentation in the verbal management of disagreement.

iv) *Dialectification:* Argumentation is appropriate only when you are able to use arguments that are able to help you arguing against another person. For resolving differences a theory on argumentation should have a set of standards. The term dialectical procedure is mentioned as a depending element on efficient arguing on solving differences.

Van Eemeren and Grootendorst identify various stages of argumentative dialogue.

i) *Confrontation*: Presentation of the problem, such as a debate question or a political disagreement.

ii) *Opening*: Agreement on rules, such as for example, how evidence is to be presented, which sources of facts are to be used, how to handle divergent interpretations, determination of closing conditions.

iii) *Argumentation*: Application of logical principles according to the agreed-upon rules.

iv) *Concluding*: When closing conditions are met. These could be for example, a time limitation or the determination of an arbiter. Note that these stages are indispensable.

Schellens uses a typology which differentiates between restricted and unrestricted argumentation schemes. Restricted schemes are limited to a certain conclusion. The group restricted argumentation schemes can be divided into three different parts:

i) *Regularity-based argumentation:* Used in support of a descriptive statement about the present, the past or the future. Argumentation is given for a proposition of a factual or descriptive nature on the basis of a regularly recurring empirical link.
ii) *Rule-based argumentation*: Used in support of a normative statement about the value of a situation or process. Arguments are given for a statement of a normative nature
iii) *Pragmatic argumentation*: Leading to a statement about the desirability of intended behaviour. A position on the desirability of a given action, behaviour or measure is advocated on the basis of its advantages and/or disadvantages.

In addition to these restricted argumentation schemes, Schellens also distinguishes three unrestricted forms; argumentation from authority, argumentation from example and argumentation from analogy. These schemas are not limited to a conclusion of a type, but have a wider application.

5.3.3.2 Applications

Argumentation theory is an interdisciplinary field which attracts attention from philosophers, logicians, linguists, legal scholars, speech communication theorists, etc. The theory is grounded in conversational, interpersonal communication, but also applies to group communication and written communication.

5.3.4 Cognitive Dissonance Theory

Leon Festinger synthesised a set of studies to distill a theory about communication's social influences. Cognitive dissonance enjoyed great popularity from the late 1950s through the mid-1970s. Theoretical problems and conflicting findings lead to temporary replacement by similar "self" theories in the early 1980s, but cognitive dissonance regained its place as the umbrella theory for selective exposure to communication by the late 1980s.

5.3.4.1 Core Assumptions

Cognitive dissonance is a communication theory adopted from social psychology. The title gives the concept: cognitive is thinking or the mind; and dissonance is inconsistency or conflict. Cognitive dissonance is the psychological conflict from holding two or more incompatible beliefs simultaneously.

Cognitive dissonance is a relatively straightforward social psychology theory that has enjoyed wide acceptance in a variety of disciplines including communication. The theory replaces previous conditioning or reinforcement theories by viewing individuals as more purposeful decision makers; they strive for balance in their beliefs. If presented with decisions or information that create dissonance, they use dissonance-reduction strategies tot regain equilibrium, especially if the dissonance affects their self-esteem. The theory suggests that

i) dissonance is psychologically uncomfortable enough to motivate people to achieve consonance, and
ii) in a state of dissonance, people will avoid information and situations that might increase the dissonance.

How dissonance arises is easy to imagine: It may be unavoidable in an information rich-society. How people deal with it is more difficult.

5.3.4.2 Applications

Dissonance theory applies to all situations involving attitude formation and change. This theory is able to manipulate people into certain behaviour, by doing so these people will alter their attitudes themselves. It is especially relevant to decisionmaking and problemsolving.

5.3.5 Contagion Theories

Contagion theories seek to explain networks as conduits for "infectious" attitudes and behaviour. Contagion theories are related to a number of theories: Structurational Theory, Symbolic Interaction, Gatekeeping, Network Theory and Analysis, Hypodermic Needle Theory. These theories all focus on the different aspects of the social construction process.

5.3.5.1 Core Assumptions

Contact is provided by communication networks in contagion theories. These communication networks serve as a mechanism that exposes people, groups, and organisations to information, attitudinal messages and the behaviours of others. Due to this exposure it increases the likelihood that network members will develop beliefs, assumptions, and attitudes similar to those of their networks. Contagion theories seek the relation between organisational members and their networks. The organisational members' knowledge, attitudes, and behaviour are related to the information, attitudes, and behaviour of others in the network to which they are linked. Factors such as frequency, multiplexity, strength, and asymmetry can shape the extent to which others influence individuals in their networks.

Contagion can be distinguished into contagion by cohesion and contagion by structural equivalence. Contagion by cohesion refers to the influence of those who had direct communication. These individuals' perceptions of self-efficacy of the new technology were significantly influenced by people who had direct communication. Contagion by structural equivalence refers to the influence of those who had similar communication patterns. These individuals' general attitudes and the use of the new technology were more influence by people who shared similar communication patterns.

5.3.5.2 Applications

Contagion theories are used to explain network members' attitudes and behaviours. Networks increase in importance and therefore the influence of the relation between members and networks can be explained by these theories. Applications are very broad, since organisations, government and certain interest groups all depend on networks.

5.3.6 Classical Rhetoric Theory

The classical rhetoric is a combination of argumentation and persuasion. Rhetoric is a blend of classical systems by among others, three ancient Greek teachers: Plato, Socrates and Aristotle. The ancient Greeks wondered about language, because they noticed that spoken or written text had a certain influence. It rapidly became apparent that the primary political skill of the age was the ability to speak effectively for one's interests. This demanded participation and demanded that citisens speak. Therefore decisions were made through deliberation and voting—both speech acts.

5.3.6.1 Core Assumptions

Rhetoric can be defined as (i) to perceive how language is at work orally and in writing, and (ii) to become proficient in applying the resources of language in their own speaking and writing. In a way every utterance of a human is rhetoric, because all human utterances are speech—acts meant to persuade.

Discerning how language is working in others' or one's own writing and speaking, one must (artificially) divide form and content, what is being said and how this is said, because rhetoric examines so attentively the how of language, the methods and means of communication, it has sometimes been discounted as something only concerned with style or appearances, and not with the quality or content of communication.

Rhetoric has sometimes lived down to its critics, but as set forth from antiquity, rhetoric was a comprehensive art just as much concerned with what one could say as how one might say it. Indeed, a basic premise for rhetoric is the indivisibility of means from meaning; how one says something conveys meaning as much as what one says.

Rhetoric studies the effectiveness of language comprehensively, including its emotional impact, as much as its propositional content.

5.3.6.2 Scope and Application

Rhetorical can be used to persuade people. The Greeks noticed that the politically crucial skill of effective public speaking can be done with (classical) rhetoric.

5.3.7 Cognitive Dissonance Theory

Leon Festinger synthesised a set of studies to distill a theory about communication's social influences. Cognitive dissonance enjoyed great popularity from the late 1950s through the mid-1970s. Theoretical problems and conflicting findings lead to temporary replacement by similar "self" theories in the early 1980s, but cognitive dissonance regained its place as the umbrella theory for selective exposure to communication by the late 1980s.

5.3.7.1 Core Assumptions

Cognitive dissonance is a communication theory adopted from social psychology. The title gives the concept: cognitive is thinking or the mind; and dissonance is inconsistency or conflict. Cognitive dissonance is the psychological conflict from holding two or more incompatible beliefs simultaneously.

Cognitive dissonance is a relatively straightforward social psychology theory that has enjoyed wide acceptance in a variety of disciplines including communication. The theory replaces previous conditioning or reinforcement theories by viewing individuals as more purposeful decision makers; they strive for balance in their beliefs. If presented with decisions or information that create dissonance, they use dissonance-reduction strategies tot regain equilibrium, especially if the dissonance affects their self-esteem. The theory suggests that

i) dissonance is psychologically uncomfortable enough to motivate people to achieve consonance, and

ii) in a state of dissonance, people will avoid information and situations that might increase the dissonance.

How dissonance arises is easy to imagine: It may be unavoidable in an information rich-society. How people deal with it is more difficult.

5.3.7.2 Applications

Dissonance theory applies to all situations involving attitude formation and change. This theory is able to manipulate people into certain behaviour, by doing so these people will alter their attitudes themselves. It is especially relevant to decisionmaking and problemsolving.

5.3.8 Elaboration Likelihood Model

Petty and Cacioppo discovered, in contrast to social judgement-involvement theory, that high levels of involvement do not invariably decrease persuasion.

5.3.8.1 Core Assumptions

The ELM is based on the idea that attitudes are important because attitudes guide decisions and other behaviours. While attitudes can result from a number of things, persuasion is a primary source. The model features two routes of persuasive influence: central and peripheral. The ELM accounts for the differences in persuasive impact produced by arguments that contain ample information and cogent reasons as compared to messages that rely on simplistic associations of negative and positive attributes to some object, action or situation. The key variable in this process is involvement, the extent to which an individual is willing and able to 'think' about the position advocated and its supporting materials. When people are motivated and able to think about the content of the message, elaboration is high.

Elaboration involves cognitive processes such as evaluation, recall, critical judgement, and inferential judgment. When elaboration is high, the central persuasive route is likely to occur; conversely, the peripheral route is the likely result of low elaboration. Persuasion may also occur with low elaboration. The receiver is not guided by his or her assessment of the message, as in the case of the central route, but the receiver decides to follow a principle or a decision-rule which is derived from the persuasion situation.

5.3.8.2 Applications

Advertisement-research (printed media, television etc.), psychological research. This theory is promising because it integrates an array of variables into a single explanation of persuasion. It addresses factors that explain why and when messages and self-motivated efforts are more or less likely to lead to attitude formation.

5.3.9 Expectancy Value Model

Expectancy value theory is directly linked to uses and gratifications theory. The theory was founded by Martin Fishbein in the 1970s.

According to expectancy-value theory, behaviour is a function of the expectancies one has and the value of the goal toward which one is working. Such an approach predicts that, when more than one behaviour is possible, the behaviour chosen will be the one with the largest combination of expected success and value.

Expectancy-value theories hold that people are goal-oriented beings. The behaviours they perform in response to their beliefs and values are undertaken to achieve some end. However, although expectancy-value theory can be used to explain central concepts in uses and gratifications research, there are other factors that influence the process. For example the social and psychological origins of needs, which give rise to motives for behaviour, which may be guided by beliefs, values, and social circumstances into seeking various gratifications through media consumption and other non-media behaviours.

Expectancy value theory suggests that people orient themselves to the world according to their expectations (beliefs) and evaluations. Utilising this approach, behaviour, behavioural intentions, or attitudes are seen as a function of:

i) *expectancy (or belief)* – the perceived probability that an object possesses a particular attribute or that a behaviour will have a particular consequence; and

ii) *evaluation* – the degree of affect, positive or negative, toward an attribute or behavioural outcome

5.3.9.1 Applications

Expectancy-value theory has proved useful in the explanation of social behaviours, achievement motivation, and work motivation.

5.3.10 Interpretative and Interaction Theories

The interpretative and interaction approach are a collection of many theories. Communication is seen an exchange of people who act with communication and interpret their real situation and form the situation and the self with interaction. These theories also describe what people do with the media. Communication must be framed in a social and cultural context.

5.3.10.1 Core Assumptions

Paul Watzlawick's Interactional View deals with interpersonal communication. His theory has five axioms that explain his view.

Axiom 1: *One cannot not communicate*: This axiom basically says that even if you are not actually talking, or perhaps not doing anything, you are still communicating. Non-verbals are a huge part of communication. Even if you are attempting to avoid speaking, you are still expressing non-verbals. Examples could be facial expressions, the way you are sitting, or your silence in general.

Axiom 2: *Human beings communicate both digitally and analogically:* Analogical communication "represents things by likeness". Non-verbal communication, for example, is classified as anological by Watzlawick. Digital communication "refers to things by name". Language is considered to be digital.

Axiom 3: *Communication = content + relationship:* Content is "what" is actually said, while relationship is "how" it is said. A few quick examples can make distinction between content and relationship more clear. If content is what is said, then relationship is how it is said. If content is computer data, then relationship is computer programme. The content and relationship make up a communication sequence.

Axiom 4: *The nature of the relationship depends on how both parties punctuate the communication sequence*: This axiom describes how each person perceives, or punctuates, a communication sequence. An example can help to clarify. Let's say that you have a conversation with a roommate. The conversation makes you upset, but you do not tell him or her your feelings. The next time that you see your roommate, you are cold to him or her. Your roommate then realises that you are upset about something. You have punctuated your feelings during the original conversation. However, your roommate thinks that you have recently become upset.

Axiom 5: *All communication is either symmetrical or complementary*: According to Watzlawick, symmetrical communication is "communication based on equal power." Complementary communication is "based on differences in power". A healthy relationship will have both types of power. Too much of one type of power can lead to possible conflicts.

The interactional view holds that there is no way to label a relationship on the basis of a single verbal statement. Interaction requires a sequence of two messages—a statement form one person, and a response from the other.

5.3.11 Language Expectancy Theory

Brooks provided a spark to begin developing the Language Expectancy Theory. He had expectations about what a source might or might not say in persuasive messages. Burgoon, Jones and Stewart added the impact of linguistic strategies. They claimed that strategic linguistic choices can be significant predictors of persuasive success. In 1995 Burgoon provided a detailed version of the formulation of the Language Expectancy Theory.

5.3.11.1 Core Assumptions

Language Expectancy Theory is a formalised model about message strategies and attitude and behaviour change. Message strategies include verbal aggressions like fear appeal, explicit opinions and language intensity which are more combat. Language Expectancy Theory assumes that language is a rule-governed system and people develop expectations concerning the language or message strategies employed by others in persuasive attempts. Expectations are a function of cultural and sociological norms and preferences arising from cultural values and societal standards or ideals for competent communication.

Language Expectancy Theory assumes that changes in the direction desired by an actor occur when positive violations of expectancies occur. Positive violations occur :

i) when the enacted behaviour is better or more preferred than that which was expected in the situation. Change occurs because enacted behaviour is outside the bandwidth in a positive direction, and such behaviour prompts attitude or behavioural change. Positive violations occur.

ii) when negatively evaluated sources conform more closely than expected to cultural values or situational norms. This can result in overly positive evaluation of the source and change promoted by the actor. Negative violations, resulting from language choices that lie outside socially acceptable behaviour in a negative direction, produce no attitude or behaviour change in receivers.

5.3.11.2 Applications

The Language Expectancy Theory explains the effect of the use of different linguistic variations on people who use persuasive messages. It is used as a theoretical framework to explain the effects of several source, message and receiver variables on message persuasiveness. Persuasive messages are used often, with this theory the impact can be described of using different intensities in language.

5.3.12 Network Theory and Analysis

The idea of social networks and the notions of sociometry and sociograms appeared over 50 years ago. Barnes is credited with coining the notion of social networks, an outflow of his study of a Norwegian island parish in the early 1950s.

5.3.12.1 Core Assumptions

Network analysis (social network theory) is the study of how the social structure of relationships around a person, group, or organisation affects beliefs or behaviours. Causal pressures are inherent in social structure. Network analysis is a set of methods for detecting and measuring the magnitude of the pressures. The axiom of every network approach is that reality should be primarily conceived and investigated from the view of the properties of relations between and within units instead of the properties of these units themselves. It is a relational approach. In social and communication science these units are social units: individuals, groups/ organisations and societies.

Rogers characterises a communication network as consisting of "interconnected individuals who are linked by patterned communication flows." A communication network analysis studies "the interpersonal linkages created by the shearing of information in the interpersonal communication structure," that is, the network.

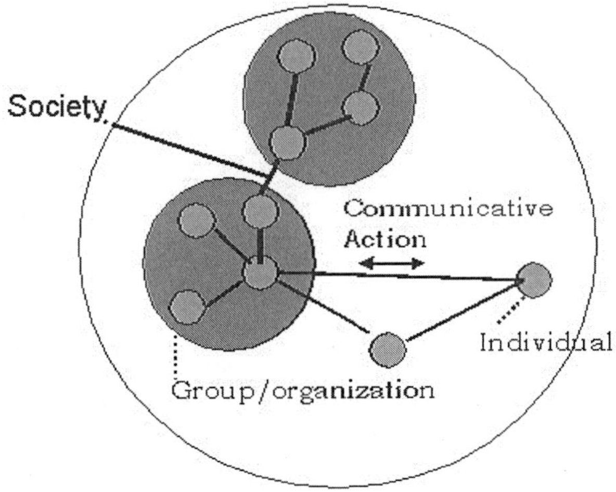

Figure 5.1. Conceptual Model of a Network Society

In general, network analysis focuses on the relationships between people, instead of on characteristics of people. These relationships may comprise the feelings people have for each other, the exchange of information, or more tangible exchanges such as goods and money. By mapping these relationships, network analysis helps to uncover the emergent and informal communication patterns present in an organisation, which may then be compared to the formal communication structures. These emergent patterns can be used to explain several organisational phenomena. For instance, the place employees have in the communication network (as described by their relationships), influences their exposure to and control over information.

Since the patterns of relationships bring employees into contact with the attitudes and behaviours of other organisational members, these relationships may also help to explain why employees develop certain attitudes toward organisational events or job-related matters. Recently there is a growing interest into why communication networks emerge and the effects of communication networks. Also, there is a substantial amount of literature available on how networkdata gathered within organisations, can be analysed.

5.3.12.2 Methods

Network analysis techniques focus on the communication structure of an organisation, which can be operationalised into various aspects. Structural features that can be distinguished and analysed through the use of network analysis techniques are for example the (formal and informal) communication patterns in an organisation or the identification of groups within an organisation (cliques or functional groups). Also communication-related roles of employees can be determined (e.g., stars, gatekeepers, and isolates). Special attention may be given to specific aspects of communication patterns: communication channels and media used by employees, the relationship between information types and the resulting communication networks, and the amount and possibilities of bottom-up communication. Additional characteristics that could, in principle, be investigated using network analysis techniques are the communication load as perceived by employees, the communication styles used, and the effectiveness of the information flows.

5.3.12.3 Applications

Thinking in terms of networks and the method of network analysis have gained ground in many disciplines, including social psychology, anthropology, political science, and mathematics, as well as communications. Network analysis generates information about the following types of network roles: the membership role, the liaison role, the star role, the isolate role, the boundary-spanning role, the bridge role, and the non-participant role. Network analysis is done in organisations, society, groups, etc. The network model encourages communication planners and researchers to use new cause/effect variables in their analysis. For example, properties of the very communication network, such as connectedness, integration, diversity, and openness.

5.3.13 Sense-making

Since sense-making has been under development since 1972, it cannot be explained in a few sentences. It is important to know that the project has been based on three central assumptions regarding communication practice:

i) That it is possible to design and implement communication systems and practices that are responsive to human needs;

ii) That it is possible for humans to enlarge their communication repertoires to pursue this vision;

iii) That achieving these outcomes requires the development of communication-based methodological approaches.

5.3.13.1 Core Assumptions

Sensemaking is an approach to thinking about and implementing communication research and practice and the design of communication-based systems and activities. It consists of a set of philosophical assumptions, substantive propositions, methodological framings and methods.

According to Weick, sense-making consists of the follwoing aspects:

i) *Grounded in identity construction*: A sense-maker is needed otherwise there won't be any sense-making, sense is in the eye of the beholder. The sense-maker is singular and no individual ever acts like a single sense-maker, each individual has a lot of identities.

ii) *Retrospective:* After a certain time the process is reflected. This is always done afterwards. This aspect, looking afterwards at a process, will depend on the success of the process.

3) Furthermore, retrospection makes the past clearer than the present or future; it cannot make the past transparent.

4) *Enactive and sensible environments*. In organisational life people often produce part of the environment they face. Action is crucial for sense-making; we cannot command and the environment will obey. Moreover, we can't predict something that will happen exact, because everything is part of a larger truth. Entity and environment are factors which influence each other. You are neither a plaything in the environment or independent. Somewhere between is the meaning.

5) *Social*: Sense-making is a social process; human thinking and social functioning are essential aspects of another. What a person does depends on others, so the direct influence is not clear. To understand sense-making is to pay more intention to sufficient cues for coordination such as generalised other, prototypes, stereotypes, and roles.

6) *Ongoing:* Sense-making never starts or stops, it is an ongoing process.

7) *Focused on and by extracted cues*: In life people are confronted with a lot of cues, too much too notice anyway. A person will only notice a few cues, because of his own filter. Your own interest and your unconsciousness depend what cues you focus on.

8) *Driven by plausibility rather than accuracy:* People are cognitively lazy, when they found an answer to the question, people stop searching. No alternatives are evaluated, while people might not even know the half of it.

In dealing with organisational issues, sense-making requires us to look for explanations and answers in terms of how people see things rather than rather than structures or systems. Sense-making suggests that organisational issues — 'strategies', 'breakdowns', 'change', 'goals', 'plans', 'tasks', 'teams', and so on are not things that one can find out in the world or that exist in the organisation. Rather, their source is people's way of thinking.

5.3.13.2 Applications

Sense-making can be used to study information seeking and use in the workplace. It can also be used for understanding deaf culture or to explore reflective thinking in nursing practice.

5.3.14 Social Identity Theory

Social Identity Theory was developed by Tajfel and Turner in 1979. The theory was originally developed to understand the psychological basis of intergroup discrimination. Tajfel et al attempted to identify the minimal conditions that would lead members of one group to discriminate in favour of the ingroup to which they belonged and against another outgroup.

5.3.14.1 Core Assumptions

In the social identity theory, a person has not one, "personal self", but rather several selves that correspond to widening circles of group membership. Different social contexts may trigger an individual to think, feel and act on basis of his personal, family or national "level of self".

Apart from the "level of self", an individual has multiple "social identities". Social identity is the individual's self-concept derived from perceived membership of social groups. In other words, it is an individual-based perception of what defines the "us" associated with any internalised group membership. This can be distinguished from the notion of personal identity which refers to self-knowledge that derives from the individual's unique attributes.

Social identity theory asserts that group membership creates ingroup/ self-categorisation and enhancement in ways that favour the in-group at the expense of the out-group. The examples (minimal group studies) of Turner and Tajfel showed that the mere act of individuals categorising themselves as group members was sufficient to lead them to display ingroup favoritism. After being categorised of a group membership, individuals seek to achieve positive self-esteem by positively differentiating their ingroup from a comparison outgroup on some valued dimension. This quest for positive distinctiveness means that people's sense of who they are is defined in terms of 'we' rather than 'I'.

Tajfel and Turner identify three variables whose contribution to the emergence of ingroup favouritism is particularly important.

i) the extent to which individuals identify with an ingroup to internalise that group membership as an aspect of their self-concept.
ii) the extent to which the prevailing context provides ground for comparison between groups.
iii) the perceived relevance of the comparison group, which itself will be shaped by the relative and absolute status of the ingroup.

Individuals are likely to display favouritism when an ingroup is central to their self-definition and a given comparison is meaningful or the outcome is contestable.

5.3.14.2 Applications

Social Identity Theory has a considerable impact on social psychology. It is tested in a wide range of fields and settings and includes prejudice, stereotyping, negotiation and language use. The theory has also implications on the way people deal with social and organisational change.

5.3.15 Symbolic Interactionism

Symbolic interactionism, formulated by Blumer is the process of interaction in the formation of meanings for individuals. The inspiration for this theory came from Dewey, which believed that human beings are best understood in a practical, interactive relation to their environment.

5.3.15.1 Core Assumptions

The theory consists of three core principles: meaning, language and thought. These core principles lead to conclusions about the creation of a person's self and socialisation into a larger community.

Meaning states that humans act toward people and things according to the meanings that give to those people or things. Symbolic Interactionism holds the principal of meaning to be the central aspect of human behaviour.

Language gives humans a means by which to negotiate meaning through symbols. Humans identify meaning in speech acts with others.

Thought modifies each individual's interpretation of symbols. Thought is a mental conversation that requires different points of view.

With these three elements the concept of the self can be framed. People use 'the looking-glass self': they take the role of the other, imagining how we look to another person. The self is a function of language, without talk there would be no self concept. People are part of a community, where our generalised other is the sum total of responses and expectations that we pick up from the people around us. We naturally give more weight to the views of significant others.

5.3.15.2 Applications

The theory is used in effective evaluating of human interaction. Different meanings can easily lead to communication problems. Problems can arise if the lines of communication are not open and assumptions are made.

5.3.16 Social Cognitive Theory

In 1941 Miller and Dollard proposed the theory of social learning. In 1963 Bandura and Walters broadened the social learning theory with the principles of observational learning and vicarious reinforcement. Bandura provided his concept of self-efficacy in 1977, while he refuted the traditional learning theory for understanding learning. The social cognitive theory is relevant to health communication. First, the theory deals with cognitive, emotional aspects and aspects of behaviour for understanding behavioural change. Second, the concepts of the SCT provide ways for new behavioural research in health education. Finally, ideas for other theoretical areas such as psychology are welcome to provide new insights and understanding.

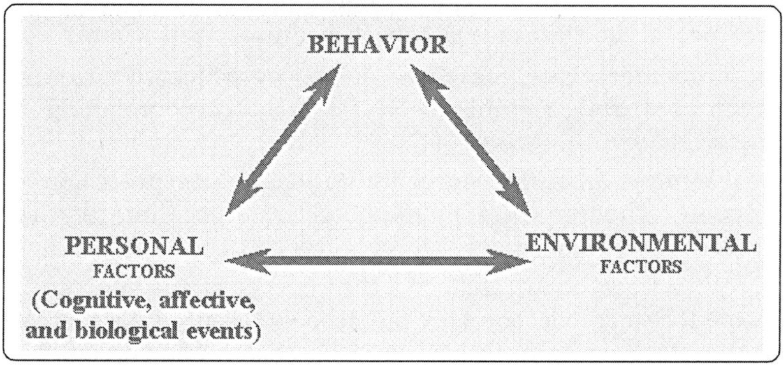

Figure 5.2. Conceptual Model of Social Cognitive Theory

5.3.16.1 Core Assumptions

The social cognitive theory explains how people acquire and maintain certain behavioural patterns, while also providing the basis for intervention strategies. Evaluating behavioural change depends on the factors environment, people and behaviour. SCT provides a framework for designing, implementing and evaluating programmes.

Environment refers to the factors that can affect a person's behaviour. There are social and physical environments. Social environment include family members, friends and colleagues. Physical environment is the size of a room, the ambient temperature or the availability of certain foods. Environment and situation provide the framework for understanding behaviour. The situation refers to the cognitive or mental representations of the environment that may affect a person's behaviour.

The three factors—environment, people and behaviour — are constantly influencing each other. Behaviour is not simply the result of the environment and the person, just as the environment is not simply the result of the person and behaviour. The environment provides models for behaviour. Observational learning occurs when a person watches the actions of another person and the reinforcements that the person receives. The concept of behaviour can be viewed in many ways. Behavioural capability means that if a person is to perform a behaviour he must know what the behaviour is and have the skills to perform it.

5.3.16.2 Concepts of the Social Cognitive Theory

— *Environment*: Factors physically external to the person; provides opportunities and social support.

— *Situation*: Perception of the environment; correct misperceptions and promote healthful forms.

— *Behavioural capability*: Knowledge and skill to perform a given behaviour; promote mastery learning through skills training.

— *Expectations*: Anticipatory outcomes of a behaviour; Model positive outcomes of healthful behaviour.

— *Expectancies*: The values that the person places on a given outcome, incentives; present outcomes of change that have functional meaning.

— *Self-control*: Personal regulation of goal-directed behaviour or performance; Provide opportunities for self-monitoring, goal setting, problem solving, and self-reward.

— *Observational learning*: Behavioural acquisition that occurs by watching the actions and outcomes of others' behaviour; include credible role models of the targeted behaviour

— *Reinforcements*: Responses to a person's behaviour that increase or decrease the likelihood of reoccurrence; promote self-initiated rewards and incentives.

- *Self-efficacy*: The person's confidence in performing a particular behaviour; approach behavioural change in small steps to ensure success
- *Emotional coping responses*: Strategies or tactics that are used by a person to deal with emotional stimuli; provide training in problem solving and stress management.
- *Reciprocal determinism*: The dynamic interaction of the person, the behaviour, and the environment in which the behaviour is performed; consider multiple avenues to behavioural change, including environmental, skill, and personal change.

5.3.16.3 Applications

The social cognitive theory is relevant for designing health education and health behaviour programmes. This theory explains how people acquire and maintain certain behavioural patterns. The theory can also be used for providing the basis for intervention strategies

5.3.17 Speech Act Theory

Speech act theory is built on the foundation laid by Wittgenstein and Austin. John Searle is most often associated with the theory. Ludwig Wittgenstein began a line of thought called 'ordinary language philosophy'. He taught that the meaning of language depends on its actual use. Language, as used in ordinary life, is a language game because it consists of rules.

5.3.17.1 Core Assumptions

According to Searle, to understand language one must understand the speaker's intention. Since language is intentional behaviour, it should be treated like a form of action. Thus Searle refers to statements as speech acts. The speech act is the basic unit of language used to express meaning, an utterance that expresses an intention. Normally, the speech act is a sentence, but it can be a word or phrase as long as it follows the rules necessary to accomplish the intention. When one speaks, one performs an act. Speech is not just used to designate something, it actually does something. Speech act stresses the intent of the act as a whole. According to Searle, understanding the speaker's intention is essential to capture the meaning. Without the speaker's intention, it is impossible to understand the words as a speech act. There are four types of speech act: utterance acts, propositional acts (referring is a type of propositional act), illocutionary acts (promises, questions and commands) and perlocutionary acts. A perlocutionary act can be used to elicit some behavioural response from the listener. Searle believes that speakers perform acts by observing two types of rules: constitutive rules or definition rules (create or define new forms of behaviour) and regulative or behaviour rules.

5.3.17.2 Applications

Speech act theory has contributed to the rules perspective in communication because it provides a basis for examining what happens when speakers use different definition and behaviour rules. By analysing the rules used by each speaker, researchers can better understand why conversational misunderstandings have occurred.

5.3.18 Theory of Planned Behaviour/ Reasoned Action

Ajzen and Fishbein formulated in 1980 the theory of reasoned action (TRA). This resulted from attitude research from the Expectancy Value Models. Ajzen and Fishbein formulated the TRA after trying to estimate the discrepancy between attitude and behaviour. This TRA was related to voluntary behaviour. Later on behaviour appeared not to be 100% voluntary and under control, this resulted in the addition of perceived behavioural control. With this addition the theory was called the theory of planned behaviour (TpB). The theory of planned behaviour is a theory which predicts deliberate behaviour, because behaviour can be deliberative and planned.

5.3.18.1 Core Assumptions

Theory of Reasoned Action suggests that a person's behaviour is determined by his/her intention to perform the behaviour and that this intention is, in turn, a function of his/her attitude toward the behaviour and his/her subjective norm. The best predictor of behaviour is intention. Intention is the cognitive representation of a person's readiness to perform a given behaviour, and it is considered to be the immediate antecedent of behaviour. This intention is determined by three things: their attitude toward the specific behaviour, their subjective norms and their perceived behavioural control.

The theory of planned behaviour holds that only specific attitudes toward the behaviour in question can be expected to predict that behaviour. In addition to measuring attitudes toward the behaviour, we also need to measure people's subjective norms – their beliefs about how people they care about will view the behaviour in question. To predict someone's intentions, knowing these beliefs can be as important as knowing the person's attitudes. Finally, perceived behavioural control influences intentions. Perceived behavioural control refers to people's perceptions of their ability to perform a given behaviour. These predictors lead to intention. A general rule, the more favorable the attitude and the subjective norm, and the greater the perceived control the stronger should the person's intention to perform the behaviour in question.

5.3.18.2 Applications

Provide useful information for the development of communication strategies. This theory is also used in evaluation studies. Other usages of the model include: voting behaviour, disease prevention behaviour, birth control behaviour, consumption prediction.

5.3.19 Uncertainty Reduction Theory

Uncertainty reduction theory (URT) was initially presented as a series of axioms (universal truths which do not require proof and theorems (propositions assumed to be true) which describe the relationships between uncertainty and several communication factors. URT was developed to describe the interrelationships between seven important factors in any dyadic exchange:

i) verbal communication,
ii) non-verbal expressiveness,
iii) information-seeking behaviour,
iv) intimacy,
v) reciprocity,
vi) similarity, and
vii) liking.

This theoretical perspective was originated by C.R. Berger and Calabrese in 1975; they drew on the work of Heider.

5.3.19.1 Core Assumptions

Uncertainty is unpleasant and therefore motivational; people communicate to reduce it. Uncertainty reduction follows a pattern of developmental stages. During the entry stage information about another's sex, age, economic or social status, and other demographic information is obtained. Much of the interaction in this entry phase is controlled by communication rules and norms. When communicators begin to share attitudes, beliefs, values, and more personal data, the personal stage begins. During this phase, the communicators feel less constrained by rules and norms and tend to communicate more freely with each other. The third stage is the exit phase. During this phase, the communicators decide on future interaction plans. They may discuss or negotiate ways to allow the relationship to grow and continue. However, any particular conversation may be terminated and the end of the entry phase. This pattern is especially likely to occur during initial interaction, when people first meet or when new topics are introduced later in a relationship.

Besides the stages in uncertainty reduction patterns makes Berger a distinction between three basic ways people seek information about another person:

i) *Passive strategies:* A person is being observed, either in situations where the other person is likely to be self-monitoring as in a classroom, or where the other person is likely to act more naturally as in the stands at a football game.

ii) *Active strategies:* We ask others about the person we're interested in or try to set up a situation where we can observe that person. Once the situation is set up we sometime observe (a passive strategy) or talk with the person (an interactive strategy).

iii) *Interactive strategies:* We communicate directly with the person. People seek to increase their ability to predict their partner's and their own behaviour in situations. One other factor which reduces uncertainty between communicators is the degree of similarity individuals perceive in each other.

5.3.19.2 Applications

Organisational communication, society. Uncertainty reduction theory also applies at the organisational and societal levels (risk society).

5.4 Theories of Mass Communication

5.4.1 Agenda Setting Theory

Agenda setting describes a very powerful influence of the media – the ability to tell us what issues are important. As far back as 1922, the newspaper columnist Walter Lippman was concerned that the media had the power to present images to the public. McCombs and Shaw investigated presidential campaigns in 1968, 1972 and 1976. In the research done in 1968 they focused on two elements: awareness and information.

Investigating the agenda-setting function of the mass media, they attempted to assess the relationship between what voters in one community said were important issues and the actual content of the media messages used during the campaign. McCombs and Shaw concluded that the mass media exerted a significant influence on what voters considered to be the major issues of the campaign.

5.4.1.1 Core Assumptions

Agenda-setting is the creation of public awareness and concern of salient issues by the news media. Two basis assumptions underlie most research on agenda-setting:

i) the press and the media do not reflect reality; they filter and shape it;

ii) media concentration on a few issues and subjects leads the public to perceive those issues as more important than other issues.

One of the most critical aspects in the concept of an agenda-setting role of mass communication is the time frame for this phenomenon. In addition, different media have different agenda-setting potential. Agenda-setting theory seems quite appropriate to help us understand the pervasive role of the media.

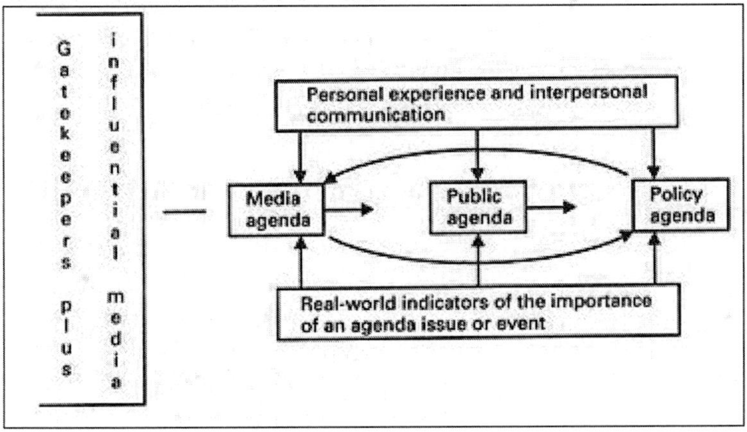

Figure 5.3. Conceptual Model of Agenda-setting Theory

5.4.1.2 Applications

Just as McCombs and Shaw expanded their focus, other researchers have extended investigations of agenda setting to issues including history, advertising, foreign, and medical news. McCombs and Shaw focused on the two elements: awareness and information. Investigating the agenda-setting function of the mass media in the 1968 presidential campaign, they attempted to assess the relationship between what voters in one community said were important issues and the actual content of media messages used during the campaign. McCombs and Shaw concluded that the mass media exerted a significant influence on what voters considered to be the major issues of the campaign.

5.4.2 Concept of Priming

Much attention in agenda-setting research, in the 80's, was focused on the concept of priming. This concept was derived from the cognitive psychological concept of priming.

Priming refers to enhancing the effects of the media by offering the audience a prior context – a context that will be used to interpret subsequent communication. The media serve to provide the audience with standards and frames of reference. Agenda-setting refers mainly to the importance of an issue; priming tells us whether something is good or bad, whether it is communicated effectively, etc. The media have primed the audience about what a news programme looks like, what a credible person looks like, etc.

5.4.3 Concept of Framing

The concept of framing is related to the agenda-setting tradition but expands the research by focusing on the essence of the issues at hand rather than on a particular topic. The basis of framing theory is that the media focuses attention on certain events and then places them within a field of meaning. Framing is an important topic since it can have a big influence and therefore the concept of framing expanded to organisations as well.

The media draws the public attention to certain topics, it decides where people think about, the journalists select the topics. This is the original agenda setting 'thought'. In news items occurs more than only bringing up certain topics. The way in which the news is brought, the frame in which the news is presented, is also a choice made by journalists. Thus, a frame refers to the way media and media gatekeepers organise and present the events and issues they cover, and the way audiences interpret what they are provided. Frames are abstract notions that serve to organise or structure social meanings. Frames influence the perception of the news of the audience, this form of agenda-setting not only tells what to think about, but also how to think about it.

Framing is a quality of communication that leads others to accept one meaning over another. It is a skill with profound effects on how organisational members understand and respond to the world in which they live. It is a skill that most successful leaders possess, yet one that is not often taught. According to Fairhurst & Sarr framing consists of three elements: language, thought and forethought. Language helps us to remember information and acts to transform the way in which we view situations. To use language, people must have thought and reflected on their own interpretive frameworks and those of others. Leaders must learn to frame spontaneously in certain circumstances. Being able to do so had to do with having the forethought to predict framing opportunities. In other words, one must plan in order to be spontaneous.

5.4.4 Cultivation Theory

Black et. al. used the metaphor of stalagmite theories to suggest that media effects occur analogously to the slow buildup of formations on cave floors, which take their interesting forms after eons of the steady dripping of limewater from the cave ceilings above. One of the most popular theories that fits this perspective is cultivation theory.

Cultivation theory (sometimes referred to as the cultivation hypothesis or cultivation analysis) was an approach developed by Professor George Gerbner, dean of the Annenberg School of Communications at the University of Pennsylvania. He began the 'Cultural Indicators' research project in the mid-1960s, to study whether and how watching television may influence viewers' ideas of what the everyday world is like. Cultivation research is in the 'effects' tradition. Cultivation theorists argue that television has long-term effects which are small, gradual, indirect but cumulative and significant.

5.4.4.1 Core Assumptions

Cultivation theory in its most basic form, suggests that television is responsible for shaping, or 'cultivating' viewers' conceptions of social reality. The combined effect of massive television exposure by viewers over time subtly shapes the perception of social reality for individuals and, ultimately, for our culture as a whole. Gerbner argues that the mass media cultivate attitudes and values which are already present in a culture: the media maintain and propagate these values amongst members of a culture, thus binding it together. He has argued that television tends to cultivate middle-of-the-road political perspectives. Gerbner called this effect 'mainstreaming'.

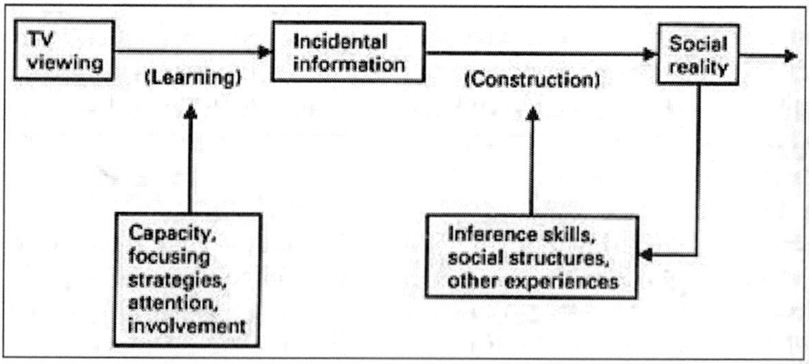

Figure 5.4. Conceptual Model of Cultivation Theory

Cultivation theorists distinguish between 'first order' effects (general beliefs about the everyday world, such as about the prevalence of violence) and 'second order' effects (specific attitudes, such as to law and order or to personal safety). There is also a distinction between two groups of television viewers: the heavy viewers and the light viewers. The focus is on 'heavy viewers'. People who watch a lot of television are likely to be more influenced by the ways in which the world is framed by television programmes than are individuals who watch less, especially regarding topics of which the viewer has little first-hand experience. Light viewers may have more sources of information than heavy viewers. 'Resonance' describes the intensified effect on the audience when what people see on television is what they have experienced in life. This double dose of the televised message tends to amplify the cultivation effect.

5.4.4.2 Methods

Cultivation analysis usually involves the correlation of data from content analysis (identifying prevailing images on television) with survey data from audience research (to assess any influence of such images on the attitudes of viewers). Audience research by cultivation theorists involves asking large-scale public opinion poll organisations to include in their national surveys questions regarding such issues as the amount of violence in everyday life. Answers are interpreted as reflecting either the world of television or that of everyday life. The answers are then related to the amount of television watched, other media habits and demographic data such as sex, age, income and education.

5.4.4.3 Applications

Cultivation research looks at the mass media as a socialising agent and investigates whether television viewers come to believe the television version of reality the more they watch it.

5.4.5 Dependency Theory

Dependency theory was originally proposed by Sandra Ball-Rokeach and Melvin DeFleur. This theory merged out of the communication discipline. Dependency theory integrates several perspectives: first, it combines perspectives from psychology with ingredients from social categories theory. Second, it integrates systems perspectives with elements from more causal approaches.

Third, it combines elements of uses and gratifications research with those of media effects traditions, although its primary focus is less on effects per se than on rationales for why media effects typically are limited. Finally, a contextualist philosophy is incorporated into the theory, which also features traditional concerns with the content of media messages and their effects on audiences. Research generated by this model had tends to be more descriptive than explanatory or predictive.

5.4.5.1 Core Assumptions

Dependency theory proposes an integral relationship among audiences, media and the larger social system. This theory predicts that you depend on media information to meet certain needs and achieve certain goals, like uses-and-gratifications theory. But you do not depend on all media equally. Two factors influence the degree of media dependence.

First, you will become more dependent on media that meet a number of your needs than on media that provide just a few. The second source of dependency is social stability. When social change and conflict are high, established institutions, beliefs, and practices are challenged, forcing you to reevaluate and make new choices. At such times your reliance on the media for information will increase. At other, more stable times your dependency on media may go way down.

One's needs are not always strictly personal but may be shaped by the culture or by various social conditions. In other words, individuals' needs, motives, and uses of media are contingent on outside factors that may not be in the individuals' control. These outside factors act as constraints on what and how media can be used and on the availability of other non-media alternatives.

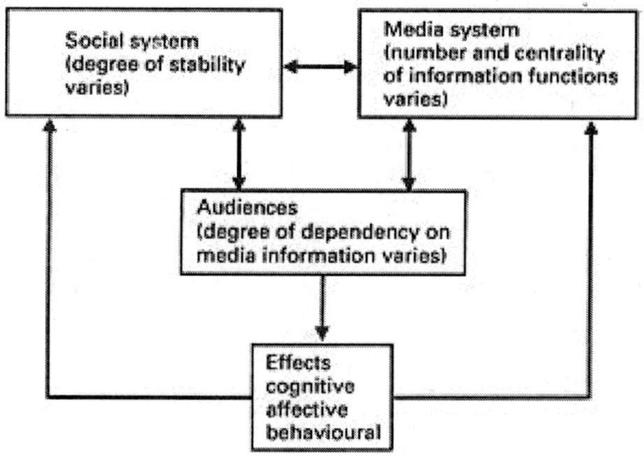

Figure 5.5. Conceptual Model of Dependency Theory

Furthermore, the more alternatives and individual had for gratifying needs, the less dependent he or she will become on any single medium. The number of functional alternatives, however, is not just a matter of individual choice or even of psychological traits but is limited also by factors such as availability of certain media.

5.4.6 Diffusion of Innovations Theory (Multi-step Flow Theory)

The original diffusion research was done as early as 1903 by the French sociologist Gabriel Tarde who plotted the original S-shaped diffusion curve. Tardes' 1903 S-shaped curve is of current importance because "most innovations have an S-shaped rate of adoption".

5.4.6.1 Core Assumptions

Diffusion research centers on the conditions which increase or decrease the likelihood that a new idea, product, or practice will be adopted by members of a given culture. Diffusion of innovation theory predicts that media as well as interpersonal contacts provide information and influence opinion and judgment.

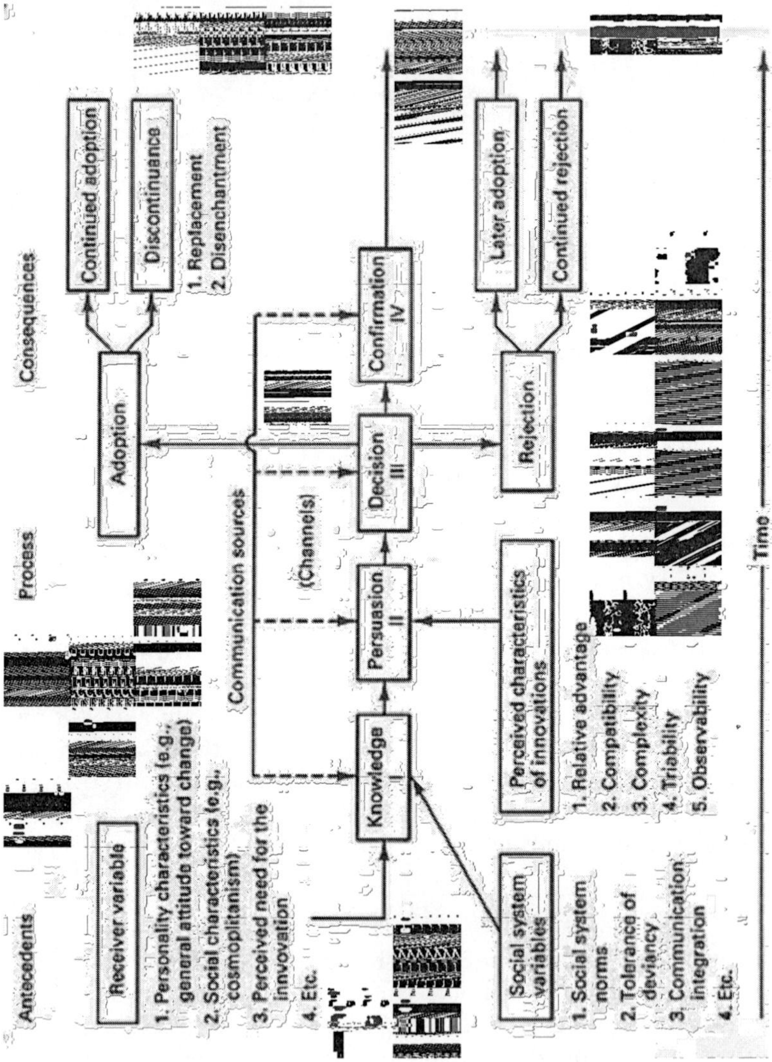

Figure 5.6. Diffusion of innovation model

Studying how innovation occurs, E.M. Rogers argued that it consists of four stages: invention, diffusion (or communication) through the social system, time and consequences. The information flows through networks. The nature of networks and the roles opinion leaders play in them determine the likelihood that the innovation will be adopted. Innovation diffusion research has attempted to explain the variables that influence how and why users adopt a new information medium, such as the Internet.

Opinion leaders exert influence on audience behaviour via their personal contact, but additional intermediaries called change agents and gatekeepers are also included in the process of diffusion. Five adopter categories are:

i) innovators,
ii) early adopters,
iii) early majority,
iv) late majority, and
v) laggards.

These categories follow a standard deviation-curve, very little innovators adopt the innovation in the beginning (2,5%), early adopters making up for 13,5% a short time later, the early majority 34%, the late majority 34% and after some time finally the laggards make up for 16%.

5.4.6.2 Methods

Some of the methods are network analysis, surveys, field experiments and ECCO analysis. ECCO, Episodic Communication Channels in Organisation, analysis is a form of a data collection log-sheet. This method is specially designed to analyse and map communication networks and measure rates of flow, distortion of messages, and redundancy. The ECCO is used to monitor the progress of a specific piece of information through the organisation.

5.4.6.3 Applications

Diffusion research has focused on five elements:

i) the characteristics of an innovation which may influence its adoption;
ii) the decision-making process that occurs when individuals consider adopting a new idea, product or practice;
iii) the characteristics of individuals that make them likely to adopt an innovation;
iv) the consequences for individuals and society of adopting an innovation; and
v) communication channels used in the adoption process.

5.4.7 Hypodermic Needle Theory (Magic Bullet Theory)

The "hypodermic needle theory" implied mass media had a direct, immediate and powerful effect on its audiences. The mass media in the 1940s and 1950s were perceived as a powerful influence on behaviour change. Several factors contributed to this "strong effects" theory of communication, including:

i) the fast rise and popularisation of radio and television
ii) the emergence of the persuasion industries, such as advertising and propaganda
iii) the Payne Fund studies of the 1930s, which focused on the impact of motion pictures on children, and
iv) Hitler's monopolisation of the mass media during WWII to unify the German public behind the Nazi party

5.4.7.1 Core Assumptions

The theory suggests that the mass media could influence a very large group of people directly and uniformly by 'shooting' or 'injecting' them with appropriate messages designed to trigger a desired response. Both images used to express this theory (a bullet and a needle) suggest a powerful and direct flow of information from the sender to the receiver.

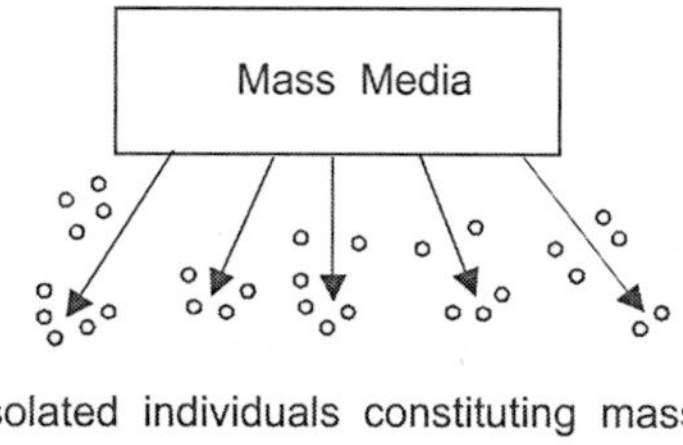

Figure 5.7. Conceptutal Model of Magic Bullet Theory Model

The bullet theory graphically suggests that the message is a bullet, fired from the "media gun" into the viewer's "head". With similarly emotive imagery the hypodermic needle model suggests that media messages are injected straight into a passive audience which is immediately influenced by the message. They express the view that the media is a dangerous means of communicating an idea because the receiver or audience is powerless to resist the impact of the message. There is no escape from the effect of the message in these models. The population is seen as a sitting duck. People are seen as passive and are seen as having a lot media material "shot" at them. People end up thinking what they are told because there is no other source of information.

New assessments that the Magic Bullet Theory was not accurate came out of election studies in "The People's Choice,". The project was conducted during the election of Franklin D. Roosevelt in 1940 to determine voting patterns and the relationship between the media and political behaviour. The majority of people remained untouched by the propaganda; interpersonal outlets brought more influence than the media. The effects of the campaign were not all-powerful to where they persuaded helpless audiences uniformly and directly, which is the very definition of what the magic bullet theory does. As focus group testing, questionnaires, and other methods of marketing effectiveness testing came into widespread use; and as more interactive forms of media (e.g.: internet, radio call-in shows, etc.)

became available, the magic bullet theory was replaced by a variety of other, more instrumental models, like the two step of flow theory and diffusion of innovations theory.

The classic example of the application of the Magic Bullet Theory was illustrated on October 30, 1938 when Orson Welles and the newly formed Mercury Theater group broadcasted their radio edition of H.G. Wells' "War of the Worlds." On the eve of Halloween, radio programming was interrupted with a "news bulletin" for the first time. What the audience heard was that Martians had begun an invasion of Earth in a place called Grover's Mill, New Jersey.

It became known as the "Panic Broadcast" and changed broadcast history, social psychology, civil defense and set a standard for provocative entertainment. Approximately 12 million people in the United States heard the broadcast and about one million of those actually believed that a serious alien invasion was underway. A wave of mass hysteria disrupted households, interrupted religious services, caused traffic jams and clogged communication systems. People fled their city homes to seek shelter in more rural areas, raided grocery stores and began to ration food. The nation was in a state of chaos, and this broadcast was the cause of it.

Media theorists have classified the "War of the Worlds" broadcast as the archetypal example of the Magic Bullet Theory. This is exactly how the theory worked, by injecting the message directly into the "bloodstream" of the public, attempting to create a uniform thinking. The effects of the broadcast suggested that the media could manipulate a passive and gullible public, leading theorists to believe this was one of the primary ways media authors shaped audience perception.

5.4.8 Knowledge Gap Theory

The knowledge gap theory was first proposed by Tichenor, Donohue and Olien at the University of Minnesota in the 70s. They believe that the increase of information in society is not evenly acquired by every member of society: people with higher socioeconomic status tend to have better ability to acquire information. This leads to a division of two groups:

a group of better-educated people who know more about most things, and those with low education who know less. Lower socio-economic status (SES) people, defined partly by educational level, have little or no knowledge about public affairs issues, are disconnected from news events and important new discoveries, and usually aren't concerned about their lack of knowledge.

5.4.8.1 Core Assumptions

The knowledge gap can result in an increased gap between people of lower and higher socioeconomic status. The attempt to improve people's life with information via the mass media might not always work the way this is planned. Mass media might have the effect of increasing the difference gap between members of social classes.

Tichenor, Donohue and Olien present five reasons for justifying the knowledge gap.

i) People of higher socioeconomic status have better communication skills, education, reading, comprehending and remembering information.

ii) People of higher socioeconomic status can store information more easily or remember the topic form background knowledge

iii) People of higher socioeconomic status might have a more relevant social context.

iv) People of higher socioeconomic status are better in selective exposure, acceptance and retention.

v) The nature of the mass media itself is that it is geared toward persons of higher socioeconomic status.

This example shows that education level or socioeconomic status made a difference in knowledge. The question was whether or not respondents felt astronauts would ever reach the moon. Those with high levels of education (based on three levels: grade school, high school and college) were more likely to agree that man would reach the moon than those with lower levels of education both at a certain point in time and over all four intervals. Most important was that the gap between levels widened over time in that the percentage of respondents in the high education level who agreed rose more than 60 percentage points over 16 years while those in the low level of education category rose less than 25 percentage points.

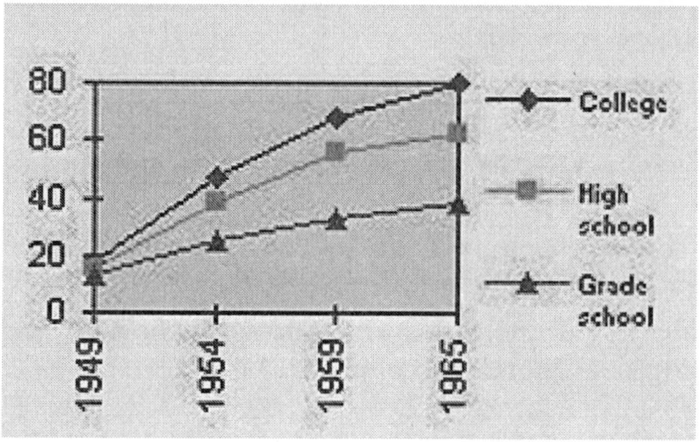

Figure 5.8. Conceptual Model of Knowledge Gap Theory

5.4.8.2 Applications

Media presenting information should realise that people of higher socioeconomic status get their information in a different way than lower educated people. Furthermore, this hypothesis of the knowledge gap might help in understanding the increased gap between people of higher socioeconomic status and people of lower socioeconomic status. It can be used in various circumstances.

5.4.9 Media Richness Theory

Media richness theory is based on contingency theory and information processing theory. First proponents of the theory were made by Daft & Lengel.

5.4.9.1 Core Assumptions

Researchers Daft, Lengel and successors propose that

communication media have varying capacities for resolving ambiguity, negotiating varying interpretations, and facilitating understanding.

Two main assumptions of this theory are: people want to overcome equivocality and uncertainty in organisations and a variety of media commonly used in organisations work better for certain tasks than others. Using four criteria, Daft and Lengel present a media richness hierarchy, arranged from high to low degrees of richness, to illustrate the capacity of media types to process ambiguous communication in organisations. The criteria are:

i) the availability of instant feedback;

ii) the capacity of the medium to transmit multiple cues such as body language, voice tone, and inflection;

iii) the use of natural language; and

iv) the personal focus of the medium.

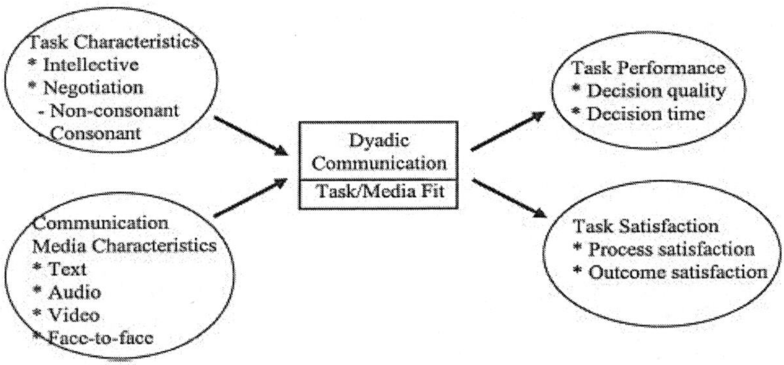

Figure 5.9. Conceptual Model of Media Richness Theory

Face-to-face communication is the richest communication medium in the hierarchy followed by telephone, electronic mail, letter, note, memo, special report, and finally, flier and bulletin. From a strategic management perspective, the media richness theory suggests that effective managers make rational choices matching a particular communication medium to a specific task or objective and to the degree of richness required by that task.

5.4.10 Medium Theory

Marshell McLuhan challenged conventional definitions when he claimed that the medium is the message. With this claim, he stressed how channels differ, not only in terms of their content, but also in regard to how they awaken and alter thoughts and senses. He distinguished media by the cognitive processes each required. McLuhan popularised the idea that channels are a dominant force that must be understood to know how the media influence society and culture.

5.4.10.1 Core Assumptions

Medium theory focuses on the medium characteristics itself (like in media richness theory) rather than on what it conveys or how information is received. In medium theory, a medium is not simply a newspaper, the Internet, a digital camera and so forth. Rather, it is the symbolic environment of any communicative act. Media, apart from whatever content is transmitted, impact individuals and society. McLuhan's thesis is that people adapt to their environment through a certain balance or ratio of the senses, and the primary medium of the age brings out a particular sense ratio, thereby affecting perception.Medium theory is an analytical theory with few empirical model building. Some of the methods used are: analysis of media characteristics and historical analysis of human perception.

Some of the metaphors used by McLuhan are: The medium is the message! The medium is the massage. We live in a mess-age. The content of a new medium is an old medium.

5.4.10.2 Applications

Medium theory examines physical, psychological and social variables as the senses that are required to attend to the medium; whether the communication is bi-directional or unidirectional, how quickly messages can be disseminated, whether learning to encode and decode in the medium is difficult or simple, how many people can attend to the same message at the same moment, and so forth. Medium theorists argue that such variables influence the medium's use and its social, political, and psychological impact.

5.4.11 Play Theory

Introduced in 1967 by William Stephenson, play theory focuses on the media user's relationship with the medium. Stephenson argued that "play" involved the ability to select among a number of products, ideas, issues, and entertainment options from the media. According to Stephenson, media content is used to engage in "convergent selectivity" — making choices about media allows us to express ourselves. Our patterns of choices provides a feeling of individuality that we use to subsequently understand ourselves. This is Stephenson's concept of "communication play," a form of self-expression that takes advantage of the various media to promote a feeling of individuality.

While Stephenson found communication play a uniquely personal experience, Davis and Baran extended the play concept into interaction endeavors. Using Goffman's definitions of play and "keyings," Davis and Baran argued that there are two types of communication play:

i) participatory play and
ii) elite dominated communication play.

Participatory play takes place when communicators are free to alter interaction to achieve their goals. On the other hand, elite dominated communication play is a passive activity. Here play exists only through making choices of what to use from existing media content.

Participatory play provides a center of interest when considering the example of computer-mediated communication. The medium of play becomes the computer-teleconnection, the content of play is determined by the participants. Thus, two types of play choices can take place during computer-mediated communication:

i) the decision to use the telelink context and,
ii) unique features of the link that provide content cues of communication play.

We can see in this perspective that much organisation based, task-centered CMC would be elite-dominated communication play, whereas the populous networks would provide a freer system of expression.

Goffman's explanation of interaction play can provide a helpful means to analyse the content cues of communication play. Goffman believed that "play" was a situation grounded on a transformation of a serious situation. Thus "play" fighting takes place with wooden swords with mimicked moves. The transformation from serious to "play" situation is rule governed and takes place as long as the participants observe the rules. Within the rules of the play situation, cues are provided that establish and maintain the transformation to play. Goffman regarded these cues as "keyings," (similar to the music metaphor) that signaled a special form of interaction based on a serious type. Among the types of behaviour that Goffman considered play are jokes, dramas, sports contests, games, simulations, practices, and role-playing.

5.4.12 Spiral of Silence

Noelle Neumann introduced the "spiral of silence" as an attempt to explain in part how public opinion is formed. She wondered why the Germans supported wrong political positions that led to national defeat, humiliation and ruin in the 1930s-1940s.

5.4.12.1 Core Assumptions

The phrase "spiral of silence" actually refers to how people tend to remain silent when they feel that their views are in the minority. The model is based on three premises:

i) people have a "quasi-statistical organ," a sixth-sense if you will, which allows them to know the prevailing public opinion, even without access to polls,

ii) people have a fear of isolation and know what behaviours will increase their likelihood of being socially isolated, and

iii) people are reticent to express their minority views, primarily out of fear of being isolated.

The closer a person believes the opinion held is similar to the prevailing public opinion, the more they are willing to openly disclose that opinion in public. Then, if public sentiment changes, the person will recognise that the opinion is less in favor and will be less willing to express that opinion publicly. As the perceived distance between public opinion and a person's personal opinion grows, the more unlikely the person is to express their opinion.

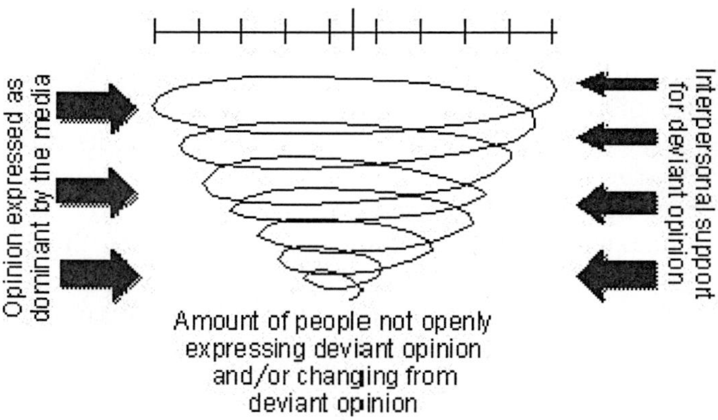

Figure 5.10. Spiral of Silence: Conceptual Model

5.4.12.2 Applications

It is related to the mass media, in such a way that mass media influences public opinion. Shifts in public opinion occur commonly and therefore this theory is used to search an explanation for behaviour (speak up or stay silent). The theory has also been criticised for ambiguity and methodological weakness, but the idea has persisted. Evidence of the spiral effect is usually small but significant.

5.4.13 Two Step Flow Theory

The two-step flow of communication hypothesis was first introduced by Paul Lazarsfeld, Bernard Berelson, and Hazel Gaudet in The People's Choice, a 1944 study focused on the process of decision-making during a Presidential election campaign. These researchers expected to find empirical support for the direct influence of media messages on voting intentions. They were surprised to discover, however, that informal, personal contacts were mentioned far more frequently than exposure to radio or newspaper as sources of influence on voting behaviour. Armed with this data, Katz and Lazarsfeld developed the two-step flow theory of mass communication.

5.4.13.1 Assumptions

This theory asserts that information from the media moves in two distinct stages. First, individuals (opinion leaders) who pay close attention to the mass media and its messages receive the information. Opinion leaders pass on their own interpretations in addition to the actual media content. The term 'personal influence' was coined to refer to the process intervening between the media's direct message and the audience's ultimate reaction to that message. Opinion leaders are quite influential in getting people to change their attitudes and behaviours and are quite similar to those they influence. The two-step flow theory has improved our understanding of how the mass media influence decision making. The theory refined the ability to predict the influence of media messages on audience behaviour, and it helped explain why certain media campaigns may have failed to alter audience attitudes an behaviour. The two-step flow theory gave way to the multi-step flow theory of mass communication or diffusion of innovation theory.

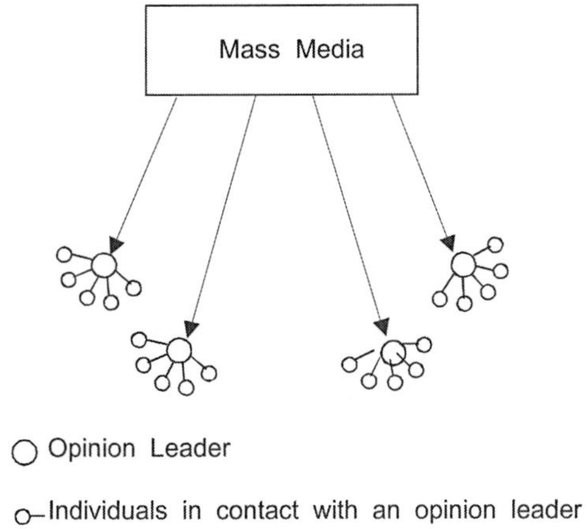

Figure 5.11. Conceptual Model of Two Step Flow Theory

5.4.14 Uses and Gratifications Theory

The uses and gratification theory was tntroduced in 1974 for by Blumler and Katz, as a reaction to traditional mass communication research emphasising the sender and the message. Stressing the active audience and user instead. Psychological orientation taking needs, motives and gratifications of media users as the main point of departure.

5.4.14.1 Core Assumptions

Uses and gratifications theory attempts to explain the uses and functions of the media for individuals, groups, and society in general. There are three objectives in developing uses and gratifications theory:

i) to explain how individuals use mass communication to gratify their needs. "What do people do with the media".

ii) to discover underlying motives for individuals' media use.

iii) to identify the positive and the negative consequences of individual media use.

At the core of uses and gratifications theory lies the assumption that audience members actively seek out the mass media to satisfy individual needs.

Uses and gratification theory suggests that media users play an active role in choosing and using the media. Users take an active part in the communication process and are goal oriented in their media use. The theorist say that a media user seeks out a media source that best fulfills the needs of the user. Uses and gratifications assume that the user has alternate choices to satisfy their need.

Uses and gratifications theory takes a more humanistic approach to looking at media use. Blumler and Katz believe that there is not merely one way that the populace uses media. Instead, they believe there are as many reasons for using the media, as there are media users. According to the theory, media consumers have a free will to decide how they will use the media and how it will effect them. Blumler and Katz values are clearly seen by the fact that they believe that media consumers can choose the influence media has on them as well as the idea that users choose media alternatives merely as a means to and end. Uses and gratification is the optimist's view of the media. The theory takes out the possibility that the media can have an unconscience influence over our lives and how we view the world. The idea that we simply use the media to satisfy a given need does not seem to fully recognise the power of the media in today's society.

Selected References

Ajzen, I., "From Intentions to Actions: A Theory of Planned Behaviour", in J. Kuhl and J. Beckman (eds.), *Action-control: From Cognition to Behaviour* Heidelberg, Springer, 1985, pp. 11-39.

Anderson, J., *The Adaptive Character of Thought*, Hillsdale, NJ: Erlbaum Associates, 1990.

Ball-Rokeach, S.J., and DeFleur, M.L., A Dependency Model or Mass Media Effects, *Communication Research*, 3, 1976, pp.3-21.

Bandura, A., "Social Cognitive Theory: An Agentive perspective. Annual Review of Psychology, 52 , 2001, pp.1-26.

Berger, C.R., and Bradac, J.J., *Language and Social Lnowledge: Uncertainty in Interpersonal Relations*, London: Arnold, 1982.

Bitzer, L.F., "The Rhetorical Situation", in *Rhetoric: Concepts, Definitions, Boundaries*, William A. Covino (ed.), Boston: Allyn and Bacon, 1995.

Blumer, Herbert, *Symbolic Interactionism: Perspective and Method*, Englewood Cliffs, NJ: Prentice-Hall, 1969.

Daft, R.L. and Lengel, R.H., "Information Richness: A New Approach to Managerial Behaviour and Organizational Design, In: Cummings, L.L. and Staw, B.M. (eds.), *Research in Organizational Behaviour* 6, Homewood, IL: JAI Press, 1984, pp.191-233.

Fairhurst, G., Star, R., *The Art of Framing*, San Francisco: Jossey-Bass, 1996.

Festinger, L., *A Theory of Cognitive Dissonance*, Stanford, CA: Stanford University Press, 1957.

Fishbein, M., "Attitude and the Prediction of Behaviour", in: Fishbein, M (ed.), *Readings in Attitude Theory and Measurement*, New York, Wiley, 1967.

Giles H., (eds.), *The New Handbook of Language and Social Psychology,* Sussex, UK, Wiley, 1997, pp. 79-102.

Griffin, E., *A first look at Communication Theory*, New York, The McGraw-Hill Companies, 1997.

Harvey, J.H., Weary, G., *Attribution: Basic Issues and Applications*, Academic Press, San Diego, 1985.

Haslam, Alexander S., *Psychology in Organizations - The Social Identitty Approach*, Sage Publications Ltd, London, 2001.

Lazarsfeld, P.F., Berelson, B., Gaudet, H., *The People's Choice: How the Voter Makes up his Mind in a Presidential Campaign*, New York, Columbia University Press, 1944.

McCombs, M.E., "The Agenda-Setting Approach", in Nimmo, D., Sanders, K. (eds.), *Handbook of Political Communication*, Beverly Hills, CA., Sage, 1982.

______________ , Shaw, D., *The Agenda-Setting Function of Mass Media*, POQ, 36, 1972, pp.176-187.

McLuhan, M., Fiore, Q., *The Medium is the Massage. An Inventory of Effects*, New York, Bantam Books, 1967.

McQuail, D., "With More Handsight: Conceptual Problems and Some Ways Forward for Media Use Research", *Communications*, 26(4), 2001, pp.337-350.

Monge, P.E., Contractor, N.S., *Theories of Communication Networks*, Oxford, University Press, 2003.

Noelle-Neumann, E., *The Spiral of Silence: Public Opinion - Our Social Skin*, Chicago, University of Chicago, 1984.

Petty, R.E., Cacioppo, J.T., *The Elaboration Likelihood Model of Persuasion*, New York, Academic Press, 1986.

Scheufele, D.A., "Agenda-setting, Priming, and Framing Revisited: Another Look at Cognitive Effects of Political Communication", *Communication Abstracts*, 24(1), 2001.

Searle, J.R., *Speech Acts: An Essay in the Philosophy of Language*, Cambridge, University Press, 1969.

Severin, W.J., Tankard, J.W., *Communication Theories: Origins, Methods and Uses in the Mass Media*, Addison Wesley Longman, 2001.

Stephenson, W., *The Play Theory of Mass Communication,* New Brunswick, NJ: Transaction Books, 1988.

Weick, K. E., *Sensemaking in Organizations*, Thousand Oaks, CA, Sage, 1995.

Williams, David Cratis, and Michael David Hazen, (eds.), *Argumentation Theory and the Rhetoric of Assent*, Tuscaloosa, U of Alabama P, 1990.

6

Models of Communication

Communication is a process that serves to connect senders and receivers of messages through space and time. Although human beings tend to be interested primarily in the study of human communication, the process is present in all living things and, it can be argued, in all things. From this we may conclude that communication is a fundamental, universal process. Rather, communication is the process of connecting. It is a collection of renewable actions that work throughout space and over time to form relationships among objects. To communicate effectively, we need to be familiar with the factors involved in the communication process. If we are aware of them, these factors will help us plan, analyse situations, solve problems, and in general do better in our work no matter what our job might be. This leads to a discussion of the communication models.

Formal communication theory (rhetorical theory) goes back 2500 years ago to Classical Greece when Plato, Aristotle, and the Sophists were speech teachers. The Greek tradition was continued and improved upon by the Romans, after which it remained static until the twentieth century. Indeed, Classical Rhetoric was and still is being taught today. However, as a result of the proliferation of mass communications via radio, movies, and television, and of empirical scientific methods, communication theory and models changed in the latter part of the twentieth century.

Several theorists have discussed the communication process in ways that have important implications for those involved in informal education programmes such as extension work. Each of the "models" that we review has a point of vital interest. Communication models come in a variety of forms, ranging from catchy summations to diagrams to mathematical formulas. They offer a convenient way to think about communication, providing a graphical checklist which one can use to create anything from a speech to a major advertising campaign.

6.1 Aristotle's Model

Aristotle, writing 300 years before the birth of Christ, provided an explanation of oral communication that is still worthy of attention. He called the study of communication "rhetoric" and spoke of three elements within the process. He provided us with this insight:

> Rhetoric falls into three divisions, determined by the three classes of listeners to speeches. For of the three elements in speech-making — speaker, subject, and person addressed — it is the last one, the hearer, that determines the speech's end and object.

Here, Aristotle speaks of a communication process composed of a speaker, a message and a listener. He points out that the person at the end of the communication process holds the key to whether or not communication takes place.

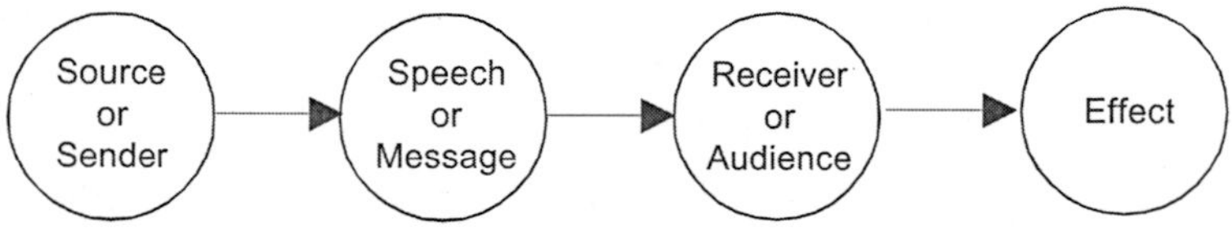

Figure 6.1. Aristotle's model

Our failure to recognise what Aristotle grasped thousands of years ago is a primary cause, if not the primary one, for communication failure. We fail to recognise the importance of the audience at the end of the communication chain.

We tend to be more concerned about ourselves as the communications source, about our message, and even the channel we are going to use. Too often, the listener, viewer, reader fail to get any consideration at all.

Aristotle's words underscore the long interest in communication. They also indicate that man has had a good grasp of what is involved in communication for a long while. So we might even wonder: If we know so much about the communication process, and if we've known it for so long, why do we still have communications problems? It's unlikely we will ever achieve perfect communication. The best we can hope for is to provide improved communication. Hopefully, we will be more aware of the process and work harder to minimise problems with communications.

6.2 Lasswell's Model

Harold Lasswell, a political scientist, developed a much quoted formulation of the main elements of communication: "Who says what in which channel to whom with what effect." This summation of the communications process has been widely quoted since the 1940s.

The point in Lasswell's comment is that there must be an "effect" if communication takes place. If we have communicated, we've "motivated" or produced an effect.

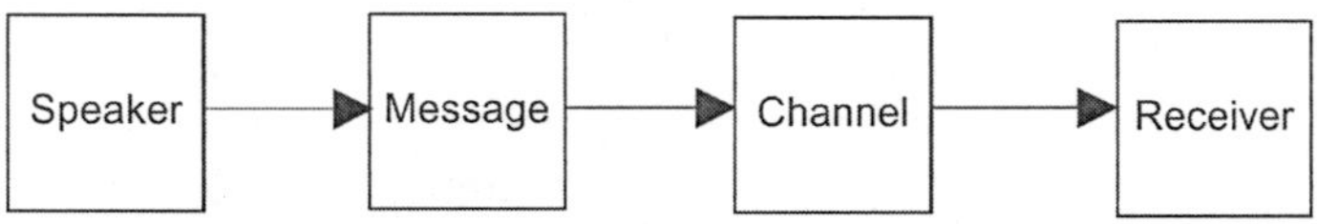

Figure 6.2.Lasswell's model

It is also interesting to note that Lasswell's version of the communication process mentions four parts — who, what, channel, whom. Three of the four parallel parts were mentioned by Aristotle — speaker (who), subject (what), person addressed (whom). Only channel has been added. Most modern-day theorists discuss the four parts of the communication process, but use different terms to designate them.

6.3 Shannon and Weaver Model

Back in 1949 Claude Shannon, an electrical engineer with Bell Telephone, and Warren Weaver, of the Rockefeller Foundation, published their book, *The Mathematical Theory of Communication*.

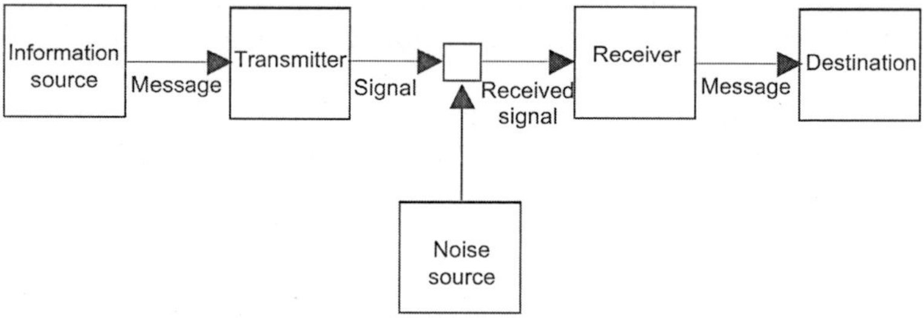

Figure 6.3.Shannon and Weaver model

Shannon and Weaver attempted to do two things:

i) reduce the communication process to a set of mathematical formulas and
ii) discuss problems that could be handled with the model.

Shannon and Weaver were not particularly interested in the sociological or psychological aspects of communication. Instead, they wanted to devise a communications system with as close to 100 per cent efficiency as possible.

The Shannon and Weaver diagram has essentially the same parts as the one formulated by Aristotle. It is true the parts have different names, and one more component — the transmitter — is included. However, this model has an interesting additional element. Shannon and Weaver were concerned with noise in the communications process. Noise, Weaver said, "may be distortions of sound (in telephony, for example) or static (in radio), or distortions in shape or shading of picture (television), or errors in transmission (telegraph or facsimile), etc."

The "noise" concept introduced by Shannon and Weaver can be used to illustrate "semantic noise" that interferes with communication. Semantic noise is the problem connected with differences in meaning that people assign to words, to voice inflections in speech, to gestures and expressions and to other similar "noise" in writing.

Semantic noise is a more serious problem or barrier to developing effective communications than most realise. It is hard to detect that semantic noise has interfered with communication. Too often the person sending a message chooses to use words and phrases that have a certain meaning to him or her. However, they may have an altogether different meaning to individuals receiving the message. In the interest of good communication, we need to work to hold semantic noise to the lowest level possible.

We should be aware that there is a semantic noise in face-to-face verbal communication just as there is static noise, for example, in radio communication.

There are other kinds of noises involved in communication as well. Keep the noise concept in mind.

6.4 Schramm's Model

Wilbur Schramm, a well-known communications theorist, developed a straightforward communications model in his book *The Process and Effects of Mass Communications*.

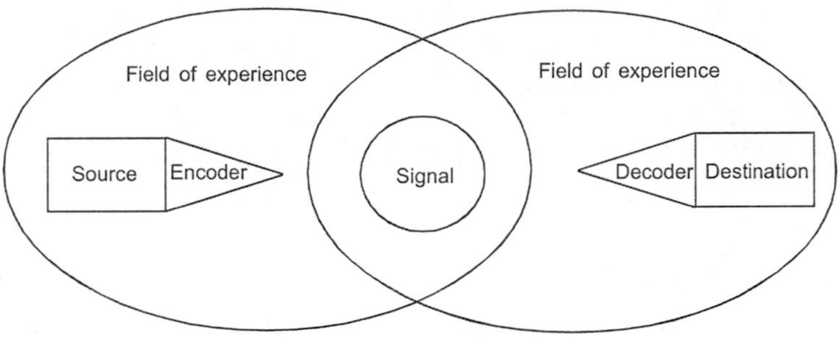

Figure 6.4.Schramm's model

In Schramm's model he notes, as did Aristotle, that communication always requires three elements — the source, the message and the destination. Ideally, the source encodes a message and transmits it to its destination via some channel, where the message is received and decoded. However, taking the sociological aspects involved in communication into consideration, Schramm points out that for understanding to take place between the source and the destination, they must have something in common.

If the source's and destination's fields of experience overlap, communication can take place. If there is no overlap, or only a small area in common, communication is difficult, if not impossible.

For many years cooperative extension service agents developed considerable skill in communicating with the large American middle class. That success is understandable. A large number of extension workers came from this middle class, and there was a large overlap between the extension communicator and the middle-class audience.

However, in the 1960s, a period of growing social awareness, many extension workers were challenged — even mandated — to work with a "disadvantaged" audience. Many of the middle-class extension workers found it difficult to communicate with a disadvantaged audience. In many cases, there was only a small overlap in the fields of experience of the source and the disadvantaged receiver.

Extension met this communications challenge to a degree by employing individuals from the target disadvantaged audience, training them, and in turn allowing them to provide the important communications linkage. Those employees are given such titles as leader aides, nutrition assistants, paraprofessionals and other like names.

6.5 Rileys' Model

W. John and Matilda White Riley, a husband and wife team of sociologists, point out the importance of the sociological view in communication in another way. The two sociologists say such a view would fit together the many messages and individual reactions to them within an integrated social structure and process. The Rileys developed a model to illustrate these sociological implications in communication.

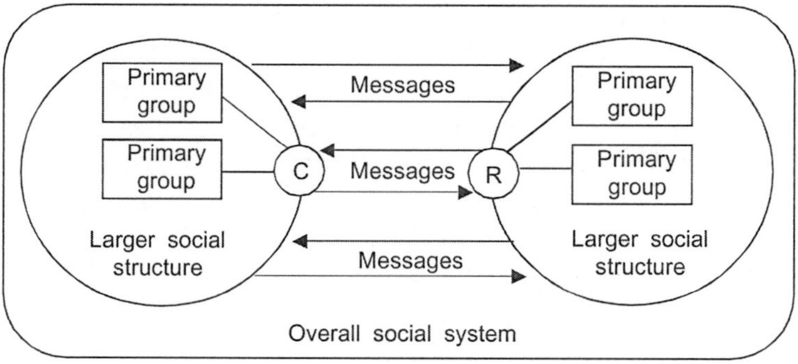

Figure 6.5. The Riley's model

The model indicates the communicator (C) emerges as part of a larger pattern, sending messages in accordance with the expectations and actions of other persons and groups within the same social structure. This also is true of the receiver (R) in the communications process.

In addition, both the communicator and receiver are part of an overall social system. Within such an all-embracing system, the communication process is seen as a part of a larger social process, both affecting it and being in turn affected by it. The model clearly illustrates that communication is a two-way proposition.

The important point the Rileys' model makes for us is that we send messages as members of certain primary groups and that our receivers receive our messages as members of primary groups. As you likely can visualise, group references may be a positive reinforcement of our messages; at other times they may create a negative force.

6.6 Berlo's Model

The final communications model that we will consider is the SMCR model, developed by David K. Berlo, a communications theorist and consultant. In his book, *The*

Process of Communication: Berlo points out the importance of the psychological view in his communications model. The four parts of Berlo's SMCR model are — no surprises here — source, message, channel, receiver.

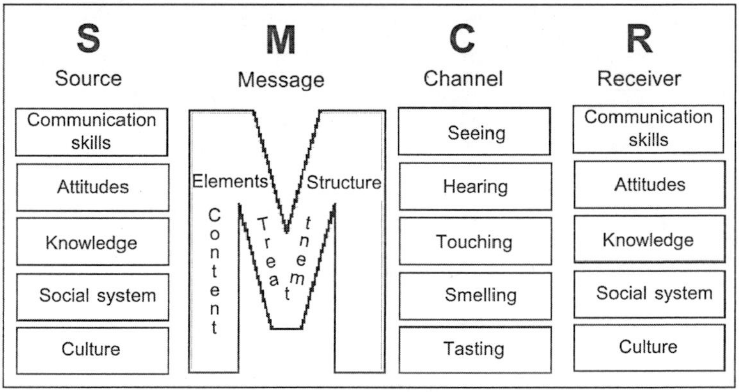

Figure 6.6. Berlo's SMRC model

The first part of this communication model is the source. All communication must come from some source. The source might be one person, a group of people, or a company, organisation, or institution such as the University of Missouri.

Several things determine how a source will operate in the communication process. They include the source's communication skills — abilities to think, write, draw, speak. They also include attitudes toward audience, the subject matter, yourself, or toward any other factor pertinent to the situation. Knowledge of the subject, the audience, the situation and other background also influences the way the source operates. So will social background, education, friends, salary, culture — all sometimes called the sociocultural context in which the source lives.

Message has to do with the package to be sent by the source. The code or language must be chosen. In general, we think of code in terms of the natural languages — English, Spanish, German, Chinese and others. Sometimes we use other languages — music, art, gestures. In all cases, look at the code in terms of ease or difficulty for audience understanding.

Within the message, select content and organise it to meet acceptable treatment for the given audience or specific channel. If the source makes a poor choice, the message will likely fail.

Channel can be thought of as a sense — smelling, tasting, feeling, hearing, seeing. Sometimes it is preferable to think of the channel as the method over which the message will be transmitted: telegraph, newspaper, radio, letter, poster or other media. Kind and number of channels to use may depend largely on purpose. In general, the more you can use and the more you tailor your message to the people "receiving" each channel, the more effective your message.

The receiver becomes the final link in the communication process. The receiver is the person or persons who make up the audience of your message. All of the factors that determine how a source will operate apply to the receiver. Think of communication skills in terms of how well a receiver can hear, read, or use his or her other senses. Attitudes relate to how a receiver thinks of the source, of himself or herself, of the message, and so on. The receiver may have more or less knowledge than the source. Sociocultural context could be different in many ways from that of the source, but social background, education, friends, salary, culture would still be involved. Each will affect the receiver's understanding of the message.

Messages sometimes fail to accomplish their purpose for many reasons. Frequently the source is unaware of receivers and how they view things. Certain channels may not be as effective under certain circumstances. Treatment of a message may not fit a certain channel. Or some receivers simply may not be aware of, interested in, or capable of using certain available messages.

6.7 Osgood and Schramm Circular Model

From the models already discussed above, you will be aware that a criticism that could be made of some of them is that they present communication as a linear process, within which the rôles of sender and receiver are clearly distinguished. Schramm stated:

> In fact, it is misleading to think of the communication process as starting somewhere and ending somewhere. It is really endless. We are little switchboard centers handling and rerouting the great endless current of information....

The Osgood and Schramm circular model is an attempt to remedy that deficiency: The model emphasises the circular nature of communication. The participants swap between the rôles of source/encoder and receiver/decoder.

The model is particularly helpful in reminding us of the process of *interpretation* which takes place whenever a message is decoded.

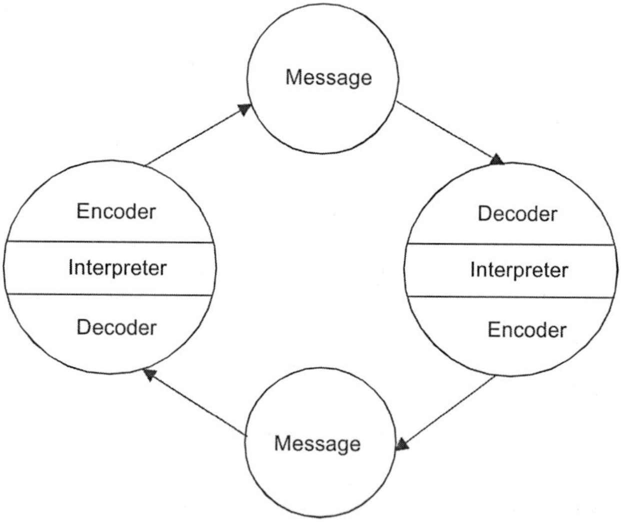

Figure 6.7. Osgood and Schramm circular model

The more mechanical models, particularly those concerned primarily with machine communication, tend to suggest that fidelity will be high as long as physical noise is reduced to a minimum or strategies (such as increasing channel redundancy) are adopted to counter the noise. This circular model reminds us that receiving a message is not simply a matter of decoding, but also of *interpreting* the message.

Whenever we receive data from the world around us, even in, say, the apparently very simple act of seeing what's in front of us, we are engaged in an active process of interpretation, not simply taking in information, but actively making sense of it. An important question is: what criteria are we using to make sense of what we are receiving? Since the criteria we use will inevitably differ from one person to another, there will always be semantic noise. If we can answer that question about our audience, then we stand a chance of communicating successfully. But it is certainly not an easy question to answer, as you will see if you take a look at Berlo's SMCR Model, which is one of the most useful models as a starting point for organising any practical work in communication.

6.8 Gerbner's General Model

Gerbner's General Model emphasises the dynamic nature of human communication. It also gives prominence to the factors which may affect fidelity.

The model shown diagrammatically is to be read from left to right, beginning at E - Event.

- — The event (E) is perceived by M (the man (sic) or machine).
- — The process of perception is not simply a matter of 'taking a picture' of event E. It is a process of active interpretation.
- — The way that the E is perceived will be determined by a variety of factors, such as the assumptions, attitudes, point of view, experience of M.
- — E can be a person talking, sending a letter, telephoning, or otherwise communicating with M. In other words, E could be what we conventionally call the Source or Transmitter.
- — Equally, E can be an event—a car crash, rain, waves crashing on a beach, a natural disaster, etc. In this

case, we could be applying the model to mass media communication, say the reporting of news.

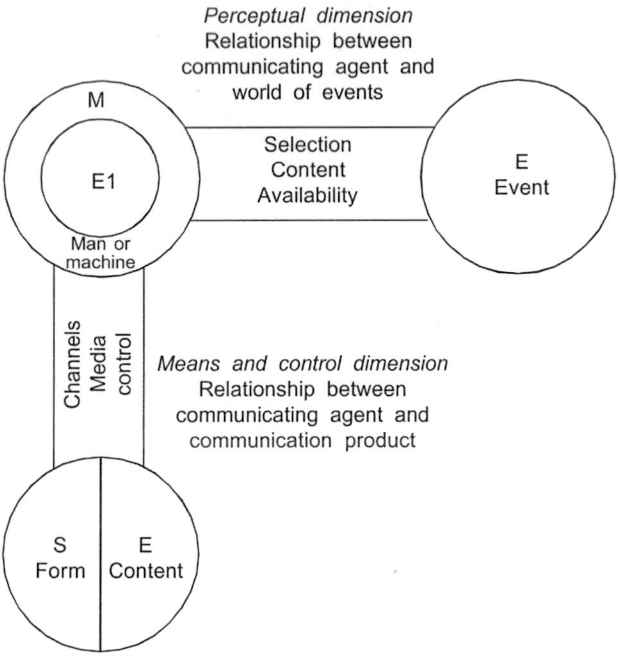

Figure 6.8. Gerbner's general Model

The model is a useful starting-point for the analysis of wide variety of communication acts. Note that the model, besides drawing our attention to those factors within E which will determine perception or interpretation of E, also draws our attention to three important factors:

i) *Selection*: M, the perceiver of the event E (or receiver of the message, if you prefer) selects from the event, paying more attention to this aspect and less to that. This process of selecting, filtering is commonly known as gatekeeping, particularly in discussion of the media's selection and discarding of events or aspects of them.

ii) *Context*: a factor often omitted from communication models, but a vitally important factor. The sound represented by the spelling 'hair' means an animal in one context, something that's not supposed to be in your soup in another. Shouting, ranting and raving means this man's very angry in one context, raving loony in another.

iii) *Availability*: how many Es are there around? What difference does availability make? If there are fewer Es around, we are likely to pay more attention to the ones there are. They are likely to be perceived by us as more 'meaningful'.

E1 and M : E1 is the event-as-perceived (E) by the man (*sic*) or machine M. In terms of human communication, a person perceives an event. The perception (E1) they have of that event is more or less close to the 'real' event. The degree of correspondence between M's perception of event E (E1) will be a function of M's assumptions, point of view, experiences, social factors etc.

Means and controls: In the next stage of the model, M becomes the source of a message about E to someone else. M produces a statement about the event (SE). To send that message, M has to use channels (or media) over which he has a greater or lesser degree of control. The question of 'control' relates to M's degree of skill in using communication channels. If using a verbal channel, how good is he at using words? If using the Internet, how good is he at using new technology and words? and so on.? 'Control' may also be a matter of access — does he own this medium? Can he get to use this medium? Think of teachers in classrooms controlling the access to communication channels, parents at home, owners of newspapers, editors of letters pages, etc.

SE: SE (statement about event) is what we would more normally call the 'message'. S stands for Signal in fact, so in principle an S can be present without an E, but in that case it would be noise only. The process can be extended ad infinitum by adding on other receivers (M2, M3, etc.) who have further perceptions (SE1, SE2, etc.) of the statements about perceived events.

6.9 Dance's Helical Model

Frank Dance's helical model related communication to a helix. The bottom of the helix is small. As the helix moves upward it becomes larger. But movement up the helix is slow; a process of circular, back-and-forth motion. In the beginning, communicators share but a small portion of themselves in their relationship. Through a slow process of give and take, their relationship develops as, little by little, they commit more of themselves.

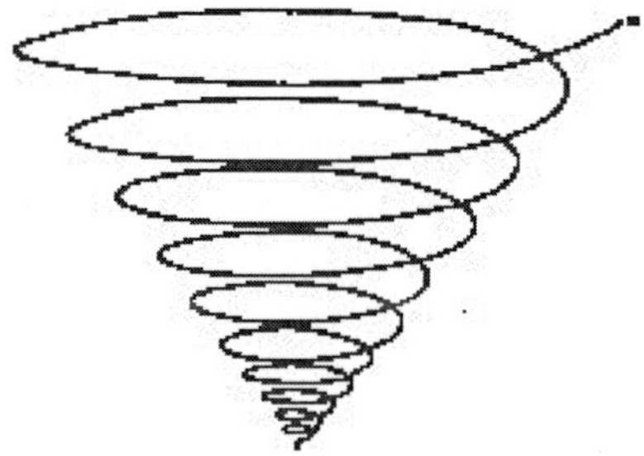

Figure 6.9. Dance's Helical model

Dance's helical model helps us to remember that the communication process is ever-changing, circular, expanding, and building upon the past.

6.10 Newcomb's Model

In 1953 Theodore Newcomb presented what was to be one of the most popular of the cognitive consistency theories. His interest lied in the general understanding of interpersonal relationships. To explore this further he reveals a concept he call orientation. Newcomb defines orientation as "a useful way of taking account of the fact of individuals' persistency's in relating themselves to things in their environment." He relates that an orientation is used synonymously with attitude.

According to Newcomb "The term orientation implies directness and selectivity." If you are oriented towards something he states you focus your attention on it instead of something else. Orientation is also characterised by it is intensity (short-tall, hot-cold). However, it displays cognitive properties as well. Newcomb illustrates this through a pair of parents. One parent could have pride and resemblance as a strong cognitive component while the other parent values personal response as the more cherished component.

Attraction is found in interpersonal relationships. (Person A is attracted to person B). Newcomb includes respect, admiration and dependence in his definition of attraction all associated with either a positive or a negative liking.

Orientation would not be complete without attitude. Person A's orientation to a non person object x is an attitude. What do attitude and attraction have to do with one another? In a relationship (attraction) where objects (X) exist, attitudes about these objects (X) formulate. Couples come up with attitudes about them (X).

To illustrate further Newcomb divides orientation into two systems - individual and collective. An individual system is complied of A's attraction to B, A's attitude toward X and B's attitude toward X perceive by A. A collective system is A and B's attitude towards each other, both A's and B's attitude toward X attributed both by A to B and B to A.

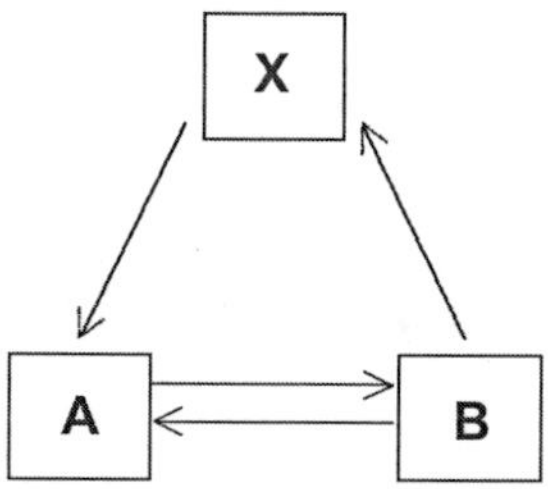

Figure 6.10. Newcomb's ABX model

The essential assumption is that communication among humans performs the essential function of enabling two or more individuals to maintain simultaneous orientation toward one another as communicators and toward objects of communication. The term "orientation" is used as equivalent to "attitude" in its more inclusive sense of referring to both cathectic and cognitive tendencies. A-B-X is regarded as a system. The essential theory posits that imbalance in part of the system creates psychological stress or pressure to change other parts of the system.

6.11 Westley and MacLean's Model

Westley and MacLean's communication model was the first to attempt to model the mass communication process specifically.

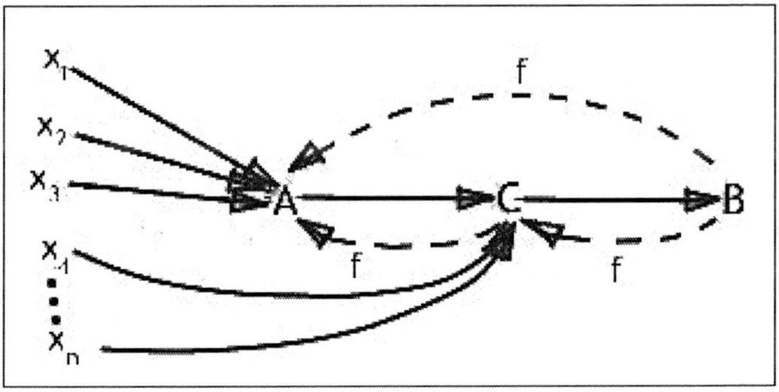

x = information source

A = sender

B = receiver

C = editorial function

f = feedback path

Figure 6.11. Westley and MacLean's model

It takes into account several factors that are especially prominent in, if not peculiar to, mass communication situations:

i) The sender (which is often a team rather than an individual) generally derives information from a variety of sources and combines it in some way to create a message.

ii) The message generally passes through some kind of editorial gatekeeper before being passed on to audiences (this again may be group, and the editorial process may have several layers, including governmental regulation of content, editors, corporation management, and investors or advertisers.

iii) The editorial functions may have direct access to relevant sources of information, some of which the sender may *not* have access to (e.g., an editor who has inside sources in the goverment or a corporation).

iv) Feedback from the audience is sometimes directed to the sender, but in many cases is directed to some part of the editorial function, who may modify or expand upon it in transmitting it to the sender.

6.12 Gatekeeping Model

Kurt Lewin was apparently the first one to use the term "gatekeeping", which he used to describe a wife or mother as the person who decides which foods end up on the family's dinner table. The gatekeeper is the person who decides what shall pass through each gate section, of which, in any process, there are several. Although he applied it originally to the food chain, he then added that the gating process can include a news item winding through communication channels in a group. This is the point from which most gatekeeper studies in communication are launched.

David Manning White was the person who seized upon Lewin's comments and turned it solidly toward journalism in 1950. In the 1970s McCombs and Shaw took a different direction when they looked at the effects of gatekeepers' decisions. They found the audience learns how much importance to attach to a news item from the emphasis the media place on it. McCombs and Shaw pointed out that the gatekeeping concept is related to the newer concept, agenda-setting.

The gatekeeper concept is now 50 years old and has slipped into the language of many disciplines, including gatekeeping in organisations. The gatekeeper decides which information will go forward, and which will not. In other words, a gatekeeper in a social system decides which of a certain commodity – materials, goods, and information – may enter the system. Important to realise is that gatekeepers are able to control the public's knowledge of the actual events by letting some stories pass through the system but keeping others out. Gatekeepers can also be seen as institutions or organisations. In a political system there are gatekeepers, individuals or institutions which control access to positions of power and regulate the flow of information and political influence. Gatekeepers exist in many jobs, and their choices hold the potential to colour mental pictures that are subsequently created in people's understanding of what is happening in the world around them. Media gatekeeping showed that decision making is based on principles of news values, organisational routines, input structure and common sense. Gatekeeping is vital in communication planning and almost al communication planning roles include some aspect of gatekeeping.

The gatekeeper's choices are a complex web of influences, preferences, motives and common values. Gatekeeping is inevitable and in some circumstances it can be useful. Gatekeeping can also be dangerous, since it can lead to an abuse of power by deciding what information to discard and what to let pass. Nevertheless, gatekeeping is often a routine, guided by some set of standard questions. The gatekeeper concept is now generally regarded as oversimplified and of little utility. It seems at first sight such an obvious concept, especially when applied to the news media, which is where you'll probably come across it most. Not everything that happens makes it into the news — well, that's hardly a revelation. !

Gatekeepers include reporters, copytasters, sub-editors, editors and, to a lesser extent, media owners. They also include the government via legislation, as well as the European Council and the United Nations, via declarations on human rights and civil liberties. They include pressure groups concerned with media output, who, while they may have no direct influence over media content, may be able to exert considerable pressure. Similar pressure will also come from political parties and from single issue groups such as Greenpeace. The concept is therefore perhaps 'of little utility' in itself, but, to the extent that it sends us off looking for all of those sources of influence on the gatekeeping process, it is a useful starting point.

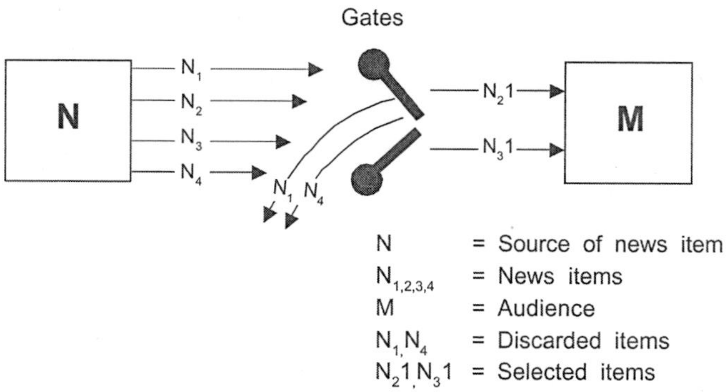

Figure 6.12. Gatekeeping model

In the graphic, N1, N2, N3 and N4 are identified as 'news items'. Doesn't that imply that 'gatekeeping' has already taken place before the gate is reached — after all, who determines that these are 'news items'? You might, in fact, also ask yourself what an 'item' is? What is a news 'event'? Is a plane crash the 'event' of the plane hitting the ground? Is it what happened before? How long before? Is it what happened after? How long after? These kinds of questions have no self-evident answer and remind us that a news 'event' is not simply 'out there' waiting to be reported. Somebody has to decide what the event is, how it is to be constructed.

6.13 Convergence Model

In Communication Networks: Toward a New Paradigm for Research, Rogers and Kincaid speak of their convergence model of communication:

> One can only know how well someone else understands a situation if the other person also shares information,

> and vice versa. After several cycles of information-exchange, the participants may shift to a new topic of discussion. [This] model of the communication process... reflects the convergent nature of mutual understanding and the cyclical nature of information exchange.

They further state:

> The convergence model represents human communication as a dynamic, cyclical process over time, characterised by (1) mutual causation rather than one-way mechanistic causation, and emphasising (2) the interdependent relationship of the participants, rather than a bias toward either the gisource" or the "receiver" of "messages". Mutual understanding and mutual agreement are the primary goals of the communication process.

Communication network analysis, according to Rogers and Kincaid, "describes the component linkages and their inter-relationships in the interpersonal communication structure. A communication network consists of interconnected individuals who are linked by patterned flows of information."

The convergence/network model of communication represents communication as a process of horizontal sharing between two or more participants within social networks. The first noticeable feature of the model is that information is shared or exchanged between two or more individuals rather that transmitted from one to the other. All participants act on the same information; none are passive receivers of information. The information can be created by the action of any participant, or it may originate from a third source such as television or radio, or a person or institution not directly participating such as church, school, non-governmental agency and so forth. The second feature of the model is that it stresses the important role of the perception and interpretation of participants, and thus draws upon the principles of semiotics and the hermeneutics, which treats understanding in terms of a dialogue or ongoing cultural conversation.

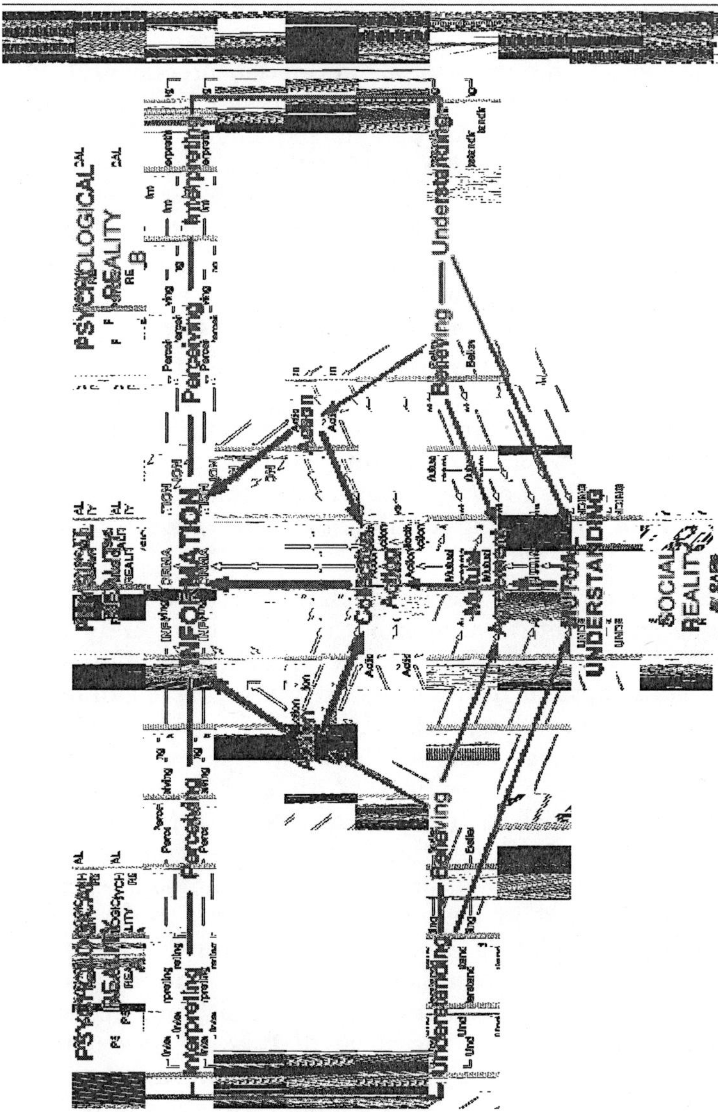

Figure 6.13.Convergence model

The third feature of the model is that it represents a horizontal, symmetrical relationship among two or more participants (A, B, ... n) that is created by sharing information. The outcomes of information processing by the participants are social — mutual understanding, agreement and collective action, as well as individual — perceiving, interpreting, understanding and believing. And finally, the model implies a continuous, cyclical process as participants take turns creating information to share with one another and then interpreting and reinterpreting its meaning until a sufficient degree of mutual understanding and agreement has been reached for collective action to take place.

"Information" is preferred over the term "message" to allow for both verbal and non-verbal information, unintended as well as intended information. For example, if women suddenly show up at a community meeting for the first time, this action by itself conveys information that can be stronger than all of the verbal comments made about "allowing women to participate."

Each participant perceives and arrives at her/his own unique interpretation, understanding and beliefs about information that is shared. Once reached, each person's understanding and beliefs can then be expressed to others. In the diagram, talking (self-expression) is one type of action that follows from, and is based on, each person's own understanding and beliefs. Any action creates new information, which potentially can be interpreted by the other participants. For instance, this means walking out of a meeting is also a form of information that can be interpreted. In a dialogue, a process of turn taking occurs as each participant seeks to clarify what others believe and understand as well as one's own understanding and beliefs. And that turn taking constitutes a minimal form of collective action: joint action in the form of two or more persons engaging in dialogue. But dialogue must mean more than just endless turn taking. The underlying assumption of dialogue is that all participants are willing to listen and change not just one of the parties. Communities that have a long history of conflict may not be able to engage even in this minimal form of collective action—talking to one another.

This turn taking (conversation, dialogue) constitutes a feedback process for each participant which, if effective, leads to a "series of diminishing mistakes—a dwindling series of under-and-over corrections converging on a goal." The common experience of "ah...so that's what you mean," indicates a process in which participants gradually converge toward a greater degree of mutual understanding and agreement (shared beliefs). The initial, relatively unique understanding and beliefs of each individual gradually become more similar and share more in common with those of others. Convergence does not imply perfect agreement, only the direction of movement.

The inherent properties of this process suggest that over time most groups will converge toward a state of greater internal uniformity, also referred to as "local culture". The convergence theory is valid in part because of the important roles played by boundaries. Within the boundaries created by the dialogue itself, convergence occurs because those who do not see an issue the same way nor agree with other participants tend to stop participating in the dialogue and then "drop out" of the group. Simply leaving a group automatically ensures greater uniformity among those who remain within the group. In communities, this process of divergence describes the formation of factions. The existence of factions/subgroups within a group (culture) implies two simultaneous processes: convergence among members within each bounded subgroup and divergence between subgroups over time. Boundaries determine who is included and who is excluded within a dialogue. Boundaries can be determined by observation and self-report, and by mapping the social networks within a community. Splitting communities into factions with different points of view reduces the overall social cohesion of a community and hence its capacity to solve mutual problems through collective action. If severe, it can bring cooperative action among groups within a community to a halt.

Ironically, dialogue itself is one of the primary means of overcoming such divisions. Effective dialogue occurs (1) when participants with differing points of view listen to one another, as indicated by paraphrasing the other's point of view to the other's satisfaction, (2) when each one acknowledges the conditions under which the other's point of view can be accepted as valid, and (3) when each one acknowledges the overlap or similarity of both points of view). But sometimes dialogue can lead to disagreement and divergence, especially when the dialogue makes it clear each individual's true interests and values are in conflict. The model depicted in Figure 1 does not show the nature of the relationships among the participants, nor does it say anything about the role of emotion, conflict and group motivation. Other models are needed to add this level of complexity. The social-change model described below considers these missing elements.

The convergence model of communication implies symmetry in the relationship of participants and equity of information sharing (action). Real groups and communities are sometimes far from this ideal. Power relationships substantially affect the communication process. Power may be exercised by means of authority (threat or use of positive and negative sanctions), influence (persuasiveness of participants), pre-existing social norms or all three. So, power and conflict represent another means for overcoming differences and opposition within a group. But even in cases where a community leader or outsider coerces recalcitrant individuals and subgroups to cooperate in a project, some minimal level of mutual understanding and agreement is still required for them to comply and engage in collective action. Negotiation represents a third means of overcoming opposition and conflict. Leaders of opposing factions can propose trade-offs and agree to compromises in order to obtain sufficient mutual agreement for collective action to proceed.

Selected References

Bittner John, *Fundamentals of Communication*, Prentice Hall, Englewood Cliffs, 1985.

Griffin, E., *A first look at Communication Theory*, New York, The McGraw-Hill Companies, 1997.

McQuail, D. and Windahl, S., *Communication Models for the Study of Mass Communications.* 2nd ed. London: Longman, 1993.

7
Verbal Communication

Verbal communication, in the form of written or oral communication, conveys more complicated and structured messages than non-verbal communication. Written communication can express highly detailed and complicated messages. It also is a form of communication that can be saved and/or stored. For example, meeting minutes often are stored for later reference if needed. Oral communication is sometimes more convenient than writing an e-mail or report. Non-verbal communication can also be combined with oral communication to increase the message's meaning. Some major forms of verbal communication are described below in brief.

7.1. Speech

Speech is an oral presentation by one person to a group (or sometimes just an individual); closely related terms include: *conversation* (infomal speech by more than one person on a topic), *debate* (formal communication between two groups holding opposing views before an audience), the academic discipline of communications. and the act of producing voice through the use of the vocal cords or other means, such as sign language, to create linguistic acts that communicate information from an initiator to a recipient.

The term speech is synonyms for the verb usage include talk, say, oral, speak, tell, oral; verbal includes written communication. In more colloquial terms, speech can be described in several different ways:

i) A linguistic act designed to convey information orally.
ii) Various linguistic acts where the audience includes more than one individual, including public speaking, oration, and quotation.
iii) The physical act of speaking, primarily through the use of vocal chords to produce voice.

However, speech can also take place inside one's head, known as intrapersonal communication, for example, when one thinks or utters sounds of approval or disapproval. At a deeper level, one could even consider subconscious processes, including dreams where aspects of oneself communicate with each other as part of intrapersonal communication, even though most human beings do not seem to have direct access to such communication.

7.1.1. Factors Affecting the Clarity of Speech

There are several factors that can affect the clarity of speech as such. Among these are:

i) Diseases and disorders of the lungs or the vocal cords, including paralysis, respiratory infections, and cancers of the lungs and throat.
ii) Diseases and disorders of the brain, including alogia, aphasias and speech processing disorders, where impaired perception of the message (as opposed to the actual sound) leads to poor speech production.
iii) Articulatory problems, such as stuttering, lisping, cleft palate, ataxia, or nerve damage leading to problems in articulation. Tourette syndrome and nervous tics can also affect speech.
iv) Problems in the perception of sound and auditory information can affect speech. In addition to aphasias, anomia and certain types of dyslexia can impede the quality of auditory perception, and therefore, expression. Hearing impairments and deafness can be considered to fall into this category.

Thus, it is clear that speech has both expressive and receptive elements. The purpose of speech can be to convey meaning or to increase social bonds between individuals and/ or groups (it is often both). For the latter shallowness is not a problem. The success of a speech act depends on numerous factors, including the presence or absence of a variety of speech disorders, the ability of the speaker to express the intended message, and the ability and willingness of the audience to play the role of recipient.

7.1.2. Speech Acts

Speaking a language is performing speech acts, acts such as making statements, giving commands, asking questions, making promises, and so on. One of the original scholars in this area, Searle, identifies four basic categories of speech acts as: utterances, propositional utterances, illocutionary utterances and perlocutionary utterances. These are not separate and independent of one another. Rather, they are similar to building blocks — humans make utterances, some of which are propositional, some of which are illocutionary, and some of which are perlocutionary. Each type of speech act are discribed below in brief.

7.1.2.1. Utterance

An utterance is a spoken word or string of spoken words. At the simplest level, to utter is simply to say a word with no particular forethought or intention to communicate a meaning. For example, if you put your hand on the hood of a car that has been sitting out in the hot sun, you might quickly pull it back while uttering the word, "Oh!" In this case, you don't *intend* to communicate meaning by this — it is simply a reflex action brought on by surprise. (Someone who hears you might take it mean something, but you did not plan on it.) Examples of "pure" utterances include such as sing-song rhymes while jumping rope or making choices (as, for example, "one potato, two potato, three potato, four..."), singing "scales" for practice, and other similar meaningless expressions.

7.1.2.2.Propositional Utterance

A more meaningful type of utterance makes reference to or describes a real or imaginary object. In the act of making a propositional utterance the speaker gains the opportunity to interact. If speaker and listener are using the same code (that is, if they speak the same language), and if both recognise the object to which the speaker is referring, then it becomes possible for them to share meanings.

Propositional utterances need not be sentences, and they do not have to intend anything. Any phrase that identifies or specifies something is a propositional utterance. It is important to see that utterances and propositions are not separate categories — a propositional utterance is a particular kind of utterance.

7.1.2.3.Illocutionary Utterances

An illocutionary utterance is spoken with the intention of making contact with a listener. Illocutionary utterances are usually sentences that contain propositional utterances, that is, they refer to things in the world — but it is their intentional nature that is of the most importance. Once it becomes clear that the speaker's intention is important to the meaning of an utterance, it can be seen that the same set of words might have different meanings depending on the speaker's intention. This leads scholars to further categorise illocutionary utterances in terms of how they communicate such intent.

7.1.2.4.Perlocutionary Utterances

Illocutionary speech acts may be intended to provide information, solicit answers to questions, give praise, and so on, but they don't necessarily require that the listener change his or her behaviour. Perlocutionary utterances, on the other hand, *do* attempt to effect a change. As with the others, perlocutionary speech acts are utterances; they include propositions, and they intend interaction with the receiver. Thus, Searle's model consists of a series of levels, each of which forms as the foundation for the levels that rest upon it.

7.1.3. Planning a Speech or Oral Presentation

Speeches and oral presentations are integral parts of communication. Public speaking allows an audience to place a face with a name. It also provides an opportunity for individuals to "stand out" and advance in their career. Similar to written communication, presentations require careful planning and preparation.

Planning a speech or presentation encompasses several steps, including determining the goal and topic, analysing the audience, developing the main statement, organising the flow of topics and support material, and determining the length and style.

Presentations generally have two main goals: to inform and/or persuade. In most situations the presentation's goal and topic are already established by the need for the presentation. For example, a project leader may need to give an informative report to his or her superiors. In this case, the presentation is informative and the topic is the project summary.

The next planning step is to evaluate the audience by addressing the following criteria. How big is the audience? Large audiences generally require a more formal presentation without much opportunity for audience interaction. Smaller audiences can be less formal and more interactive. What is the audience's composition, such as gender, age, and ethnicity, for example? What is the audience's motivation for attending? Is attendance required or optional? What is the audience's probable reaction to the presentation? If the presentation is about company downsising, then the probable audience reaction will be fear and anger. Addressing the probable reaction in the planning stages increases the chances of a successful presentation.

What is the level of knowledge of the audience? The level of detail and complexity given in the presentation should correlate to the audience's level of interest and motivation. If the audience is attending the presentation for a project summary, a detailed analysis is not necessary even though the audience may have the appropriate technical background. Finally, what is the relationship between the audience and the speaker? The presentation tone will be different if the audience is comprised of immediate co-workers and friends versus supervisors and/or strangers.

The main statement should inform the audience of the presentation's topic and scope. In the beginning, the speaker needs to identify the presentation's goal. In other words, where is the speaker taking the audience and why?

To guide the audience, the presentation topics should be sequenced logically. The presentation also should be interesting to hold the audience's attention. This can be accomplished by explaining why the presentation topic is important and how the topic personally affects the audience.

Finally, the presentation should close with a brief summary of the main points and a restatement of the purpose. If the audience is expected to formulate a decision or incorporate the presentation material into future actions, the speaker should provide the audience with some guidance as to what to do next.

Prior to the speech or presentation, supporting material or data pertinent to the purpose of the speech or presentation should be compiled. Convincing or supporting information is helpful in communicating the message.

How long should the speech or presentation be? If there is a predetermined time limit, then the speech or presentation must be designed accordingly. However, being allotted 30 minutes, for example, does not mean the presentation or speech must necessarily consume the entire time. An audience is likely to react negatively if a speech or presentation that lasts 30 minutes could have been done adequately in 20 minutes. Which presentation style should be employed?

The style is dependent on the purpose and environmental setting for the presentation. If the purpose, for example, is to present a technical paper at a national conference, then a formal style would be appropriate. If the audience is small and/or comprised of co-workers, an informal presentation style may be appropriate. An informal style also would be appropriate if the presentation involves audience interaction with the presenter. A formal presentation style would be appropriate for larger audiences and/or when the audience comprised superiors or strangers. In a formal presentation, the speaker may stand behind a podium and possibly on a stage. The speaker in an informal presentation may simply stand in front of or mingle with the audience.

7.2. Writing

Writing is a process which may refer to two activities: the inscribing characters on a medium, with the intention of forming words and other lingual constructs that represent language and record information, or the creation of information to be conveyed through written language. (There are some cavets to this rule. The use of a typewriter to record information is generally called typing, rather than writing.) The English word "writing" referes to both activities equaly, and often both activities occur simulatiously; however one may write while doing only one of the activities.

7.2.1. Writing Systems

In order for writing to occur a system must exist that allows for it. Most writing systems can be broadly divided into three categories: logographic, syllabic and alphabetic. As an interesting aside, historians draw a distinction between prehistory and history with the advent of writing systems. The cave paintings and petroglyphs of prehistoric peoples can be considered the precursor of writing systems, but cannot be considered as such because they relied heavily on oral tradition in order to be understood.

7.2.1.1. Logogramic

A logogram is a single written character which represents a complete grammatical word. The vast array of logograms and the memorisation of what they mean are the major disadvantage of the logographic systems over alphabetic systems. While most languages do not use wholly logographic writing systems many languages use some logograms, Arabic numerals being a prime example. The most important (and, to a degree, the only surviving) modern logographic writing system is the Chinese one, whose characters are used, with varying degrees of modification, in Chinese, Japanese, Korean, Vietnamese, and other east Asian languages.

7.2.1.2. Syllabic

As logographic writing systems use a single symbol for an entire word, a syllabary is a set of written symbols that represent (or approximate) syllables, which make up words. A symbol in a syllabary typically represents a consonant sound followed by a vowel sound, or just a vowel alone. Syllabaries are best suited to languages with relatively simple syllable structure, such as Japanese. Other languages that use syllabic writing include Mycenaean Greek (Linear B) and Native American languages such as Cherokee. Several languages of the Ancient Near East used forms of cuneiform, which is a syllabary with some non-syllabic elements.

7.2.1.3. Alphabetic

An alphabet is a small set of letters—basic written symbols—each of which roughly represents or represented historically a phoneme of a spoken language. In a perfectly phonological alphabet, the phonemes and letters would correspond perfectly in two directions: a writer could predict the spelling of a word given its pronunciation, and a speaker could predict the pronunciation of a word given its spelling. As languages often evolve independently of their writing systems, and writing systems have been borrowed for languages they were not designed for, the degree to which letters of an alphabet correspond to phonemes of a language varies greatly from one language to another and even within a single language.

7.2.3. Forms of Written Communication

There are many forms of written communication such as letters, resumes, memos, reports, and proposals. The writing process generally follows a series of steps. First, what is the purpose of the message? Is it informative or persuasive? Second, who is the audience? Is the audience composed of co-workers or strangers, for example? Is the audience familiar with the topic and what will their probable reaction be? It is generally advisable to anticipate the audience's questions and provide enough information as practical. Third, the appropriate communication medium is selected based on the purpose and audience. The most common forms of written communication are memos, letters, reports, and proposals.

Memos are typically internal documents that communicate a brief message. They are typically one-page documents, which are normally directed to many people; however, the audience could be a single person.

Letters are more formal documents that are typically sent to other people or organisations. They are generally one to two pages in length and printed on company letterhead.

Reports are a form of written communication conveying facts, data, and other technical information. Reports can communicate the results of a project or experiment.

Proposals are similar to reports. However, they are generally persuasive in nature as opposed to objectively communicating factual information. Proposals can be a few pages to several hundred pages in length. A proposal typically asks for approval or support of an idea or project.

After the communication medium has been selected, the author needs to organise and compose the message. In the organisation process, the author identifies the main points of the message to be communicated. In other words, the author identifies what information he or she wants the audience to receive and remember. It is generally advisable for the author to develop an outline starting with a main idea and supporting ideas. A coherent outline forms the framework for a coherent message. A well-organised and -crafted message will be easier and shorter for the audience to read, thereby making the audience more likely to accept it as opposed to dismissing it. It is important to remember that the audience will infer the author's tone and mood from the message. The author does not have the luxury of reading the message and using non-verbal communication. Due to an author's poor choice of words or writing style, readers often infer the wrong impression from a message. This happens frequently with e-mails. E-mails are generally drafted quickly and little attention is given to how the reader interprets the words and writing style. For example, the reader may think the author is angry when he or she is not. An author should choose the level of words and style appropriate for the audience and message.

There are three basic sentence structures: simple, compound, and complex. A simple sentence has one subject and one predicate, such as "Car prices have risen in the past year." A compound sentence consists of at least two main ideas or clauses. Coherent and fluid paragraphs increase the communication's effectiveness. Paragraphs are typically a group of sentences that all relate to one main idea. They contain a topic sentence, which is supported by the remaining sentences in the paragraph. The topic sentence, which can be a question, provides a summary of what the paragraph will discuss. For fluid communication, paragraphs must be arranged coherently to prevent confusion. There also must be smooth transition from one paragraph to the next. The transition can be a word, sentence, or paragraph. The final step in the writing process is editing. Editing consists of rewriting, grammar and spell checking, and proofreading. The key to good writing is rewriting. Depending on the type of writing, a few revisions may be adequate or 10-20 revisions may be necessary. The communication quality increases with the number of revisions.

Good writers are not always naturally gifted. They rewrite several times to perfect their message. Good writers are also typically good readers. In other words, people who read frequently usually are better writers than people who do not. Word processing and e-mail software packages can check for spelling mistakes. However, there are situations where software will not catch a mistake such as "to or too." Checking grammar can be more difficult, but many word processing software packages come with some form of grammar checking.

Some common grammar errors to be aware of are subject-verb agreement, voice, and tense. A singular subject, for example, requires a singular verb, such as "the car travels fast", not "the car travel fast." The two types of voice, referring to verbs, are active and passive. For example, in the active voice, "teenagers like to drive fast cars." In the passive voice, "Fast cars are typically driven by teenagers." The voice needs to be consistent throughout the message. Tense refers to past, present, and future.

Usage of visual aids can also improve the effectiveness of written communication. It can express some messages more simply and clearly than words. They can highlight specific points and, if appealing to the eye, can be persuasive. Visual aids generally consist of tables, charts, pictures, and maps. They provide another avenue for communicating a message. Tables are generally applicable for displaying data, particularly numerical data. It is cumbersome to read data in paragraph form. Line charts and bar charts are typically used to illustrate data with respect to time such as stock market results. These charts also can be used to compare two or more variables over time. Flow charts typically illustrate a sequence of steps or processes.

7.3. Verbal Communication and Language Development

Communication is no less than the transfer of consciousness beyond the body. The process of this transfer is realised essentially in the following stages:

i) focus on a given part of the content of consciousness;

ii) selection of an element to be communicated;

iii) rendering that element discrete (i.e., articulation);

iv) formalising it (i.e., adapting it to the experience of the community);

v) linearising it (i.e. organising the already discrete and formalised element into a one-dimensional sequence);

vi) encoding it in language (i.e., verbalising it).

Obviously, the original form of the element of consciousness changes or is somewhat compromised at each stage of the process.

7.3.1. Language as a Technology

We do not ordinarily regard language as a technology. The spoken word, its primary form, is, after all, "the product of our bodies." The words of Michael Polanyi should at least cause us to ponder the matter: "We have seen that in all applications of a formalism to experience there is an indeterminacy involved, which must be resolved by the observer on the ground of unspecifiable criteria. Now we may say further that the process of applying language to things is also necessarily unformalised: that it is inarticulate. Denotation, then, is an art, and whatever we say about things assumes our endorsement of our own skill in practising this art." Polanyi suggests that existing human experience has a continuous character, that it is not disjunctive, and therefore the application of formal (linguistic) rules to it requires of the applier the same kind of art as the application of any other kind of technology. In this sense, language, even in its primary (spoken) form can be seen as a technology, whose function—as with all other communication technologies—also results in losses.

7.3.2. Written Language

Everyone regards writing as a perfect technology if communtion. There are two types of writing: Haas uses the Greek words pleremic and cenemic to describe these two types. Pleremic writing has little in common with language: such writing actually cuts through language, creating direct contact between writing and the things it represents, ignoring acoustic language altogether. Cenemic writing, for its part, records only phonetic, not semantic, information. Syllabaries, consonant alphabets and phonetic alphabets belong to this category. Phonetic alphabets were born in the eighth century BC, when the Greeks completed the Phoenician consonant alphabet with signs for vowels. In a sense, the phonetic alphabet was the highest product of acoustic language-analysis: it could appear only when the acoustic disaggregative process in language had reached a relatively high level.

Writing is not a perfect communication technology: not only can it not convey extra-linguistic communication devices, but it is also incapable of recording supra-segmental resources in acoustic language use. In principle it can indeed record segmental resources, but in practice a great deal depends on the acoustic memory of the reader. Another important shortcoming of writing is its lack of interactivity. This was recognised as early as Plato, who wrote in the *Phaedrus*, that written texts "maintain a solemn silence." "If you ask them what they mean by anything," Plato adds, "they simply return the same answer over and over again." The imperfections of writing increase the perfection of language.

These two imperfections of writing significantly influenced the written use of language, and communication in general. The fact that writing could not register either suprasegmental language elements or the extralinguistic elements of communication obliged human writers to incorporate everything they wanted to say into segmental language elements. Accordingly, the widespread practice of writing significantly impoverished the arsenal of extralinguistic means of communication and also suprasegmental means, while vastly enriching the store of segmental resources, which had to carry the full weight of the message. This circumstance, along with the lack of interactivity, both in the acoustic dimension and in the semantic dimension of human language, forced a steady and profound process of disaggregation.

Writing did not allow for the process that Goody and Watt call "direct semantic ratification", which in primary orality served to reaffirm the significance of the words used. Accordingly, it was essential to separate out the complex meanings of words in primary orality and to assign a separate segmental linguistic sign to each signifying element. These signifying elements had to be clearly outlined, concentrated to their essence, and freed of phenomenological components. An obvious outcome of this process was the proliferation of word forms, and at the same time written language became more abstract.

7.3.3. Orality and Literacy

This process of abstraction touched not only written language, but also spoken language, above all because of the high prestige that written language gradually acquired in human society. The possibility that it could be written down imbued spoken language with a certain prestige: for this reason, people began to speak forms of language that could be readily written.

At the same time, spoken language also had its influence on written language, primarily because spoken language remained quantitatively dominant in human communication. As a result, language use could be described as spoken or written in two ways: in terms of its medium or in terms of its concepts.

Medium posits opposition between the sound of speech and the graphic signs of writing; the conceptual-cognitive dimension sets language that is fashioned through speech and heavily reliant on context, over against abstract language planned and fashioned through writing, the 'algebra of speech'. This in turn makes possible the emergence of rich variants that combine elements of written and spoken language.

Until the middle of the twentieth century, writing was the only widely and effectively functioning communication technology. The sequential appearance of telephony, radio, the phonograph, and means of recording, storing and transporting human speech in its full acoustic nature and completeness challenged the position of writing, although for a long time this challenge was not remarked.

As early as 1933, Bloom Field foresaw the possible disappearance of writing: "We may expect that at some time in the future our social organism will reach a degree of co-ordination and flexibility where a concerted change becomes possible, or else that mechanical devices for reproducing speech will supersede our present habits of writing and printing." However, because of the then general view that writing had nothing to do with language, he did not delve deeper into the subject.

The turning-point in communication technology came with the appearance and gradual expansion of television. Because of its multimedia capability, television can almost flawlessly recreate the conditions of face-to-face communication: it is capable of conveying all three dimensions of such communication: segmented linguistic resources, suprasegmental linguistic resources, and extralinguistic communication resources. Accordingly, segmented linguistic resources, and, along with them, discrete signs, are losing their relative monopoly within the field of communication.

7.3.4. Secondary Orality

Ong has named this new era of communication "secondary orality." In 1982 he wrote, "This new orality has striking resemblances of a communal sense, its concentration on the present moment, and even its use of formulas. But it is essentially a more deliberate and self-conscious orality, based permanently on the use of writing and print, which are essential for operation of the equipment and for its use as well". Two decades later, this view of the "basic" role of writing and print in secondary orality seems rather too optimistic. The rapid expansion of functional illiteracy confirms the supposition that a significant part of the adult population can live without reading and writing after leaving school.

However, the twentieth-century revolution in communication technology does not consist only in the emergence of means of recording and transmitting human speech and therefore the suprasegmental dimension of communication that writing cannot convey. The tape recorder or phonograph and radio in this respect "corrected" one shortcoming of writing. But an equally important event in the history of communication was the process that has been called the 'iconic turn' or 'pictorial turn' which made possible the recording and transfer of extralinguistic means of communication, thereby "correcting" an additional shortcoming of writing.

This turn began in the nineteenth century with the invention of photography. Joyce named photography, in a happy turn of phrase, "automatic writing", and found that a photograph was "a rival, and perhaps a usurper, of the word, whether written or spoken." Pictures accordingly compete not only with writing, but with language itself, primary thinking takes place through sensory perception, among which pride of place goes to visual perception, i.e., pictures. One might also say that as the phonograph and the radio corrected shortcomings, imperfections, in writing, photography corrects shortcomings and imperfections in language itself.

For a long time people could make pictures only at a low level of efficiency: making a picture required extended work by people with exceptional talent. And the pictures that resulted had a serious deficiency: they could not be reproduced in the same form. William Ivins points out in his *Prints and Visual Communication*, that Lessing, writing about the Laokoon, not only had not seen the sculpture itself, but also, given the availability of pictures at the time, could not have had a faithful image of its true appearance.

In the early years of human existence the inability to produce iconic signs describing elements of consciousness forced people to accept as a means of communication a symbolic system of acoustic signs (spoken language) and later its written variation, namely, writing.

Further stages in the iconic turn following the development of photography were film, television, and finally computer-generated and computer-processed pictures: the production of pictures is growing steadily more perfect and simpler. As a result, data and information of a visual character can be communicated in their original form, without first going through the distorting and simplifying process of disarticulation, abstraction, formalisation, symbolisation and linearisation, all of which are a prerequisite of linguistic communication.

The ability to avoid distortion and simplification both improves communication and renders it more comfortable, though at the same time the process of analysis, a necessary accompaniment of linguistic communication, falls away. Finally, communication by pictures makes it possible to send messages that the sender has not disarticulated, indeed may not understand.

The iconic or pictorial turn partially or completely eliminates this need to disarticulate, and, if Polanyi is right, the current direction in the evolution of communication will of necessity lead to a reduction in the human capacity to think.

7.3.5. Post-literacy

More accurately than the term "secondary orality", the term "post-literacy" best characterises the communication of the present day: although spoken language is going through a major revival, what matters is not so much the revival as the fact that writing is losing its position. It is not that, in the era of post-literacy, everyone is forgetting how to read and write. Post-literacy is characterised by the fact that "the dominance of the printed book as the medium of communication has become challenged by the rise of the new, electric and electronic media." And this situation describes more or less the entire twentieth century. In his lectures on Greek literature, given at Basel in 1874-75, Nietzsche complains that literature is concerned with "the written products" of the various peoples, rather than devoting itself to the "spoken products". In the works of Heidegger the words Rede and Sage occur frequently, making a clear link to the use of spoken language.

The greatest rebel against writing, however, was Wittgenstein. His rebellion had its roots not in philosophical considerations, but rather in the fact that he was dyslexic, as Jaakko Hintikkahas demonstrated. The Hungarian scholar Nyíri further explains that Wittgenstein was unsuccessful in ordering his thoughts in uninterrupted linear sequence, the norm for the printed book. The thoughts appearing in his works are rendered as a complicated and complex network of relationships.

7.3.6. Language without Writing

Post-literacy does not result in the complete disappearance of writing: human inventions used over a long period never wholly disappear (harness racing and equestrianism continue to flourish as sports in the age of the automobile). Speech, having made itself independent of writing "will drown out everything else," declares Flusser. "CD's, cassettes and speaking pictures" cry and whisper constantly into human ears. He finds that the collapse of the control associated with written language will lead inevitably to the complete barbarisation of language.

Flusser is probably right that non-written language must of necessity lose those characteristics that it has acquired from writing-in fact characteristics thrust upon it by writing. These characteristics are above all the acoustic and semantic traits made necessary by written use and written use only. McLuhan says that "print," i.e., writing widely applied, "altered not only the spelling and grammar but the accentuation and inflection of languages, and made bad grammar possible." In post-literacy the possibility of grammatical error again disappears: one can see the beginning of such disappearance in the growing elasticity of language rules and the expansion of linguistic tolerance.

Writing fixes and materially objectifies linguistic material, and printing in turn further emphasises its fixity and objectivity. This explains why fixed written texts have become the basis of the humanities. With the use of computers for writing, texts have lost their material objectivity, and their fixity has also been compromised. A text published through print remains constant, and we can refer to it even at a chronological distance of several centuries, but a text published on the internet can change even on a daily basis: the author can continue to correct, improve and rewrite it.

On the one hand this capability constitutes an advantage for scholarship, but on the other hand the complete loss of continuity overturns the operations of the scholarly life as these have been known up to now. There appears to be no good solution to this dilemma. There are so many advantages to web publishing—minimal financial investment, technical simplicity, and easy, ongoing and almost cost-free access for all potential consumers of the text—that it is difficult to imagine any other solution than adaptation of the scholarly life to the mechanisms and operating principles of the new technology.

7.3.7. Emergence of Hypertext Language

The ordinary form of existence of electronic text—hypertext—enables closer proximity of written text to the multi-dimensionality of face-to-face communication, first because hypertext can contain links with other texts, thus reducing the severe one-dimensional linearity of written text, but, more importantly, because such links can incorporate pictures as well (including moving pictures), along with sounds, thereby creating actual multimediality. Written texts are always virtually multimedial: good literary texts have always sought to create, and indeed succeeded in creating, the illusion of sensation in all the senses of the reader. In the present moment it therefore seems that the typical future form of textuality will be the hypertext.

Hypertext is the form in which texts will survive, but we should not ignore the fact that such survival requires concessions and compromises. Text, which in the era of print culture—until the development of iconic turn—was practically the exclusive transporter of communication, must now yield its monopoly position and be satisfied with conveying a half or a third of the traffic. Probably even this share will decline with the expansion, sophistication and simplification of the technical means of electronic processing of picture and sound.

It seems, then, that the loss of position of writing—and also of language—is inevitable. The only question is how this will affect human thought and human capacity for thought. To put the question more succinctly: Could human capacity for thought survive if language slipped from under it? There are also positive ways of answering the question. Flusser, for example, writes that "... departure from writing is possible in one of two directions: backwards to pictures or forward to calculation." Elsewhere he explains matters further: "After we have moved beyond the alphabet, thinking will become emancipated from speech, and other, non-linguistic means of thought will begin to develop at unbelievable speed."

Pictures are a more comfortable and more convenient form of communication that the segmented linguistic form called words. And examples show that an easier and more convenient mode of communication can dislodge one that is less comfortable and convenient. Thus the segmented linguistic resources that followed the invention of writing almost completely dislodged the suprasegmental linguistic resources, leaving only third-rate auxiliary functions for the once richly endowed sign languages. So it is not merely theoretical hypothesis to suggest that a similar dislodgement could occur to the segmented linguistic resources as well.

To avoid a disaster in this area, communication strategies would be required that gave particular emphasis to communication technologies, with special consideration of the ways in which a given technology might affect language and its use. We must positively discriminate in order to advantage those technologies whose use will have a positive effect on language.

7.4. Barriers to Verbal Communication

7.4.1. Language Barriers

i) *Vocabulary*: The vocabulary and its extent must be limited to the range that the listeners can understand. Otherwise you might as well be talking in a foreign language.

ii) *Jargon*: It is so easy to pick up the jargon of the organisation or the discipline, but if the listeners do not come from the same environment, the jargon is not only not understood, but annoying.

iii) *Ambiguity:* Be careful that you say what you mean, not simply what you mean to say. Extra care is essential when multi-cultures form the audience in view of differing meanings to some words and sayings.

i) *Rambling*: Keep KISS (Keep it Simple) in mind, and avoid the long, vague rambling speech. Otherwise there is the danger of the audience stopping listening or even falling asleep.

i) *Unusual words*: If the words are unfamiliar to you, ensure that you are using the best word, the right word, pronounced correctly.

7.4.2. Psychological Barriers

i) *Pressures*: All sorts of pressures are working on members of an audience, and these can detract and distract from listening fully to what is said. Work, health, domestic, money, learning, social, and other pressures can all have an effect.

ii) *Mood* : Listeners who are easily affected by the mood they are in, may be in such a mood that listening to you may not be a priority.

iii) *Enforced attendance* : Not every learner attends a training programme voluntarily. If they are attending because they were told to, they are unlikely to be in a receptive mood and will, perhaps, even actively resist learning.

iv) *Fear*: Fear can be a strong motivator for listening and learning, but, if it is too strong, it becomes a barrier to listening and learning, the fear being uppermost in the person's mind.

v) *Shyness:* The learner has overcome the first shyness barrier by actually attending. If something is not understood, however, the shyness may prevent a question with the result that what follows is lost.

vi) *Aggression:* This may be linked with enforced attendance, or an on-the-spot dislike of you, the learning environment, or the other learners. It usually exhibits itself by an aggressive expression that is developed rather than listening to what you are saying.

vii) *Resistance to learning*: The reasons for this attitude can be many: enforced attendance, failure to see the reason for the training, various dislikes, and so on. "I do not intend to learn" can sometimes be broken down by involvement or an interesting presentation or activity, but often it stays throughout the session.

viii) *Know-it-all:* One of the common types of resistance to learning, particularly by long-serving employees who have been sent on the training against their wishes. If this is indeed the case, it is more effective to try to use their experience within the group than to try to react to the attitude.

ix) *Too old to learn* : This is usually an attitude developed by those who are frightened to learn or otherwise do not want to learn. Research has shown that, unless older people have allowed their minds to degenerate, they are often, because of a wealth of experience, better learners than many younger people.

x) *Status differences:* Sometimes the learners are at different status levels within the organisation. Unless the group is well established, the higher level members may resist to avoid making fools of themselves in front of their juniors, who themselves do not want to take the risk of showing themselves up in front of their bosses.

xi) *Mind not on the learning*. If the learner's mind is still on what has been left at work or on other worries—responsibility for making arrangements for a variety of events, interview coming up, and so on—full attention is not paid to the learning.

7.4.3. Environmental Barriers

i) *Noise, heat, cold, ventilation, space available:* All these aspects of the environment can get in the way of listening and learning. Sometimes they can be resolved and the barrier is broken; at other times nothing can be done and they may remain as barriers.

i) *Interruptions/work intrusion:* Interruptions of whatever nature, but particularly if they bring work into the learning environment, affect listening and learning. Most can be avoided by preliminary precautions.

i) *Restricted time*: Learning requires a variable length of time to be effective-time to fit in the material of the event, time for different learners to assimilate material, time for the trainer to put over the material effectively, and so on. If there is a time restriction, this has a detrimental effect on both the trainer and the learner.

7.4.4. Speech Barriers

i) *Unskilled speaker*: An unskilled speaker uses methods and techniques that are not the most effective with which to make impact on the listeners. Too many hesitations, verbal noises, mannerisms, and so on are noted by the listeners, who may take more notice of these than of what is being said. There may be an element of sympathy for the inexperienced speaker, but lack of skill is unlikely to be approved.

ii) *Accent*: At one time regional accents were not acceptable for many areas of public speaking. This has now been discounted, but if the accent is too strong, it may not be understandable. The use of dialect words, however, should be avoided since these may not be widely understood.

iii) *Manner*: Speakers may not be able to completely control their overall manner, but usually this can be modified somewhat for the period required. A patronising manner is soon recognised and rejected by the listeners. Aggression from the speaker results in either withdrawal or returned aggression, neither of which is conducive to good communication. An abrasive manner has a similar effect. Speakers can usually modify the first two; the last one is more difficult since speakers may not even be aware of this aspect of their natural manner.

iv) *Attitude*: This aspect of the speaker is often not self-recognised, but nevertheless may have an effect on the extent of listening and acceptance. The speaker's prejudices may emerge unconsciously—racism, sexism, and so on--and even personal views that ignore or reject the views of others without reason or argument. The speaker may be judgemental, making decisions or forcing opinions without seeking other options, and, perhaps because of these two aspects and other internal motivation, may be overdirective. Trainers have to be aware of these possible attitudes in themselves and, if present, modify their approaches accordingly. The latter aspect is particularly important in the training field in which the emphasis is more and more on learner-centred rather than trainer-centred control.

v) *Lack of knowledge:* The converse of knowing it all and letting everybody be aware of this is demonstrating that the speaker's knowledge of the subject is limited or incomplete. The listener, particularly in a learning situation, has every justification in rejecting someone who has obviously not undertaken sufficient care in preparation in order to know the subject. Naturally nobody knows everything and at times the trainer will admit some lack of knowledge, making a firm promise to find out. But if this becomes an over frequent admission, credibility is soon lost.

7.5. Power of Listening

Listening is one of the most important factor in verbal communication. It accounts for a major part of the time spent communicating. Poor listening skills can result in miscommunications and costly errors in terms of lost time and money. To be a good listener a person must first be motivated to listen. People are generally motivated if the communication is job related and/or if there is some interest in the communication. Generally, higher motivation results in better listening. Being a good listener requires a person to focus on the content as opposed to the delivery style. This is referred to as content listening. Regardless of whether the presenter's communication style is entertaining or dry, it is the content of the message that counts. For example, a person with poor communication skills may convey an important message, whereas a person who is entertaining may be easy to listen to but has nothing important to say.

Another important part of being a good listener is not jumping to conclusions, thereby deferring evaluation to the end. Often, a speaker may arouse emotions within the listener. This may cause the listener to stop listening and start formulating a response before the entire message is absorbed. Premature evaluation can seriously inhibit the listener's ability to understand the true meaning of the message.

A good listener gives non-verbal or verbal feedback to the speaker. For example, making eye contact with the speaker can mean the listener acknowledges the message. No eye contact can mean the listener has lost interest or disagrees with the message. Verbal feedback can express recognition, agreement, and disagreement. A listener may verbally indicate receipt of the message with agreement or disagreement. In general, feedback should be constructive, timely, coherent, and impersonal. Feedback needs to be helpful rather than harmful, and practical. It has to relate to something within the speaker's realm of control. Feedback needs to occur soon after the message is sent or it is not very effective. Also, feedback loses its meaning if it is viewed as personal. If a speaker views feedback as personal, he or she may ignore it completely.

7.5.1. Barriers to Listening

i) Hearing difficulties and seating position

ii) Speed of thought, being ahead of the speaker

iii) Prejudice against speaker's apparent background, culture

iv) Speaker's apparent experience

v) Different views from speakers

vi) Difficulties of language and jargon
vii) Undefined reaction against speaker
viii) Wanting to speak yourself
ix) Internal environmental distractions
x) External distractions
xi) Incongruent verbal and non-verbal behavior
xii) Heard it all before
xiii) Not interested in subject (and determined not to be)
xiv) Only present because of being sent
xv) Wanting to hear only what you want to hear
xvi) Assuming what is being said
xvii) Emotive words and phrases ("with respect," etc.)
xviii) Daydreaming
xix) Other things on your mind
xx) Tiredness

Selected References

Burgoon Michael, et.al., *Human Communication,* Sage Publications, London, New Delhi, 1994.

Carey, James. W., *Communication as Culture: Essays on Media and Society*. Winchester, Massachusetts, 1989.

Deetz, Stanley A., *Democracy in an Age of Corporate Colonization: Developments in Communication and the Politics of Everyday Life*. Albany, 1992.

John Powell, *Will the Real Me Please Stand Up?: 25 Guidelines for Good Communication*, Thomas More Publishing,1995.

Pearce, W. Barnett. Communication and the Human Condition. Carbondale, Illinois, 1989.

Suzette Haden Elgin, *Genderspeak: Men, Women, and the Gentle Art of Verbal Self-Defense.* John Wiley & Sons Inc., Third Avenue, New York, 1993.

Watzlawick, Paul, et.al., *Pragmatics of Human Communication: A Study of Interactional Patterns, Pathologies, and Paradoxes.* New York, 1967.

Bibliography

Ajzen, I., "From Intentions to Actions: A Theory of Planned Behaviour", in J. Kuhl and J. Beckman (eds.), *Action-control: From Cognition to Behaviour* Heidelberg, Springer, 1985, pp. 11-39.

Anderson, J., *The Adaptive Character of Thought*, Hillsdale, NJ: Erlbaum Associates, 1990.

Argyle, Michael, *Bodily Communication*, Methuen & Co., 1978.

Arnold, Carroll C., and John Waite Bowers, (eds.), *Handbook of Rhetorical and Communication Theory*, Boston, 1984.

Arnold Jeffrey, *The Big Book on Small Groups*, Downers Grove, Ill., InterVarsity Press, 1992.

Ball-Rokeach, S.J., and DeFleur, M.L., A Dependency Model or Mass Media Effects, *Communication Research*, 3, 1976, pp.3-21.

Bandura, A., "Social Cognitive Theory: An Agentive perspective. Annual Review of Psychology, 52 , 2001, pp.1-26.

Barkai, John L., "Nonverbal Communication from the Other Side: Speaking Body Language", *San Diego Law Review*, p 101-25, Jan, 1990.

Barker, Steve, et al., *Good Things Come in Small Groups*, Downers Grove, Ill.: InterVarsity Press, 1985.

Barnouw, Erik, et.al., (eds.), *International Encyclopedia of Communications*, New York and Oxford, 1989.

Barrett, E., NetLibrary Inc., *Sociomedia, Multimedia, Hypermedia, and the Social Construction of Knowledge*, Boulder, Colo.: NetLibrary Inc. 1999.

Baym, et al., "Social Interactions Across Media", *New Media Society*.2004; 6: 299-318.

Beal, George M., et al. "Communication Impact," Rural Sociology Report No. 41. Department of Sociology and Anthropology, Iowa State University, Ames, Iowa. 1967.

Beebe, Steven A., and John T. Masterson, *Communicating in Small Groups: Principles and Practices*, New York: HarperCollins, 1993.

Berger, Charles R., and Steven H. Chaffee, (eds.), *Handbook of Communication Science*, Newbury Park, California, 1987.

Berlow, D. K., *The Process of Communication: An Introduction to Theory and Practice*, New York: Holt, Rinehart, and Winston, 1960.

Bittner John, *Fundamentals of Communication*, Prentice Hall, Englewood Cliffs, 1985.

Bitzer, L.F., "The Rhetorical Situation", in *Rhetoric: Concepts, Definitions, Boundaries*, William A. Covino (ed.), Boston: Allyn and Bacon, 1995.

Blanck, P. D., (ed.), *Interpersonal expectations: Theory, research, applications*, Cambridge University Press. 1994.

Blumer, Herbert, *Symbolic Interactionism: Perspective and Method*, Englewood Cliffs, NJ: Prentice-Hall, 1969.

Burgoon Michael, et.al., *Human Communication,* Sage Publications, London, New Delhi, 1994.

Burgoon, J., Stern, L. A. & Dillman, L., *Interpersonal adaptation: Dyadic interaction patterns*, Cambridge University Press, 1995.

Carey, James. W., *Communication as Culture: Essays on Media and Society*. Winchester, Massachusetts, 1989.

Daft, R.L. and Lengel, R.H., "Information Richness: A New Approach to Managerial Behaviour and Organizational Design, In: Cummings, L.L. and Staw, B.M. (eds.), *Research in Organizational Behaviour* 6, Homewood, IL: JAI Press, 1984, pp.191-233.

Daiute, C., Damon, W., *The Development of Literacy through Social Interaction*, San Francisco: Jossey-Bass, 1993.

Deetz, Stanley A., *Democracy in an Age of Corporate Colonization: Developments in Communication and the Politics of Everyday Life*. Albany, 1992.

DeVito, J. A., *Messages: Building interpersonal communication skills*, NY: Longman, 1999.

Donna Bellafiore, *Interpersonal Conflict and Effective Communication*, DRB Alternatives, Inc., 2004.

Duncan, Barry, *Mass Media and Popular Culture*, Toronto: Harcourt, Brace, Jovanovich, 1988.

Ellis, Donald G. Crafting Society: Ethnicity, Class, and Communication Theory. Mahwah, New Jersey, 1999.

Fairhurst, G., Star, R., *The Art of Framing*, San Francisco: Jossey-Bass, 1996.

Farace, R. V., Monge, P. R., Russell, H.M., *Communicating and Organizing*, Reading, MA: Addison-Wesley, 1977.

Festinger, L., *A Theory of Cognitive Dissonance*, Stanford, CA: Stanford University Press, 1957.

Fishbein, M., "Attitude and the Prediction of Behaviour", in: Fishbein, M (ed.), *Readings in Attitude Theory and Measurement*, New York, Wiley, 1967.

Giles H., (eds.), *The New Handbook of Language and Social Psychology,* Sussex, UK, Wiley, 1997, pp. 79-102.

Griffin, E., *A first look at Communication Theory*, New York, The McGraw-Hill Companies, 1997.

Harper, Robert, *Nonverbal Communication*, Wiley, 1980.

Harvey, J.H., Weary, G., *Attribution: Basic Issues and Applications*, Academic Press, San Diego, 1985.

Haslam, Alexander S., *Psychology in Organizations - The Social Identitty Approach*, Sage Publications Ltd, London, 2001.

Hauser, Marc D., *The Evolution of Communication*, Cambridge, Massachusetts, 1996.

John Powell, *Will the Real Me Please Stand Up?: 25 Guidelines for Good Communication*, Thomas More Publishing,1995.

Kalbfleisch, P. J., and Cody, M. J., (eds.), *Gender, power, and communication in human relationships*, Lawrence Erblaum and Associates, 1995.

____________, *Interpersonal Communication: Evolving Interpersonal Relationshsips*, Lawrence Erblaum and Associates, 1993.

Knapp, M. L., and Hall, J. A., *Nonverbal communication in human interaction*, Harcourt Brace College Publishers, 1997.

Laswell, H.D., "The Structure and Function of Communication in Society", in L. Bryson (ed.), *The Communication of Ideas,* New York: Harper, 1948.

Lazarsfeld, P.F., Berelson, B., Gaudet, H., *The People's Choice: How the Voter Makes up his Mind in a Presidential Campaign*, New York, Columbia University Press, 1944.

Leathers, D, *Successful Nonverbal Communication: Principles and Applications*, Allyn & Bacon, 1997.

Leeds-Hurwitz, Wendy, *Communication in Everyday Life: A Social Interpretation*, Norwood, New Jersey, 1989.

Mattelart, Armand, *The Invention of Communication*, Translated by Susan Emanuel, Minneapolis, 1996.

McCombs, M.E., "The Agenda-Setting Approach", in Nimmo, D., Sanders, K. (eds.), *Handbook of Political Communication*, Beverly Hills, CA., Sage, 1982.

_____________ , Shaw, D., *The Agenda-Setting Function of Mass Media*, POQ, 36, 1972, pp.176-187.

McCroskey, J.C., *An Introduction to Rhetorical Communication*. Englewood Cliffs, NJ: Prentice-Hall, 1968.

McLuhan, Marshall, *Understanding Media: The Extensions of Man*, New York, 1964.

_____________, Fiore, Q., *The Medium is the Massage. An Inventory of Effects*, New York, Bantam Books, 1967.

McQuail Dennis, *Communication*, Longman, London and New York, 1984.

_____________ and Windahl, S., *Communication Models for the Study of Mass Communications*. 2nd ed. London: Longman, 1993.

_____________, "With More Handsight: Conceptual Problems and Some Ways Forward for Media Use Research", *Communications*, 26(4), 2001, pp.337-350.

_____________, *Mass Communication Theory: An Introduction*, London, 1994.

Miller, G. R., and Fudge, K., *Handbook of interpersonal communication,* Thousand Oaks, CA: Sage, 1994.

Monge, P.E., Contractor, N.S., *Theories of Communication Networks*, Oxford, University Press, 2003.

Noelle-Neumann, E., *The Spiral of Silence: Public Opinion - Our Social Skin*, Chicago, University of Chicago, 1984.

Parenti, Michael, *Inventing Reality: The Politics of the Mass Media*, New York: St. Martin's Press, 1986.

Pearce, W. Barnett. Communication and the Human Condition. Carbondale, Illinois, 1989.

Penalosa, F., *An Introduction to the Sociology of Language*, Rowley, MA: Newbury House, 1981.

Peters, John Durham, *Speaking into the Air: A History of the Idea of Communication*, Chicago, 1999.

Peters, D., *Speaking into the Air: A History of the Idea of Communication*, Chicago and London, University of Chicago Press, 1999.

Petty, R.E., Cacioppo, J.T., *The Elaboration Likelihood Model of Persuasion*, New York, Academic Press, 1986.

Pilotta, Joseph J., and Algis Mickunas, *Science of Communication: Its Phenomenological Foundation*, Hillsdale, New Jersey, 1990.

Radcliff, C. J., "Interpersonal communication with library patrons: Physician-patient research models", *RQ, 34* (4), pp. 497-506, Summer, 1995

Rogers, Everett M., *A History of Communication Study: A Biographical Approach*, New York, 1994.

Roloff , M. E. , Miller, G. R., (eds.), *Interpersonal Processes: New Directions in Communication Research*, Newbury Park, CA: Sage, 1987.

Rothenbuhler, Eric W., *Ritual Communication: From Everyday Conversation to Mediated Ceremony*, Thousand Oaks, California, 1998.

Rothwell, J. Dan., *In Mixed Company: Small Group Communication*, Philadelphia, Harcourt Brace, 1992.

Ruben, B. D., Stewart, L. P., *Communication and Human Behavior,* Boston, Allyn and Bacon, 1998.

Scheufele, D.A., "Agenda-setting, Priming, and Framing Revisited: Another Look at Cognitive Effects of Political Communication", *Communication Abstracts*, 24(1), 2001.

Schiller, Dan., *Theorizing Communication: A History*, New York, 1996.

Schrank, Jeffrey, *Understanding Mass Media*, Toronto, Copp Clark, 1986.

Searle, J.R., *Speech Acts: An Essay in the Philosophy of Language*, Cambridge, University Press, 1969.

Segerstrale, U., and Molnar, P., (eds.), *Nonverbal Communication: Where Nature Meets Culture*, Lawrence Erblaum and Associates, 1997.

Severin, W.J., Tankard, J.W., *Communication Theories: Origins, Methods and Uses in the Mass Media*, Addison Wesley Longman, 2001.

Stephenson, W., *The Play Theory of Mass Communication,* New Brunswick, NJ: Transaction Books, 1988.

Taylor, O. L., (ed.), *Nature of Communication Disorders in Culturally and Linguistically Diverse Populations*. San Diego, CA: College Hill Press, 1986.

Taylor, Talbot J., *Mutual Misunderstanding: Scepticism and the Theorizing of Language and Interpretation*, Durham, North Carolina, 1992.

Watt, J. H., Van Lear, C. A., (eds.), *Dynamic Patterns in Communication Processes,* Thousand Oaks, CA: Sage, 1996.

Watzlawick, P., Beavin, J., Jackson, D., *Pragmatics of Human Communication.* NY: Norton, 1967.

Watzlawick, Paul, et.al., *Pragmatics of Human Communication: A Study of Interactional Patterns, Pathologies, and Paradoxes.* New York, 1967.

Weick, K. E., *Sensemaking in Organizations*, Thousand Oaks, CA, Sage, 1995.

Westley, Bruce H. and Malcolm S. MacLean Jr."A Conceptual Model for Communications Research," *in Dimensions in Communication*. James H. Campbell and Hal W. Helper- (eds.). Belmont, Calif: Wadsworth Publishing Co., 1965.

Williams, David Cratis, and Michael David Hazen, (eds.), *Argumentation Theory and the Rhetoric of Assent*, Tuscaloosa, U of Alabama P, 1990.

Wilmot, W. W., *Relational Communication,* New York, McGraw-Hill, 1995.

Wood, J. T., *Relational Communication: Continuity and Change in Personal Relationships,* Belmont, CA: Wadsworth, 1995.

Index